Development, Environment and Migration

AF763812

This book brings the discourses around social justice and sustainable development back into focus by looking at India's mining sector and the state's frameworks for economic development. The chapters in this volume analyse mining practices in the mineral-rich areas of eastern India through various case studies and highlight their immense human and environmental costs.

This volume critically analyses selected mining projects in India that have resulted in large-scale displacements, impoverishment and environmental degradation. It identifies the gaps in policy, its implementation, and the lack of safeguards which threaten the socio-economic and ecological ways of life and the livelihoods of the local communities. Based on documents, reports, interviews and field observations, this book engages with the issues surrounding the mining sector, e.g., land acquisition, land use and degradation, the politics of compensation, policies, agitation and social mobilisation, health and agriculture, livelihood and gender. It further provides an assessment of local political economies and offers suggestive frameworks for inclusive growth in this sector.

This book will be of interest to students and researchers exploring the disciplines of development studies, sociology, law and governance, human ecology and economics.

S. Irudaya Rajan is Professor at the Centre for Development Studies, Thiruvananthapuram, Kerala. He is Editor of the two Routledge series India Migration Report (annual) since 2010 and South Asia Migration Report (biennial) and is the founder and Editor-in-Chief of the journal *Migration and Development*.

Debabrata Baral is Assistant Professor at Bennett University. He has also worked in research projects funded by British Academia, DFID, ICSSR. His research aims at identifying and addressing the gaps in the idea of development and governances. His research interests are located in the fields of development studies, social movements and corporate social responsibility. He has studied various aspects of the mining sector during his doctorate and post-doctorate study at Jawaharlal Nehru University, New Delhi.

Development, Environment and Migration

Lessons for Sustainability

Edited by S. Irudaya Rajan
and Debabrata Baral

Routledge
Taylor & Francis Group
LONDON AND NEW YORK

First published 2020
by Routledge
2 Park Square, Milton Park, Abingdon, Oxon OX14 4RN

and by Routledge
52 Vanderbilt Avenue, New York, NY 10017

Routledge is an imprint of the Taylor & Francis Group, an informa business

© 2020 selection and editorial matter, S. Irudaya Rajan and Debabrata Baral; individual chapters, the contributors

The right of S. Irudaya Rajan and Debabrata Baral to be identified as the authors of the editorial material, and of the authors for their individual chapters, has been asserted in accordance with sections 77 and 78 of the Copyright, Designs and Patents Act 1988.

All rights reserved. No part of this book may be reprinted or reproduced or utilised in any form or by any electronic, mechanical, or other means, now known or hereafter invented, including photocopying and recording, or in any information storage or retrieval system, without permission in writing from the publishers.

Trademark notice: Product or corporate names may be trademarks or registered trademarks, and are used only for identification and explanation without intent to infringe.

British Library Cataloguing-in-Publication Data
A catalogue record for this book is available from the British Library

Library of Congress Cataloging-in-Publication Data
A catalog record for this book has been requested

ISBN: 978-1-138-56531-9 (hbk)
ISBN: 978-0-367-50477-9 (pbk)
ISBN: 978-1-003-04998-2 (ebk)

Typeset in Sabon
by Apex CoVantage, LLC

Dedicated to those invisible, unrepresented masses
of society who have been bearing the cost
of development projects

Contents

Figures

Tables

Contributors

Debabrata Baral is Assistant Professor at Bennett University.

Narendra Kumar Behera is Assistant Professor at Larambha College, Odisha.

Garima Kirti is a law student at ILS Law College, Pune.

Saswat Kishore Mishra is a doctoral student at Department of Humanities and Social Sciences at Indian Institute of Technology at Kharagpur, West Bengal.

R.K. Kumbhar is Assistant Professor at Sambalpur University, Odisha.

Pulak Mishra is Associate Professor at Department of Humanities and Social Sciences at Indian Institute of Technology at Kharagpur, West Bengal.

Sujit Kumar Mishra is Associate Professor in Council of Social development, Hyderabad.

Suravee Nayak is a doctoral student at Centre for Development Studies, Kerala.

Ramya Ranjan Patel is Assistant Professor at Dyal Singh(E) College, University of Delhi.

S. Irudaya Rajan is Professor at the Centre for Development Studies, Kerala.

Dinabandhu Sahoo is a doctoral student at National Institute of Technology
Sujata Sahu is a doctoral student at Sambalpur University, Odisha.

S.N. Tripathy is Professor at Gokhale Institute of Politics and Economics at Rourkela, Odisha.

Himanshu Upadhyaya is Assistant Professor at Azim Premji University.

Preface

This volume can be seen as an effort, to fill in a piece, of the large jigsaw puzzle known as 'sustainable development'. At the national level (various governments) and at the international level (various international organisations, e.g., UNDP, UNEP, etc., to name a few), are trying to evolve a consultative-legislative framework to balance the interrelationship between commodity production, legislative framework and the concerns of the impacted peoples. We definitely applaud the Indian government efforts to bring in social-environmental equity in the mining sector. For example, the Ministry of Mines, Government of India, has quite comprehensively identified the structural framework around which sustainable mining operations should operate, to quote,

> Mining that is financially viable; socially responsible; environmentally, technically and scientifically sound; with a long term view of development; uses mineral resources optimally; and, ensures sustainable post-closure land uses. Also one based on creating long-term, genuine, mutually beneficial partnerships between government, communities and miners, based on integrity, cooperation and transparency.

Definitely legal provisions and constitutional promises are there to safeguard the interest of the impacted people. But with the emergence of aggressive local resistances, social movements and so forth against various mining sector projects highlight the presence of gaps or loopholes in the respective policies or promises. Hence a contemporary research on the mining sector becomes extremely relevant. This academic volume tries to outline the various socio-economic, administrative, legislative, environmental and other lesser-known gaps that are associated with various mining projects which have eventually started to become dominant contexts of contentions. This volume strongly believes that by revisiting, reflecting and acknowledging the local aspirations and concerns and by incorporating them within the dominant policy debates and challenges to inclusive growth or sustainable development can be addressed. This book advocates that social policy should be treated not only as a method but also as a methodology for various welfare economies or developmental states. Social policy rather than public policy should be the way forward. This book attempts to contribute to the policy debates on the mining sectors.

Acknowledgements

We show extreme gratitude to Indian Council for Social Science Research and International Development Research Council for funding the international conference titled 'Development-Induced Displacement and Migration, Land acquisition and Resettlement' that was hosted at Centre for Development Studies, Thiruvananthapuram, in 2016. This edited volume is one of the academic outcomes from the conference.

We highly appreciate the contribution of all the academic and administrative staff at Centre for Development Studies, Kerala, and at Jawaharlal Nehru University, Delhi, for their hard work in bringing out *Development, Environment and Migration* in its present form.

1 Introduction

Mining sector and the idea of development: challenges, policies and possibilities

S. Irudaya Rajan and Debabrata Baral

Mining sector and sustainable development goals

The buzz around sustainable development is growing in the contemporary era. But it is not a new phenomenon. It has been emerging and finding its place in various policy documents that have been governing and influencing policies and programmes of nation-states. Mostly, the political awareness and advocacy at large scale was done by few international organisations. For example, in 1972, the United Nations Conference on the Human Environment was held in Stockholm. Popularly known as the 'Stockholm Declaration', it outlined the framework for sustainability. To quote,

> Principle 2: Natural resources of the earth, including the air, water, land, flora and fauna and especially representative samples of natural ecosystems, must be safeguarded for the benefit of present and future generations through careful planning and management.
>
> (United Nation, 1972: 2)

But, the re-emphasise on sustainable development emerged during 1987 through the World Commission on Environment and Development, popularly known as 'Brundtland Report'. This report was formulated by the prime minister of Norway in 1987 in consultations with 172 nations. The report was titled, 'Our Common Future'. It argued for sustainable development to be a global agenda. To quote,

> Meeting the needs of the present without compromising the ability of future generations to meet their own.
>
> (World Commission on Environment and Development, 1987: 37)

An overt emphasis on environment as a key constituent of sustainable development was re-introduced in 1992. The Rio Declaration on Environment and Development in 1992 outlined the principle of achieving sustainable development. To quote,

> Principle 4: In order to achieve sustainable development, environment protection shall constitute an integral part of the development process and cannot be considered in isolation from it.
>
> (United Nations, 1992: 1)

> While, it was only in September 2015, India, along with other 193 member states, had signed and adopted the 'Agenda 2030' at the UN Sustainable Development summit for achieving sustainable development. On 1 January 2016, the era of sustainable development came into effect. Seventeen sustainable development goals (SDGs)1 were laid out, and a time frame of fifteen years was set to achieve the goals.
>
> (United Nations, 2015)

Here one need to note that, as per the white paper[2] submitted by Columbia Centre on Sustainable Investment, the mining sector has the potential to influence all the 17 SDGs. For example, the mining activities have an impact on the environment sustainability as it impacts the land, water, climate and flora which people are dependent on. Second, it impacts social inclusion, as its activities impact local communities by either bringing then economic opportunities or challenging their economic opportunities. Third, it influences economic development by generating economic opportunities, construction of new infrastructure, etc. To quote,

> Historically, however, mining has contributed many of the challenges that the SDGs are trying to address – environmental degradation, displacement of populations, worsening economic and social inequality, armed conflicts, gender-based violence, tax evasion and corruption, increased risk for many health problems, and the violation of human rights. In recent decades, the industry has made significant advances in mitigating and managing such impacts and risks, by improving how companies manage their environmental and social impacts, protect the health of their workers, achieve energy efficiencies, report on financial flows, and respect and support human rights.
>
> (Columbia Centre on Sustainable Investing, 2016: 3)

Sustainable development in India: the interplay between political institutions and political environment

On 19 July 2017, NITI Aayog of India voluntarily presented its 'National Review on implementation of SDGs' at the United Nations High Level Political Forum 2017. It presented its review report on seven specific goals, these are, Goal 1, to end poverty and all its forms everywhere; Goal 2, to end hunger, achieves food security, improves nutrition and promotes sustainable agriculture; Goal 3, to ensure healthy lives and promotes well-being for all ages; Goal 5, to achieve gender equality and empowers all women and girls; Goal 9, to build resilient infrastructure, promotes inclusion and sustainable industrialisation and fosters innovation; Goal 14, to conserve and sustainably use the oceans, seas and marine resources; and Goal 17, to revitalize the global partnership for sustainable development. Apart from the national government, there are other state governments who have developed their own vision for achieving the SDGs, such as Assam, Andhra Pradesh, Bihar, Haryana, Maharashtra, Kerala, Karnataka, Tamil Nadu, Punjab and Madhya Pradesh (NITI Aayog, 2017).[3] Definitely one sees actions and activities regarding the realisation of SDG by 2030. But it would be unfair if it is not pointed out that India has been experimenting with the idea of sustainable development for a long time. For example, in the year 2005, a high-level committee was set up under the chairmanship of planning commission to review the National Mineral Policy. The committee recommended for 'sustainable development Framework' by referring it to the work done by 'International Council of Mining and Metals' and 'International Union for the Conservation of Nature and Natural Resources'. This eventually led to the development of a working definition of sustainable development for the mining sector in India. To quote,

> Mining that is financially viable; socially responsible; environmentally, technically and scientifically sound; with a long term view of development; uses mineral resources optimally; and, ensures sustainable post-closure land uses. Also one based on creating long-term, genuine, mutually beneficial partnerships between government, communities and miners, based on integrity, cooperation and transparency.
>
> (ERM India and Ministry of Mines, Government of India, 2011: 6)

Mining sector in India: the interplay between economic orientation and political institutions

This section, tries to locate the ways the private sector and state looks at mining activities. Here a reference to Polanyi theoretical premise becomes quite relevant. He had theorized the interrelationship between the modern nation-state and the modern market economy. He argued that a powerful modern state is required to bring forth changes in the social structure that is conducive to competitive capitalist economy (Polanyi, 1944).

Now, coming back to India, for long, mining has become a priority for the state. The National Mineral Policy 2006 stated that mining could provide genuine development opportunities for indigenous populations. This argument was resounded even by the corporate sector. FICCI (2013) report states that mining contributes to the GDP. It stated that every 1 per cent increase in mining would lead to 0.5 per cent increase in GDP. India is in a good position for mining and quarrying activities; it captures the fourth position in coal and seventh position in iron ore reserves. The value of mineral production was 16,3907 crores in India during 2010 and 2011. In addition, to facilitate the growth of mining, the Mines and Minerals (Development and Regulation) Act, 1957, was replaced by the Mines and Minerals (Development and Regulation) Bill, 2011. The bill aimed to provide 'sustainable mining' and 'local area development'. To facilitate the mining activities, the eleventh five-year plan outlined the impediments for the mining and quarrying activities. In the context of India, mining can be linked and associated with the idea of growth. The Mines and Minerals Bill, 2011, claims that mining can provide local area development. Here one can argue that the corporate sector and the state had similar views on the mining projects. But apart from the immense interest in establishing the mining sector, there are also certain safeguards that have been incorporated within various plans and policies to facilitate the establishment and acceptance for various mining projects. The next section outlines it in great details.

Mining sector and inclusive development in India: a review

In India, the mining sector is facilitated through the Mines and Minerals (Development and Regulation) Act, 1957; Mineral Concession Rules (MCR), 1960; Mineral Concession and Development Rules (MCDR), 1988; Mines Act, 1952; Mines Rules, 1955; State Minor Mineral Concession Rules, Offshore Areas Mineral (Development and Regulation) Act, 2002; Offshore Areas Mineral Concession Rules, 2006; National Mineral Policy, 2008; National Mineral Exploration Trust; Mining Tenement System (MTS); Sustainable Development Framework (SDF), Coordination-cum-Empowered Committee; and notification of 31 minerals as minor minerals, increasing the royalty amount prescribed to the state for major minerals. Apart from this, there are safeguards assured to the people impacted by the mining projects through the MMDR Act, District Mineral Foundation and its subsection 'Pradhan Mantri Khanij Kshetra Kalyan Yojana, Rehabilitation and Resettlement Policy 2007 and the amended Land Acquisition Act of 2014. But irrespective of this, there has been a rise of aggressive local resistance challenging the establishment of various mining projects in India. Here, one is intrigued to understand why people are resisting the development projects when government through its various 'principles', 'promises' and 'policies' safeguards their interests? If one talks about safeguards, then the constitution of India should be the first reference point before any analysis. To quote,

> The constitution of India has guaranteed certain Fundamental Rights to the citizens of India and enunciates certain Directive Principles of State Policy, in particular, the state shall strive to promote the welfare of the

people by securing and protecting as effectively as it may a social order in which justice, social, economic and political, shall be the institutions of the national life and shall direct its policy towards securing, among other things:

(a) that all citizens, men, women, equally, have the right to an adequate means of livelihood;
(b) that the ownership and control of the material resources of the community are so distributed as best to sub serve the common good; and
(c) that the operation of the economic system does not result in the concentration of wealth and means of production to the common detriment.[4]

(Ministry of Human Resource Development, Government of India, 2016: 1)

Apart from the constitution of India, the National Mineral Policy, 2006, talks about safeguarding and enhancing the ecosystem. The policy aims at maintaining the natural capital. There are two statutes, viz., the Forest (Conservation) Act 1980 and the Environment (Protection) Act 1986, which lays down the law that must be followed in the development of mines. A criticism that has been made is that the two statutes have a preoccupation with two concerns, namely, compensation for diversion of forest land to non-forest use in various forms (including compensatory afforestation) and the need for environment impact studies prior to the grant of environmental clearances. While, the best practice internationally goes much beyond these concerns. Worldwide, mining interventions are becoming increasingly sophisticated. Mining practice should ensure natural capital. National Mineral Policy (2007) suggests, to quote,

> 'to ensure that the critical natural capital is maintained, that ecosystems are enhanced where possible, and that mineral wealth contributes to net environmental continuity'.
>
> (Planning Commission, Government of India, 2006: 68)

To add, the National Mineral Policy, Report of the High Level Committee, 2006, talks about further safeguards. To quote,

> Safeguards -11
>
> Land is often used without the consent of the indigenous people. Mining companies should act as if consent to gain access to land is required even when the law of the land does not require this. In making decisions, the cultural circumstances of the local people and loss of access to common resources should be kept in mind. Where resettlement takes place, companies need to ensure that living standards are not

> diminished, that community and social ties are preserved, and that they provide fair compensation for loss of assets and economic opportunity. Responsibility for ensuring the long-term well being of resettled communities needs to be defined and monitored. Environmental mining and other interests should be considered along with the interests of the poor and politically marginalised who live in these areas.
>
> (Planning Commission, Government of India,[5] 2006: 69)

Even, in principle, Rule 54 and 55 of the Mineral Concession Rules of 1960 essentially lays the procedure for grievance redressal. It clearly states that any aggrieved person can appeal to the central government. And the central government can exercise its revisionary power to, 'confirm', 'modify' or 'set aside' the impugned order[6] (Ministry of Mines, Government of India, 2005).

Since the mining projects require large-scale land acquisition, hence the Ministry of Rural Development in its Right to Fair Compensation and Transparency in Land Acquisition, Rehabilitation and Resettlement (Social Impact Assessment and Consent) Rules 2014 outlines certain safeguards or measures. In addition, the National Rehabilitation and Resettlement Policy, 2007, also assures safeguards. To quote,

> In case of a project involving land acquisition on behalf of a requiring body,-
>
> (a) The requiring body shall give preference to the affected families – at least one person per nuclear family- in providing employment in the project, subject to the availability of vacancies and suitability of the affected person for the employment;
>
> (b) Wherever necessary, the requiring body shall arrange for training of the affected persons, so as to enable such persons to take on suitable jobs;
>
> (c) The requiring body shall offer scholarships and other skill development opportunities to the eligible persons from the affected families as per the criteria as may be fixed by the appropriate Government;
>
> (d) The requiring body shall give preference to the affected persons or their groups or cooperatives in the allotment of outsourced contracts, shops or other economic opportunities coming up in or around the project site, and
>
> (e) The requiring body shall give preference to willing landless labourers and unemployed affected persons while engaging labour in the project during the construction phase.
>
> (Ministry of Rural Development, Government of India, 2007: 51)

To add, further, the National Rehabilitation and Resettlement Policy, 2007, even aims to minimise displacement, adequately rehabilitate affected families, protect weaker sections of society, provide better standards of living to the affected families, integrate the plans of rehabilitation with development and have a harmonious way for land acquisition. To quote,

> 2.1 The objectives of the National Rehabilitation and Resettlement Policy are as follows,
> (a) to minimise displacement and to promote, as far as possible, non-displacing or least displacing alternatives.
> (b) to ensure adequate rehabilitation package and expeditious implementation of the rehabilitation process with the active participation of the affected families.
> (c) to ensure that special care is taken for protecting the rights of the weaker sections of society, especially members of the Schedule Caste and Schedule tribes, and to create obligations on the state for their treatment with concern and sensitivity;
> (d) to provide a better standard of living, making concerted efforts for providing sustainable income to the affected families;
> (e) to integrate rehabilitation concerns into the development planning and implementation process; and
> (f) where displacement is on account of land acquisition, to facilitate harmonious relationship between the requiring body and the affected families through mutual cooperation.
>
> (Ministry of Rural Development, Government of India, 2007: 35)

Earlier, The Land Acquisition Act, 1894, of the Ministry of Law and Justice, Government of India and the National Mineral Policy, Report of the High-Level Committee, 2006, talks about safeguards in the context of land. Even the outdated, The Land Acquisition Act of 1894 states, to quote,

> Hearing of objections –
> (1) Any person interested in any land which has been notified under section 4, sub-section (1), as being needed or likely to be needed for a public purpose or for a Company may, [within thirty days from the date of the publication of the notification], object to the acquisition of the land or of any land in the locality, as the case may be.
> (2) Every objection under sub-section (1) shall be made to the Collector in writing, and the Collector shall give the objector an opportunity of being heard [in person or by any person authorized by him in his behalf] or by pleader and shall, after hearing all such objections and after making such further inquiry, if any, as he thinks necessary, [either make a report in respect of the land which has been notified under section 4, sub section (1), or make different reports in respect of different parcels of such land, to the appropriate Government, containing his recommendations on the objections, together with the record of the proceedings held by him, for the decision of that Government]. The decision of the [appropriate Government] on the objections shall be final.

(3) for the purpose of this section, a person shall be deemed to be interested in land who would be entitled to claim an interest in compensation if the land were acquired under this Act.

(Ministry of Law and Justice, Government of India, 1985)

While, the redrafted Land Acquisition Policy of 2014 also outlines the role of the government. To quote,

19 Roles and responsibilities of the appropriate Government for consent process.

(1) the appropriate government shall notify and publish the date, time and venue of Gram Sabhas, Panchayats, or Autonomous District Council meetings (in cases where Gram Sabha does not exist or has not been constituted) and affected land owners meetings for obtaining the consent and organise public awareness campaigns to encourage participation of the affected land owners in the consent processes.

(2) the appropriate Government shall ensure that the following are provided at least three weeks in advance to every member from whom consent is sought, in the local language, namely:-

(a) a copy of the draft SIA report (if readily available) in the local language;

(b) initial package being offered for compensation and Rehabilitation and Resettlement;

(c) a list of the rights currently enjoyed by the village and its residents under revenue laws, Forest Rights Act and other legislations;

(d) a written statement signed by the District Collector, certifying that there will be no consequences, if consent is denied for a project stating that any attempt to coerce or intimidate in order to obtain consent shall be illegal; and

(e) contact details of the officer or authority along with official telephone number to be contacted in case of any attempt to coerce for signing the declaration of consent process.

(3) The District Collector or any official appointed by the District Collector shall attend the Gram Sabhas, Panchayats or Autonomous District Councils (in cases where Gram Sabha does not exist or has not been constituted) and land owners meetings.

(4) The appropriate Government shall ensure that all the documents relating to Social Impact Assessment are made available to the affected land owners and all requests for information are provided within seven days.

(Ministry of Rural Development, Government of India, 2014: 24)

The presence of the safeguards itself symbolizes that the state is aware that its model of development could create 'wider disparity in the society'. Policy debates should be looked through the concepts developed by Mayer and Ingram. They used the concepts of 'Insider and Outsider' in order to understand the complex relationship between social movement, state and public policy. Insiders are those located firmly within governmental institutions; by virtue of being most proximate to the policymaking process, they are most strategically located to determine the contours of public policy. Insiders are state bureaucrats, politicians and others who, quite literally, write public policy. In sharp contrast, outsiders are those at least one step removed from the formal governing process; nonetheless they try to influence the formulation, content and implementation of public policy by engaging in contentious politics. To do so, grassroots activists, associations of all sorts and the networks that surround them engage in what is called 'outsider claims making'. They do so in response to the existing public policy or to shape the formulation of new policy. With these key players in place, understanding the development and implementation of public policy has most often required examining when and how outsiders mobilise to pressure insiders to write some types of public policies and not others (Meyer et al., 2005: 117–118). Hence this book attempts to identify whether the 'outsider' concerns are addressed and incorporated within various plan and policies or have been ignored.

Mining sector and the human-ecology perspective: lesson for sustainable development of natural resources and inclusive growth

Apart from economic orientation, mining projects has to be looked from the human-ecology perspective. The influence of external environment on life, livelihood and social structures cannot be ignored. Of late mining sector has become a priority in this paradigm of development. But at the same time, mining as development projects have been aggressively criticized, for not being inclusive of the immediate local community or being harmful to the environment. From the policy perspective, there are safeguards guaranteed to the people impacted by these mining projects. But still the rise of aggressive social movements puts a question mark on the inclusiveness and the effectiveness of these safeguards. It is in this context, that the *first* chapter will outline and review various programs, policies and promises that facilitate the mining projects and even assure safeguards to the impacted people. *Second*, this volume will also outline resistances that have emerged, challenging various mining projects in India. *Third*, this volume reviews selected development projects, from both the macro perspective as well as through selected case studies. It aims to outline the various 'human' and 'environment' costs as well as identify the 'governance gaps' which challenge the inclusiveness of these development projects. Chapters selected in the volume are based on reviews of the local political economy and political ecology. This volume aims at providing suggestive framework for inclusive growth.

A lot has been said and debated on the impact of the so-called 'idea of development' on local communities in India. At the same time, these impacts are quite undermined. Literature suggests that over the years, development has been increasingly threatening the socio-economic, cultural and ecological ways of the local communities. This phenomenon exists across the world, and the 'development communities' seem to share several common characteristics. Within this background, this chapter is an attempt to depict the vicious cycle of different factors confronted by a development community in the process of development. The second chapter compiles different issues such as land and its politics of compensation, politics of agitation, externalities in terms of health and agriculture, accident and mine closure and the issue of livelihood by pooling it from six different case studies of Odisha. It attempts to analyse the impacts of development on the development communities. Evidence based on review of documents and reports, interviews with project officials and field observations have pointed to a separation of 'equity' from the entire regulatory mechanism. There is a question on the 'inclusivity' of the development communities with respect to equity and justice in the entire development process.

The role of neoliberal strategy of development in facilitating the profit-seeking behaviour of the corporates cannot be undermined. The lands that have been acquired for the development project was once a source of livelihood for the tribals. It was also serving the purpose of collateral, fall-back resources. It had also acted as a means of economic and social power through which citizens can claim their rights. Hence the land acquisition initiated for the development projects resulted not only in the permanent loss of livelihood but has also negatively impacted the achievement in human development among the tribes. Hence, the third chapter examines, *first*, the impact of mining-induced displacement on human development among the rural tribal households of Odisha. While the secondary data (mostly time series) collected from MCL offices have shown an optimistic picture of growth among the tribes, the primary data collected from the field survey shows quite a dismal result with regards to tribals' income, employment, land possession, agricultural and livestock production, physical assets, labour disposition, housing, health, education and other civil rights in the post-displacement period. *Second*, this chapter further argues that the haphazard implementation of the compensation and rehabilitation and resettlement policy marginalised the tribes. This chapter provides perspective on mining-induced development and displacement by reviewing and analysing the issues and concerns of tribes impacted by mining projects in Odisha.

Development projects often displace people from their habitat. This involuntary displacement of people from their productive assets and homes, due to industrial or infrastructure projects, has been one of the social issues that have caused intense debate among academics, social activists and planners.

Literature suggests that tribes are the most impacted who are forced to migrate to new areas. The scheduled tribes constituted about 8.6 per cent of the total population of the country according to a 2011 census. But it is quite alarming to learn that the tribes constitute around 55.16 per cent of total displaced people. Does this imply a sort of victimisation of the tribes in the context of development? Studies on the displacement, rehabilitation and resettlement, particularly in the context of tribal society in Odisha, have been done extensively. The fourth chapter is based on secondary sources of data and provides an outline regarding the problems, prospects and impact of mining industrialisation on the tribes of eastern India (Orissa). This chapter aims at giving some policy suggestion. It urges that rehabilitation policy for the tribes should safeguard their means of livelihood.

Odisha is one of the poorest states in India, though richly endowed with mineral resources. To alleviate poverty, the government of Odisha primarily relies on mineral-based industrialisation policy. In the last decade, it has speeded up the process of mineral-based industrialisation policy and has signed 89 MOUs until 2011. The government presupposes that it will create employment, generate revenue and bring overall development of all the regions and social groups, including the tribals, since those industries are primarily located in the tribal belt. In this context, the fifth chapter aims to understand, first, how these industries absorb the local tribal population and, *second*, the impacts of these large-scale land acquisitions (*grabbing*) in terms of displacement, livelihood and environment. This chapter argues that these mineral-based industrialisation policies initiate the process of underdevelopment. It looks like the availability of mineral resources acts like a *curse* for those regions and its tribal population.

Does gender segregation operate in the mining sector? Globally, the mining sector has been severely criticized due to its gender segregation of the workforce. Advocacy groups and organizations clearly stated the importance of gender equality in achieving 'Sustainable Development'. Chapter six, will first, review the Women Workforce and the Mines Act 1952 to outline the status of the women in the mining sector of India. It also maps the status of women in the extractive industry at the global level. The chapter further outlines the various socio-economic and legislative contexts that promote gender segregation of workers. The chapter further suggests ways of addressing exclusionary practices in the mining sector.

Since independence, large-scale development projects such as multipurpose river valley projects, large industrial projects, linear projects and mining of coal, iron, bauxite, etc. have been undertaken in India at a greater scale to support economic development. This process has received further stimulus in the era of neoliberalisation through expansion of domestic and foreign private investment. The process of development entails land acquisition, involuntary displacement, rehabilitation and resettlement. Odisha is a resource-rich state. The establishment of different development projects resulted in uprooting millions of people. Despite the formulation of resettlement and rehabilitation policy by the state, mostly a vast majority of the displaced people have not been better off. The project beneficiaries have benefited at the cost of displaced people. There have been a number of studies on involuntary displacement by various scholars. Among them, Michael M. Cernea has extensively studied the socio-economic impact under 'Impoverishment Risks and Reconstruction Model'. The affected people face impoverishment risks such as landlessness, joblessness, homelessness, marginalisation, food insecurity, increased morbidity, loss of common resources and social disarticulation that result in a loss of socio-cultural resilience. Three fourths of those displaced in India over five decades still face an uncertain future. The resettlement process assumes to be complete once compensation is paid to the affected people and relocated to a new resettlement site without any consideration to their economic restoration and better off. The seventh chapter is based on extensive field study to different categories of projects which have come up in western Odisha at different time periods, such as Hirakud Dam, Ib Thermal Power Station, Mahanadi Coalfield Ltd. and Vedanta Aluminium Ltd. and tries to focus on the conditions of the displaced people due to these development projects. The chapter argues that for the affected people, development has turned out to be 'de-development'.

What fails development projects? The rise of aggressive social movements against the establishment of numerous development projects in contemporary definitely points out that the idea of development needs to address certain gaps. But the point is: what are the gaps? How does one identify these gaps? It is in this context the chapter takes into account the case of Posco-India Transit Camp to understand the perception of people on Posco-India Project. In this context, the eighth chapter will, *first*, outline the social history regarding the establishment of Posco-India Transit Camp. *Second*, this chapter will take into account the lived experienced of people residing in the transit camp. Third, with reference to the lived experience of people, this chapter reviews the safeguards that are prescribed to the people in various policies and plan documents. This chapter argues that livelihood concerns employment opportunity, political mobility, inter-group conflicts, political difference and governance gaps are the contexts which formulated and reformulated the perceptions of the people with reference to the development projects. And mostly the governance gaps are the primary reasons for the failure of the development projects. Data for this chapter was collected using semi-structured interviews using random snowball and purposive sampling methods.

Given the widespread coal extraction to fuel rapid industrialisation to energise the country, displacement seems an inevitable part of India's growth story. Literature suggests that perspective on development-induced displacement has been mainly done through a risks and reconstruction (IRR) model. While displacement due to coal mines has been extensively studied from the gender and environment perspective, the present chapter attempts to analyse the impact of the rapidly growing coal capitalism on the social lives of the displaced people of Talcher, Odisha. Chapter nine employs the Marxian framework of social reproduction of labour. The chapter highlights the process around which the coal capitalism was founded and how it created conditions for the establishment of a market-based economy. Due to this, the young generations were socially reproduced to join the labour force of the capitalist system and thus became part of coal capitalism. It has been found that the livelihoods and social life of the displaced people have been altered in such a way that they are forced to depend on the capitalist industries by becoming both unit of production and its consumer. Although it is widely debated in academics that the impact of displacement is multidimensional, this chapter emphasizes the impact of displacement on the social coordinates, given the fact that displacement leaves a long-standing social cost as part of everyday survival for the displaced people. The study is based on the fieldwork carried out in four villages of Talcher. Both quantitative and qualitative data has been collected, and basic tools of statistics have been adopted for analysis, taking an approach of a case-control study. The chapter brings out the organic narratives of the displaced people and narrates the forceful intervention by the capitalistic forces by introducing market mechanisms, which changes the social structures of the displaced people in Talcher.

Acquisition of land for mining directly benefits its owners who generally belong to higher castes and are literates. However, the extent of benefits accrued may differ across the owners. The difference in benefits is dependent on their size of landholding, amount of land given up and compensation received, their education level, the provision for jobs, etc. In this context, the ninth chapter attempts to examine how the socially marginalised communities are included in mining-led development initiatives and explore its implications for further land acquisition. The tenth chapter uses primary data collected from the vicinity of Talcher Coalfields, the second-largest producer of coal in the country, situated in Angul district of the Indian state of Odisha. Attempts towards the acquisition of land for mining in the region in recent years have faced severe protests by various social groups. The sample households were selected following a proportionately stratified random sampling procedure. Using descriptive statistics and applying the ordinary least squares (OLS) method of estimation, the chapter finds that mining-based development initiatives do not necessarily lead to financial inclusion of the socially marginally households, particularly when there is provision of employment in the mines only for the landowners. Since many of the socially marginalised households lack ownership rights over land, they suffer from limited employment opportunities in the mining enterprises. In addition, asymmetries in bargaining power, access to information and capabilities further limit the scope of reaping the benefits of mining. Hence, socially inclusive mining and smooth economic transitions require imparting higher and quality education to the members of these households and development of the skills, providing greater access to information and widening the scope of employment beyond the landowners.

The contemporary idea of development that waves the Indian state of Odisha as an upshot of neoliberalism leads to the forceful displacement and impact livelihoods of Adivasis communities by the state mediation. The state developmentalism results in a chain reaction process of impoverishment, inequalities, planet of slums, gentrification and forceful assimilation of Adivasis in the emerging social structure. Adivasis resist this move, making alliances with various civil and political societies, raising the issues of livelihoods, exploitation and development intervention. Drawing from Patricia Hill Collins' Marxian notion of class and its class and indigeneity (Adivasis) intersection, the ninth chapter explores how class and class-based exploitation is reproduced in Kalinga Nagar Industrial Complex in neoliberal period. This reproduction of class and its exploitation leads to a class-based resistance movement that shapes the trajectories of state developmentalism. The chapter, based on one year of ethnographic fieldwork and case studies, explores colonial and neoliberal forms of exploitation in Kalinga Nagar. Interviews and group discussions with affected and displaced people, movement leaders, activists and other members involved in the movement were conducted during the fieldwork. Secondary sources of data such as district gazetteer and settlement reports are used to trace the colonial form of exploitation in the territory. The eleventh chapter seeks to highlight how colonial and post-colonial class-based exploitation has an important role to play in the neoliberal resistance movement in Kalinga Nagar. It illustrates collective mobilisation, demands and strategies behind and beyond the resistance movement. Further, it reflects upon how resistance movement affects the trajectories of development in Kalinga Nagar Industrial Complex. The chapter argues that Adivasis resistance not only forced the state to formulate resettlement policies, but it also has influenced the state for proper implementation of the policies. The chapter can contribute to the understanding of state developmentalism and exploitation in colonial and neoliberal places.

Land rights are quite complex zones in constitutional spaces. Property rights have been reviewed from the right to development of community, its abuse by the government by exercising the provision of eminent domain, its implications on multitude of individual rights, and conducting a time- and area-specific study to find the impact of development-induced displacement on land and livelihood. The themes the twelfth chapter will attempt to explore are, *first*, land to be an indispensable element for the fundamental right to life, even though the right to property has been eroded from the fundamental rights under the constitution of India. *Second*, it also questions the state power on eminent domain at a moral as well as the legal level. The chapter takes the social economic and political perspective for the interpretation of law and takes development-induced displacement and its impact on individual rights as the context of study. *Third*, the chapter infers that development-induced displacement being termed a 'necessary evil' is just a façade. Since land rights are so interwoven with right to life, it cannot be touched upon except with minimal disturbance to human life and dignity. The way the state exercises its prerogative of eminent domain leads to a compromise of human life and dignity. *Fourth*, the way the state exercises its power is different than the legislative debates on land rights. Hence revisiting the legislative debates will help to synchronise right to land without compromising developmental needs. The chapter explores the journey of land rights within Indian legal framework while measuring the role each of legislature, executive and judiciary in arriving at its conclusions.

The thirteenth chapter analyses a few audit reports from comptroller and auditor general of India, the constitutional audit institution dealing with the land acquisition and resettlement processes. It examines the cases where land is acquired for industrial development and subsequently allotted by State-level Industrial Development Corporations (SIDCs). India's supreme audit institute has made detailed comments on the bureaucratic deviations that constrain the safeguards available to landowners and undue favours that are granted by industrial development corporations to corporate entities. But there is a very little analysis of these audit findings by social scientists and public policy researchers. Hence this chapter will, *first*, review a few of the audit findings pertaining to West Bengal, Goa and Kerala. It also discusses at length the performance audits on land acquisition and rehabilitation policy in case of Odisha. The reports published by the comptroller and auditor general of India on the process of land acquisition and implementation of resettlement and rehabilitation has revealed serious gaps at the level of governance, but this knowledge hasn't so far entered the social action litigation literature. This chapter is written with a hope that anthropology and public policy researchers would start looking at these audits reports, which should sharpen the academic discourse on internal displacement and rehabilitation. By reviewing audit findings, this chapter tries to engage with the gap that exists between the policy and its implementation.

Concluding critical observations

First, this volume stresses the role of the state in achieving inclusive citizenship, sustainable development, addressing local resistances, etc. Garner and Zad had earlier stated that the state laws, policies and practices shape the context of a movement. The state can repress and criminalize, accept and tolerate or encourage and facilitate various forms of movement organisation, strategy and tactics. States can also sponsor quasi-movements or countermovements, foster clienteles or co-opt movements. States can even redefine the categorical identities that compromise the membership existing or potential movements (Garner and Zald, 1987: 312). While the role of the state post-1970 increased in the economy, the state was now both the guarantor of the market and also manager of the economic activities. The growth in the role of the state had multiplied the number of social actors whose existence and opportunities seemed to be linked partially to political decision-making mechanisms. The change in the role of the state had promoted the growth of collective identities; it also mobilized people around their interest, and it could also lead to their segmentation (Porta and Diani, 2006). The boundaries between insiders (i.e., policymakers) and outsiders (i.e., social movement actors and organisations) are getting fuzzy (Meyer et al., 2005: 118). To quote Porta and Della,

> State action is capable of producing collective actions in at least two ways: by fixing the territorial limits of political action (i.e. setting borders); and by facilitating or blocking the development or the growth of certain social groups – depending on the priorities of public policy, and in particular on the destination of public spending.
>
> (Porta and Diani, 2006)

Lastly, the safeguards, the plans and policies and its associated sustainable framework definitely suggest that the era of sustainable development has already begun. But the local resistances against this mining sector do convey a different story. Here one wonders the relevance of Sachs (2010) views on sustainable development. To quote,

> No development without sustainability, no sustainability without development' is the formula which establishes the newly formed bond. "Development" emerges rejuvenated from the liaison, the ailing concept gaining another lease of life. This is nothing less than the repeat of a proven ruse: every time in the last thirty years when the destructive effects of development were recognized, the concept was stretched in such a way as to include both injury and therapy. For example, when it becomes obvious, around 1970, that the pursuit of development actually intensified poverty, the notion of "equitable development" was invented so as to reconcile the irreconcilable: the creation of poverty with the abolition of poverty. In the same vein, the Brundtland Report incorporated concern for environment into the concept of development by erecting "sustainable development" as the conceptual roof for both violating and healing the environment.
>
> (Sachs, 2010: 28)

Notes

1 As per the United Nations, the seventeen goals that need to be achieved were to quote, '(i) end poverty in all forms everywhere. (ii) end hunger, achieve food security and improved nutrition and promote sustainable agriculture, (iii) Ensure health lives and promote well being for all. (iv) Ensure inclusive and equitable quality education and promote life long leaning opportunities for all. Quality Education, (v) Achieve gender equality and empower all women and girls. (vi) ensure availability and sustainable management of water and sanitation for all. (vii) ensure access to affordable reliable, sustainable and modern energy for all. (viii) promote inclusive and sustainable economic growth and decent work for all (ix) Build resilient infrastructure, promote sustainable industrialisation and foster innovation, (x) reduce inequality within and among cities (xi) make cities inclusive, safe, resilient and sustainable, (xii) ensure sustainable consumption and production patterns, (xiii) Take urgent action to combat climate change and its impact (xiv) conserve and suitably use the oceans, seas and marine resources, (xv) suitable manage Forests, combat desertification, halt and reverse land degradation, halt biodiversity loss, (xvi) promote Just, peaceful and inclusive societies, (xvii)revitalise the global

partnership for sustainable development'. These sustainable goals were listed at the United Nations website, www.un.org/sustainable development/globalpartnerships,

2 The white paper was submitted to the World Economic Forum. It's titled 'Mapping Mining to the Sustainable Development Goals: An Atlas'. The Columbia Centre on Sustainable Investment, United Nation Development Program, United Nation Sustainable Development Solution Network and the World Economic Forum jointly prepared the report. The report is available at tp://unsdsn.org/wpcontent/uploads/2016/11/Mapping_Mining_SDGs_An_Atlas.pdf.

3 The Voluntary National Review report on the implementation of sustainable development goals was presented by NITI aayog at the United Nations High-level Political Forum in 2017. The documents were downloaded from http://niti.gov.in/writereaddata/files/Final_VNR_report.pdf on 22 March 2018.

4 Source: Government of India's resolution while setting up the planning commission of the government of India Cabinet Secretariat Resolution in New Delhi, 15 March 1950.

5 National Mineral Policy. Report of the High-Level Committee. Published by Government of India, Planning Commission, New Delhi, 2006.

6 Quoted from 1/24/2009-Rc-1, Government of India, Ministry of Mines. Dated 16 December 2009. www.orissaminerals.gov.in/Download/Government_Delegation_Act.pdf. Accessed 24 March 2014 at 1.31 p.m.

References

Columbia Centre on Sustainable Investment. (2016). *Mapping Mining to the Sustainable Development Goals*. World Economic Forum.

ERM India and Ministry of Mines, Government of India. (2011). *Sustainable Development Framework for the mining sector in India – A report by the Ministry of Mines*. ERM India.

FICCI. (2013). *Development of Indian Mining Sector – The way Forward*. New Delhi: Ficci Mines and Metals Division.

Garner, R. A., & Zald, M. N. (1987). The Political Economy of Social Movement Sectors. In M. N. Zald, & M. J. D, *Social Movements in an Organizational Society: Collected Essays*. (pp. 293–318). New Brunswick, NJ: Transaction Publishers.

Meyer, D., Jennes, V., & Ingram, H. (2005). *Routing theOpposition: Social Movements, Public Policy, and Democracy,*. Minnesota: University of Minnesota Press.

Ministry of Human Resource Development, Government of India. (2016,). *Constitutional Provision*. Retrieved March 23, 2020 from Constitutional Provision, Governmnet of India, Ministry of Human Resource Development: https://mhrd.gov.in/directive_principles_of_state_policy_article-39

Ministry of Law and Justice, Government of India. (1985). *THE LAND ACQUISITION ACT, 1894 (As modified up to the Ist September, 1985)*. New Delhi: Ministry of Law and Justice.

Ministry of Mines, Government of India. (2005). *Mineral Concession Rules, 1960 (As amended up to 26th July, 2012)*. Nagpur: Controller General, Indian Bureau of Mines.

Ministry of Rural Development, Government of India. (2007). *The National Rehabilitation and Resettlement Policy, 2007*. Department of Land Resources, Land Reforms Division. New Delhi: Ministry of Rural Development.

Ministry of Rural Development, Government of India. (2014). *Right to Fair Compensation and Transparency in Land Acquisition, Rehabilitation and Resettlement*

(Social Impact Assessment and Consent) Rules, 2014. Department of Land Resources. New Delhi: Ministry of Rural Development.

NITI Aayog. (2017). *Voluntary National Review Report on the implementation of Sustainable Development Goals*. New Delhi: Niti Aayog.

Planning Commission, Governmnet of India. (2006). *National Mineral policy Report of the High Level Committee*. Delhi: Government of India.

Polanyi, K. (1944). *The Great Transformation*. New York: Farrar and Rinehart.

Porta, D. D., & Diani, M. (2006). *Social Movements: An Introduction, 2nd Edition*. USA: Wiley-Blackwell.

Sachs, W. (2010). *The Development Dictionary. A Guide to Knowledge as Power*. London: Zed Books.

United Nations. (1972). *Declaration of the United Nations Conference on the Human Environment,*. Stockholm: United Nations.

United Nations. (1992). *Report of the United Nations Conference on Environment and Development (Rio de Janeiro, 3–14 June 1992)*. United Nations Publication.

United Nations. (2015). *The sustainable Development Agenda*. Retrieved March 23, 2020 from Sustainable Development Goals: https://www.un.org/sustainabledevelopment/development-agenda/

World Commission on Envionment and Development. (1987). *Our Common Future*. Oxford University Press.

Part I

Development, displacement and dispossession

Macro Perspectives

2 When I listened to the voices of development communities

Sujit Kumar Mishra

Introduction

I met Mr Thibu, a victim of an Ultra Mega Power Plant in Odisha located in the district of Sundargarh, sometime in February 2015. He was appointed as a temporary child caretaker at the district magistrate's house. When asked, he revealed that he had left the job long ago and now owns Rs. 27,00,000. Out of that huge amount of money, he has saved Rs. 4,00,000 for his daughters' marriage and also has bought a new two-wheeler for his wife. He told me he had enough money to spend his life lavishly; he could afford any kind of food and drinks. On inquiring further, I got to know that he received Rs. 27,00,000 as compensation for the land he left for the Ultra Mega Power Plant Project. The second case is of Mr Thakur, a temple priest who happened to be a victim of the same project. He received quite a handsome amount as compensation for the loss of his land. He planned to marry his girl off in a grand ceremony. They are the people, however, with a first stage of monetary economy (where the mode of exchange is solely money) who are basically under the illusion/spell of economic prosperity much before actually entering into such a category. Without having sound ideas about the quantum of compensation received from the state, being victims of 'Demonstration Effect', these people spent the money in unproductive ways. The examples depicted are the actors of the so-called development process. Mathur (1995) calls them 'development refugees'. The practice of putting the development communities[1] 'alone' continues to be a reality in India despite strong institutional interventions to prevent such issues. Within this backdrop, I started the chapter to describe a path of these actors in different stages (described through different issues) of the development process and the regulatory mechanisms available for their interest. The rest of the chapter is followed by the historical context of regulatory mechanisms available to address the issue of development-induced displacement. The third section deals with a detailed section on study areas and methodology. Subsequently an overview of different important issues like land and politics of land compensation, political economy of compensation, livelihood, the issue of agitation, externalities, accidents and mining closures are discussed. The last section refers to a summary and conclusion.

Historical context and regulatory framework

'Development' and 'Making Development Happen' consists of different stages: First Stage (identification of place, cost-benefit analysis, land acquisition, displacement and rehabilitation); Second Stage (externalities in the form of livelihood, agriculture, health and accident, etc.); and Third Stage (closure in case of mining project and the issue of livelihood). A link can be established in these three stages only through the development communities. In each and every stage, the issue is different, but the actor is the same. Each stage has its own importance in the development process.

While talking about the first stage, it is a notable fact that the institutional mechanisms such as Land Acquisition Act and Rehabilitation Policy are there to address only to the people who lose their lands, whereas ignoring a large number of livelihood losers (Mishra, 2011). It is a key feature of the Land Acquisition Act that it empowers the state to acquire private land when required and to compensate the owner of the land for the involuntary acquisition. However, as a matter of great concern, the Land Act creates a distinction between two categories of people: those who reside on a private land and those who reside on a common or state-owned land. Tribal and landless people happen to come under the latter category. These people, the landless and tribal, generally are highly dependent upon the village commons, forest and forest products and shifting agriculture to earn a living. Apart from this, the large landholders employ these landless people on their lands on wages. Thus, it makes a sense that these landless people, either directly or indirectly, earn their living from land, similarly as the displaced people in the former category do. Thukral (1988)'s work on Narmada Dam project clearly stated about the ignorance of the displaced people about the quantity and quality of land to be acquired for the dam. To this, underestimation and incorrect information about them by the project authority added more vulnerability to their lives. Sharma (1986) also put a question on the rehabilitation measures made for the persons displaced by dam projects in India.

The next stage, or second stage, basically deals with the externalities in the forms of agriculture, health, livelihood and accident. In particular, it is the development communities (i.e., affected/displaced people) receiving the negative externalities/impacts in terms of ill health (Mishra, 2009, 2015), loss of valuable production of food grain and problems in finding a suitable employment (Mishra and Pujari, 2008; Mishra, 2012). There is hardly any scope for these communities in the established institutional mechanisms to address their issues. A study of Mishra and Mishra (2014) sheds light on the mining accidents and the consequent death of people in Mahanadi Coal Field Limited (MCL) of Odisha. The people in the locality (mining communities) are not only badly affected in terms of health, but also uprooted and lose their livelihood due to the poor management of such mines. There is a scope for a member of each agricultural land losing family to get a job in the rehabilitation policy of the mining authority. This idea of job allocation to a member of the affected family leaves the others in the family to be dependents since they neither own a piece of land nor have a job for themselves. There is another group of people who were landless before, but they started working on those patches of land, and unfortunately those lands are also acquired now. So in the face of nonavailability of other livelihood options for these communities, they have taken to an immediate alternative, i.e., collecting coal. The Indian Mines Act, 1952, stipulates some guidelines for the health and safety of the workers. However, the act does not give any reference to the people (especially mining communities) residing in the vicinity of the mines. On the face of any accident/death met by an employee of the mines, one of the family members of him/her is offered the job. However, the only possible mechanism available for these villagers is an *ex gratia* amount.

Apart from this, an important issue (third stage) which has not received proper concern over a period of time in India is 'mining closure and the issue of livelihood' in India. It is the mining communities who suffer a lot due to the closure as they derive their livelihood from it directly or indirectly. Also the local economy in the vicinity area largely depends on the mining activities. Hence, mine closure affects the communities in a large number of ways. Government of India's National Policy, 1993,[2] and subsequently the new National Mineral Policy, 2008,[3] emphasizes the issue of rehabilitation and mine closure. Both these polices are not silent about the mining communities (though they mentioned very less about the 'dependent communities'). Nevertheless the guideline to conduct the mine closure is almost silent about the 'dependent communities' or 'mining communities'. Largely it can be said that the institutional frameworks should give more rooms to the mining communities, as these are the people who always bear the cost where the other group shares the benefit of development. These are the communities who suffer in two different stages: first during the land acquisition for establishment of the project and second during the closure of the project. Basically these communities are the net losers of the development process.

Study area and methodology

The study is based on three different stages for collation of information: (a) primary fieldwork; (b) collection of information like reports, awards of land acquisition officers, various investigative reports and magazines from time to time; and (c) discussions with officials and local leaders from the field area and focus-group discussions with people. The information presented in the present chapter is from six different projects of Odisha, selected on the basis of different issues, i.e., (i) land and politics of compensation from two irrigation projects (Rengali Dam and Harabhangi Project of Odisha); (ii) politics of agitation from a power plant project (Ultra Mega Power Plant, Odisha); (iii) externalities in terms of health and agriculture from one mining project (MCL, Basundhara and Odisha); (iv) accident from one mining project (MCL, Garjanbahal and Odisha); and (v) mine closure and the issue of livelihood from a lead mines (Hindustan Zinc Limited [HZL], Sargipalli and Odisha).

Findings of the study

Land and politics of compensation

Since large sections of people rely on their agricultural land, either directly or indirectly, to earn their living, it serves a major part in the rural economy. Nevertheless, the doctrine of 'eminent domain' makes it possible for the state to acquire any kind of private land for public purpose (Ramanathan, 2011). On one hand, compensation is the only possible option available for the land losers; on the other, the state keeps silent on the issue of livelihood losers. We have a clear distinction here categorizing[4] the people into the following types: (i) household possessing land with legal right; (ii) people possessing land without legal right; (iii) tenant households; and (iv) landless households. So far as the issue of compensation concerned, the Land Acquisition Act addresses only the first category of people. The act is completely silent about the rest. In order to identify the issue of land and politics of compensation, two case studies are taken from two major irrigation projects in Odisha, namely Rengali Dam and Harabhangi Project.

Political economy of compensation

With regard to the payment of compensation in Rengali Dam, agricultural lands in the submersible villages are divided into seven different categories, taking into consideration the factors like geographical situation, quality and level of the land, productive capacity, moisture retention capacity, etc. (Government of Orissa, 1978; Mishra, 2002).[5] The classification is made on the basis of crop production in different cropping seasons—Kharif and Rabi. They are Sarad (1, 2 and 3); Goda (1, 2 and 3); and Patita. Some years ago, people grew paddy in the Sarad varieties land, and the Goda land was meant for the Rabi crops. The last category of land, i.e., Patita, is not suitable for any kind of cultivation.

The Land Acquisition Act, 1894, provides that the compensation for the loss of a piece of land can be made according to its market value, which is purely based on the sale deed of the land. There was no sale deed available for the ousted of the Rengali Dam project. So the second-best possible option was to determine the compensation amount according to the market value of the annual yield of paddy. There was again another problem in this. There were no reliable figures of annual yield of paddy for different types of land available. So the figures of normal annual yield for different types of land supplied by the Bureau of Statistics and Economics were decided to be taken to fix the market value in an arbitrary way. From our conversation with the displaced, we got to know that more than 80 per cent of people had no knowledge of the land-valuation process. Even more, the displaced were not allowed to enter the negotiation process so they could ensure a good bargain for their lost lands.

Table 2.1 offers an overview of the land acquired and the trend of compensation paid to the affected people. One common issue here to be noticed is that in each and every old village, besides rayati land (the private land over which there is legal ownership), people enjoyed the benefits of ample amount of government-encroached land. Old villages used to have more common properties. Common property resources were not entitled to any compensation. However, in the present times, there is a considerable loss of common properties in comparison to the pre-displacement situation owing to the new resettlement colonies.

The government norm provides that the chief source for land revenue (LR) is the rent of 'rayati' land. The collection of LR was a special feature of Rengali Dam. The same collection was inclusive of the compensation head. The land acquisition officer had sent the estimate of revenue of the land for 25 years of the rayati land, which got submerged due to the construction of this dam. After the sanction of the amount, the land acquisition collector deducted the amount under LR head from the compensation and deposited the amount at the nearest treasury in favour of LR. The amount was later transferred to the Revenue Department.

Furthermore, there was a huge time gap between the date of land acquisition and final date of payment in both the case study areas. Even more, there is a more shocking part in the Land Acquisition Act. The act states that a person is supposed to stop all productive activities on the land on receipt of the 4 (1) notification. This period of frictional unemployment, the period between the 4 (1) notification and the shift period are too hard for the displaced people to imagine their livelihood. Therefore, this is the only reason they spend all their compensation money on consumption as the marginal propensity to consume of the poor people is more.

Politics of 'land for land' as compensation

The rehabilitation policy approved by the state of Odisha cannot be denounced completely (Mishra, 2005). It treats all the affected people equally. On account of Rengali Dam construction, the suffered people (irrespective of loss of land or livelihood) have been distributed homestead land of 0.50 acre each. The best part of it is that the house site areas of all the people have increased to a large extent. People used 0.05 to 0.10 acre to build their houses, and the rest parts were being used as kitchen gardens. According to the government norms, out of 0.50 acre, 0.02 acre is tax-free.

Table 2.1 Land Acquisition and the Quantum of Compensation to the Displaced People of Rengali Dam

S. No	*New village*	*Old village*	*Total land acquired (acre)*	*Encroached land (acre)*	*Land identified for compensation by the government (acre)*			*Land revenue for 1 year (Rs.)*	*Land revenue for 25 years (Rs.)*	*Total compensation (Rs.)*
					Rayati land	*Settable encroachment*	*Total*			
1	Siding	Old Siding	502.79	351.65	151.14	10.52	161.66	760	19001	12,70,183
2	Chargachia	Banar	1925.69	1580.39	345.30	98.03	443.33	1437	35947	18,22,195
3	Pendrakhole	Ranjabahal	NA	NA	260.66	73.67	366.95	807	20177	23,13,489
		Gambhariposhi	193.34	166.41	26.93	16.39	43.32	65.04	1626	2,70,770
4	Badadangaghat	Kandsor	1258.45	985.33	273.12	–	273.12	457	11446	23,26,049
5	Barkotia	Bahadaposhi	825.13	547.74	277.30	16.37	293.76	1250	31265	17,32,116
		Jharkilinda	256.01	–	256.01	–	256.01	899.59	22489	16,86,347
		Susulei	NA	NA	164.64	59.33	223.97	964	24106	13,14,369
6	Bhaliadihi	Kesala	821.95	520.31	301.64	89.61	391.25	782.96	19574	25,26,921
		Jharaihi	752.38	493.29	259.09	75.65	334.74	504.56	12614	13,86,617
		Kousalibahal	NA	NA	149.01	140.01	389.51	853.40	21335	28,50,667
		Jandadihi	325.75	NA	NA	NA	325.75	NA	NA	5,64,715

Source: Government of Orissa (1983)

In some cases, the homestead land is distributed into three to four different plots (Government of Orissa, 2000). If such is the case, people's suffering worsens, having one plot located inside the village and another near the forest or the hills. So people cannot concentrate more on those lands.

Another major issue in the policy is the provision of reclaimed agricultural land. Each family where land has been acquired for the project could be provided with either three acres of reclaimed irrigated land or six acres of reclaimed un-irrigated land. The average legal landholding of the displaced people increased from 3.85 to 4.34 acres (Mishra, 2005). Though the average landholding increased tremendously on account of the implementation of this policy, the operational landholdings decreased because these lands were highly infertile in nature and were provided by cutting reserve forest. Now, even after 30 years of displacement, they are still unable to cultivate the whole land. Out of six acres, people cultivate in three to three-and-a-half acres. A large number of people were found unhappy with the quality of land they were offered in compensation. Scattered land has added to the vulnerability of displaced people, consequently adding to their plights. In some of the resettlement colonies, the number of patches has even increased to seven (table 2.2). Hence, a single cultivator cannot pay his/her full attention on all the patches of land in one cultivating season.

Yet another most important issue is the provision of irrigated land as compensation. Irrigated lands are divided into two broad categories: (i) irrigated head and (ii) irrigated tail. While irrigated head areas are situated adjacent to the canal, irrigated tail areas are much farther away from the canal and, in most cases, at the end part of the canals. While the irrigated head areas are suitable for both Rabi and Kharif crops, irrigated tail areas are suitable only for Rabi crops. But in classification of irrigated and un-irrigated land, both the types of villages (irrigated head and irrigated tail) are coming under irrigated villages. However, the numbers of resettlement colonies nearer to the irrigated head area are very fewer. On the contrary, most of the colonies are situated nearer to the irrigated tail areas. Here, discrimination is quite evident with regard to the irrigated tail village, as these villages are more

Table 2.2 Distribution of Land in the Resettlement Colonies

S. No	*Name of the study villages*	*Maximum number patches of land distributed (number)*
1	Badadangaghat (I)	07
2	Pendrakhole (I)	06
3	Bhaliadihi (I)	06
4	Siding (UI)	05
5	Chargachia (UI)	07
6	Barkotia (UI)	06

Source: Field Work; I: Irrigated; UI: Un-irrigated

or less the same as the villages, where people have received six acres of unirrigated land as compensation. Therefore, on average, these people lose three acres of land each. In this context, the issues of equity (Singh et al., 2000) and intergenerational equity (Wood, 2011) can be questioned for the welfare of the development communities.

Livelihood: a gender glance

Joblessness is one of the major factors which has been heavily responsible for the impoverishment of the displaced people because due to acquisition of land and displacement of people, there is tremendous loss of employment opportunities (Ota, 1996; Cernea, 1997). In this study, to assess as to what extent joblessness has affected the impoverishment of the displaced people in the relocated sites has been examined by taking four indicators. The detail is given in table 2.3.

Alternatively the same exercise has been tried in the present study with a special reference to gender. The reduced number of days of work from over 180 days to 160 days is the major change in women's work lives. The workplace distance was also increased on average from two to six kilometers. Though the wages are paid in time, they are not matching to those of men (table 2.4).

Table 2.3 Status of Livelihood in Harabhangi Irrigation Project

S. No	*Parameters*	*Status*	
		Before	*After*
1	Average number of days a man gets work	300 days	300 days
2	Per cent of households cultivating their own land	92.5	3.0
3	Per cent of households engaged in unskilled wage work	–	31.7
4	Farm wage earners	27.0	0.9

Source: Field Work

Table 2.4 Status of Livelihood in Harabhangi Irrigation Project with a Gender Glance

S. No	*Parameters*	*Status*	
		Before	*After*
1	Average number of days a woman gets work	> 180 days	160 days
2	Average distance of workplace in kilometres	02	06
4	Women are paid on time	Yes	Yes
5	Women get wage rate equal with male	No	No

Source: Field Work

The issue of agitation and development projects

Agitation is an integral part of any development intervention. The trend of agitation is very common in the available literature on development-induced displacement in India (Saxena, 2009; Baboo, 1991; Supakar, 2004; Nath and Agrawal, 1987; Oza, 1997; Rao, 2006; Banerjee, 2006). My personal observations, along with interviews conducted with different categories of people, led to the conclusion of this important issue, conducted through an explorative survey carried out in the Ultra Mega Power Plant in Sundargarh District of Odisha.

The major development projects in India, like the construction of big dams, are known for development-induced conflicts; appropriation of lands and displacement of settlements lead to disputes between the stakeholders, and sometimes it results in mobilisation of local people for protests and agitations. Hirakud, Rengali, Narmada, Polavaram, Vedanta movement, Ultra Mega Power Plant and Kalinganagar are some of the instances widely known for such conflicts. The problems concerning the rehabilitation policies and compensation to the affected people (likely to be) serve as the highlights of these protests and agitations. Moreover, there are certain issues related to the implementation, monitoring, transparency (sharing of information at the grassroots level) and decision-making power at various levels of the project.

The construction of Ultra Mega Power Plant[6] with a capacity of 4,000 megawatts in Odisha (in Sundargarh district) was also not an exception to the agitation history against large development projects of the state of Odisha. In this case, though the project authority conducted three consecutive gram sabhas to discuss the objectives of the project, rehabilitation policy and the land acquisition, nothing was discussed during any of the gram sabha sessions. The people to be displaced were confused about the Rehabilitation Policy, 2006, of the government of Odisha (Government of Orissa, 2006). However, a few people raised questions regarding their entitlements during the agitation, their eligibility in getting shares in the plant, the process of land valuation, etc. They demanded a written assurance from the district administration for providing employment to the affected people. Two major issues emerged from those discussions on agitation: (i) asymmetry of information between two agents (in this case, between the project authority and the development communities) and (ii) skewed participation of the development communities in the bargaining process. Beginning from the Hirakud Dam until the construction of Ultra Mega Power Plant, a number of considerable issues puzzled the development communities: (i) what is compensation? (ii) who will receive compensation? (iii) who will decide the amount of compensation? (iv) how much will the amount of compensation be? (v) why will the state offer compensation for the betterment of others?

Externalities[7] *and the development communities*

Agriculture[8]

Despite coal mines earning huge revenue for the country, the implementation of these mines in the rural areas has a large number of externalities. The two very important externalities are in the form of reduced agricultural production and the issue of ill health. The result is based on the data collected from a sample of 140 households of 3 mining villages and 52 households from 1 non-mining village in MCL, Basundhara, Odisha.

Impact on agriculture

The Basundhara coal mining area has primarily been an agrarian economy. A majority of people derive their livelihood from agriculture and some of them from livestock. After the establishment of the mine, there has been a gradual shift from agriculture to nonagricultural activities in the mining villages. Rice is the dominant crop in both types of surveyed villages. The area under rice crop constitutes nearly 73.8 to 89.1 per cent in these villages. The production of paddy per acre of land is 6.3 quintals in the mining villages and 9.2 quintals in non-mining villages. In mining villages, one notices significant decline in production of paddy. Compared to 2001 (before mining started), the current year production levels are 60.6 per cent and 98.7 per cent, respectively, in mining and non-mining villages, showing 29.4 per cent production loss in the mining villages. At the level of cultivating households, the loss of production is 100 per cent for more than 28.6 per cent cultivators in mining villages, whereas in non-mining villages it is found to be nil (table 2.5). The main reason is the deposition of coal dust on the vegetation, which prevents proper growth of the crops.

Area under cultivation shows that now agriculture is not an important activity in the mining villages. And the yield per acre shows the losses are substantial (as it is 9.2 quintal in non-mining villages and 6.3 quintal in the mining villages). Hence the difference in yield between these two types of villages

Table 2.5 Extent of Production in the Study Villages

S. No	*Detail*	*Villages*	
		Mining	*Non-mining*
1	Percentage of paddy area	73.8	89.1
2	Average production of paddy per acre	6.3	9.2
3	Percentage of current year production to before mining production	60.6	98.7
4	Percentage of households with 100 per cent loss	28.6	Nil

Source: Field Survey

is found to be 2.9 quintals. The market value of one quintal of paddy is around Rs. 850. So the loss of income in mining villages is Rs. 2465 per acre.

Impact on livestock and animal husbandry

Livestock rearing was considered an important livelihood opportunity of the people staying in the vicinity of Basundhra coal mine, as it used to support by providing additional income for most of the villagers. The climate and topography were suitable for this livestock to sustain in these areas.

The respondents reported about the possession of livestock, especially cows, buffaloes, goats and poultry, 'before mining' and 'after mining' scenario. There is an adverse impact found in the case of cows and buffaloes due to pollution of mining activities. This situation is more precarious in the case of possession of goats and poultry. The dependence of landless, marginal and, to a certain extent, the small households on animals like goat and poultry for supporting their livelihood in the vital stage are evident from the composition of this livestock. These huge impacts can be attributed to two factors: (i) coal dust on all the green vegetation for which they are suffering from digestion problem and (ii) livestock forced to drink contaminated water from sources like river, ponds and borewells. The net impact of all these factors leads to massive death of livestock.

Impact on health

A large number of people complained that they have suffered from many waterborne diseases like skin diseases, arthritis and joint pains. However, a majority of them is airborne like eye allergy, malaria, cold, fever, etc. In the control village, the main health problems are fever and malaria. Consumption of water has a direct relation to human disease. It is water, which can cause some diseases within a human body. Following suggestions from a hydrologist and a geologist,[9] water samples were taken from only one mining village, as the results will not vary among these three study villages given their similar physical nature to verify the level of pollution.

Table 2.6 presents an outcome of the water samples tested at the National Institute of Technology Laboratory of Rourkela, Odisha. Here in all the cases, the test outcomes are found to be more than the normal range in the mining village. An imbalanced P^H has been observed in the water used by the households of mining villages. An imbalanced P^H affects all cellular activity in the body, leading to the development of degenerative diseases.[10] In samples taken from the borewell, almost all the parameters show above-normal range, indicating severe pollution level in the groundwater[11] due to coal mining pollution in the mining village, which is a resettlement colony for the displaced people of MCL, Basundhara.[12] People perceived the hard nature of water, which very much has an impact of the higher alkalinity value appearing from the water sample in the mining village. Digestion problems are very

Table 2.6 Water Samples in Mining and Non-Mining Villages of the Study Area

Village	*Water sample*	*P^H^*	*Electrical conductivity (mho/m)*	*Total dissolved solids (mg/l)*	*Alkalinity (mg/l)*	*Total hardness (mg/l)*	*Calcium (mg/l)*	*Magnesium (mg/l)*	*Arsenic (mcg/l)*
	Normal Range[13]	*6.8–7.5*	*0.005–0.05 (mho/m)*	*500 mg/l*	*75*	*60–180*	*60 mg/l*	*14 mg/l*	*0.05*
Tikilipara (Mining)	**Borewell**	6.616	881×10^{-6}	746.7	98.7	196	123.3	2	0.004
	Pond	6.55	185×10^{-6}	104.8	67.5	49	24.14	72.8	0.004
	Open Well	6.664	218×10^{-6}	117.7	105.3	84	63.2	23.9	0.006
Tihuria (Non-mining)	**Borewell**	6.144	439×10^{-6}	268.1	87.6	98	62.4	46.5	0.023
	Pond	7.24	217×10^{-6}	104.5	85	48	46.4	4.7	0.035
	Open Well	6.432	582×10^{-6}	331.2	52.1	123	76.5	1.6	0.012

Source: National Institute of Technology Laboratory, Rourkela, Odisha

much correlated with the hard nature of water. Interestingly, the borewell and pond sample from the control village has also revealed high alkalinity.

Mining and accident

This case study is based on an accident that took place in the Basundhra-Garjanbahal area of Sundargarh district of Odisha. In this accident, 14 people belonging to development communities were killed as a result of the sudden collapse at the Kulda Open-Cast Coal Mine (Mishra and Mishra, 2014). The deceased people were the members of the development communities, living in the vicinity of the mining areas. They used to derive their livelihood by collecting small pieces of coal from the overburden and selling it to the people for their private consumption. They were the mining-affected people and lost their livelihood on the land acquisition of the MCL, Basundhara-Garjanbahal area.

Odisha's experience with MCL authorities can be used to highlight some of these issues. It has been pointed out that MCL did not accept the victims as their workers, thereby excluding many mining workers from availing themselves of the benefits distributed through settlements that evolved from different institutional mechanisms. During the process of settlement, the management claimed that they had been warning people against getting closer to the dump, but the local people and activists denied this and pointed that there was neither any notice nor any mark or fence erected to prevent local people from entering the dump yard. Besides this, it was also brought out to notice that both height and slope of the dump exceeded the permitted limit and that the slope was found extremely steep and dangerous. This was a threat to the lives of local people who regularly went to the dump yard to collect coal. It has been noticed that the local people – who got displaced and lost their land, homes and livelihood without being left with any other alternatives – were not informed about this hazardous place, and the concerned authorities failed in managing the risks involved in the place.

This example of Odisha highlights several issues related to the way the risk was poorly managed and the cost incurred on common people. Thus, poor people were forced to bear the cost of development in terms of the negative externalities of mining activities such as polluting the water and air, noise pollution, health degradation, loss of agricultural production, livelihood and displacement were rarely taken into account. Hence, present benefits of development will become costly and unsustainable at the cost of other resources/communities and future generations.

Mining closure and the development communities

This case study has been conducted in the closed lead mines called HZL Sargipalli of the state of Odisha. The results based on data collected from a sample of 500 different types of stakeholders of Hindustan Zinc Limited, Sargipalli, of the state of Odisha, India, of 24 mining villages. On the basis of the collated information such as secondary data and reports, different stakeholders at primary level and interviews with direct and indirect employees of the mine, these show negative impact of closure in terms of decreased purchasing power of the people and underemployment (e.g., a skilled labour working as a daily wage earner). The middle- and upper-age group people are commuting from their villages in search of livelihood and largely became the victims of vulnerability. The major impact is found to be on the losses of livelihood of small businesses like cycle-repairing shops, grocery shops, weekly market and hotels. The chapter also gives an indication of a special voluntary retirement scheme (VRS) of the employees which was a conspiracy, and some middlemen were confusing the common man. These particular development communities were the victim of development in two different ways, first the acquisition of land and second the closure of the project. The closing down of mining activities influenced the local economy adversely. The weekly market was the biggest market of the area. The purchasing power of the people decreased because of the closure of the mining activities. People took loan under different schemes implemented by the government and produced lots of milk for their livelihood. However, the sudden closure made them vulnerable as they could not repay the loan properly. Due to lack of proper care, the cattle also died after some time, and they entered into an interlocked credit market. Many more migrated to Goa to get engaged in fishing, and the other migrated to Gujarat to work in textile industries and remain there for six to seven months. The government schemes meant for people are not properly implemented.

Conclusion

Through this chapter, I tried to portray multifaceted issues associated with the other side of development, though development is intended for growth of the country. The multifaceted issues discussed in this present chapter through different case studies are (i) land acquisition; (ii) political economy of compensation; (iii) agitation; (iv) livelihood; (iv) externalities in the form of agriculture and health; (v) accident and finally (vi) closure. The thread, which connects all these issues, is the development community as it features in the entire discussion. In this backdrop, a simple question can be raised: who is a sustainable development community? In this context, one can think about the concept of 'equity' and 'intergenerational equity' to make a simple development community into a sustainable development community. Equity is nothing but equality in terms of quality of life and standard of living (in an egalitarian manner) whereas intergenerational equity is sustaining the equality in the future in the changed environment, i.e., nobody will be worse off because of a change. Let's see the development community, which features prominently in this discussion and their status of sustainability.

To start with the issue of compensation and land, a larger proportion of the people who did not have land were not a part of the compensation process. Those were basically the scheduled tribe and the landless communities. However, evidence is there where some of the economically sound people (generally the land-cultivating caste called 'Chasa') went to the court and claimed compensation for change of business[14] to a new place, and very surprisingly, the court sanctioned Rs. 15,000 in favour of the petitioners. At this crucial process, where just compensation is the backbone of the resettlement process, the study finds the separation of equity from the entire regulatory mechanism. The same trend has been observed in all the issues, e.g., agriculture, health, livelihood, accident and closure. Nevertheless in the post-constitution era, the activities in terms of act, policy and schemes have increased. The material and intellectual investment are also found to have increased. But the outcome is not satisfactory since the status of the development communities has not been changing as expected. They are still the same as they were 60 years ago. In the entire process, the study finds a weaker link between the community and the state in terms of participation in the development process, the capacity to negotiate with the state to determine the level of acceptance, etc. Hence, there is a need to create a system which will negotiate with the state by exploring how community perception and concerns reflect in the development policy in India and what mechanisms need to be evolved to make the current policies sustainable with emphasis on social justice and equity.

Notes

1 Development community is that community who always pay the cost of development. For example, these are the people thrown from their habitats when the development projects are land-based (largely irrigation projects); in case of mining projects, they are the one who receives cost in the form of externalities: agriculture, health and livelihood (Mishra 2007). Veiga et al. (2001) call them as mining community and define them 'as a community where the population is significantly affected by a nearby mining operation'.

2 National Mineral Policy, 2008, (for non-fuel and non-coal minerals) Government of India, Ministry of Mines http://mines.nic.in/writereaddata/Content/88753b05_NMP2008[1].pdf. Accessed 15 August 2015.

3 Ibid. Accessed 15 August 2015.

4 See Reddy (1992).

5 Also available in http://ir.inflibnet.ac.in:8080/jspui/handle/10603/1503/browse?type=author&order=ASC&rpp=20&value=Mishra%2C+Sujit+Kumar. Accessed 15 August 2015.

6 See Akundy and Mishra (2012).

7 Externality is defined as third-party (or spill-over) effects arising from the production and/or consumption of goods and services for which no appropriate compensation is paid. Externalities cause market failure if the price mechanism does not take into account the full social costs and social benefits of production and consumption. Externality may be positive or negative. For detail, see Mishra (2012b).

8 For detail, see Mishra (2012b).
9 See Mishra (2012a, 2012b).
10 See http://avalonhealthinfo.com/articles/acid-water-may-be-harmful-to-your-health.html. Accessed 9 January 2012.
11 See Reddy and Behera (2006) on water pollution in the industrial belt of Andhra Pradesh.
12 See Mishra (2012) for a detailed discussion on coal mine externality and water pollution.
13 See Reddy and Behera (2006).
14 Land Acquisition Case No. 52, Court of the Civil Judge, 4 May 1999.

References

Akundy, A. and S. K. Mishra. (2012). People's Responses to the State Policies of Resettlement–The Case of Ultra Mega Power Plant in Orissa. *Journal of Socio-Economic Development*, vol. 14, no. 2, pp. 202–214.

Baboo, Balgovind. (1991). State Policies and People's Response: Lessons from Hirakud Dam. *Economic and Political Weekly*, vol. 26, no. 41, pp. 2373–2379.

Banerjee, P. (2006). Land Acquisition and Peasant Resistance at Singur. *Economic and Political Weekly*, vol. 41, no. 46, pp. 4718–4719.

Cernea, M. M. (1997). The Risks and Reconstruction Model for Resettling Displaced Populations. *World Development*, vol. 25, no. 10, 1569–1587.

Government of Orissa. (1978). *BahumukhiJatiyaYojana, Rengali Dam Project*. Cuttack: Government of Orissa Press.

Government of Orissa. (1983). *Valuation of Land*. Sambalpur: Office of Land Acquisition, Rengali Project.

Government of Orissa. (2000). *Land Acquisition Status in Rengali Dam*. Orissa: Rengali Dam Site.

Government of Orissa. (2006). Orissa Resettlement and Rehabilitation Policy, 2006. *The Orissa Gazette*, no. 651, Baisakha 25, 1928.

Mathur, H. M. (1995). *Development, Displacement and Resettlement: Focus on Asian Experiences*. New Delhi: Vikas Publishing House Private Limited.

Mishra, P. P. (2007). *Resource Extraction Externalities: A Socio-Economic Analysis of Coal Mining in Orissa*. Ph. D Thesis, University of Hyderabad, India.

Mishra, P. P. and S. K. Mishra. (2014). Coal Mining and Local Livelihoods. *Economic and Political Weekly*, vol. 49, no. 8, pp. 25–26.

Mishra, P. P. and A. K. Pujari. (2008). Impact of Mining on Agricultural Productivity: A Case Study of the Indian State of Orissa. *South Asia Economic Journal*, vol. 9, no. 2, pp. 337–350.

Mishra, S. K. (2002). *Development and Displacement: A Case Study of Rengali Dam in Orissa, India*. Ph. D Thesis, University of Hyderabad, India.

Mishra, S. K. (2005). Impact of Rehabilitation Policy and Low Crop Yield: A Case Study of Rengali Dam in Orissa, India. *Economic and Political Weekly*, vol. 40, no. 60, pp. 2688–2691.

Mishra, S. K. (2009). *Estimation of externality costs of electricity generation from coal: An OH-Market extension dissertation*. PhD thesis, The Ohio State University, United States of America.

Mishra, S. K. (2011). Compulsory Land Acquisition in Orissa: Policy and Praxis. In S. Choudhry, V. Dhagamwar, J. M. Kujur, R. Mangalekar, P. P. Mishra (Eds.),

Development-Induced Displacement, Rehabilitation and Resettlement in India: Current Issues and Challenges. Abingdon, Oxon: Routledge, pp. 75–90.

Mishra, S. K. (2012). Coal Mining Externalities: A Study of Basundhara Coal Field of India. *Hyderabad Social Development Papers*, vol. 1, no. 1, pp. 1–28.

Mishra, S. K. (2015). Putting Value to Human Health in Coal Mining Region of India. *Journal of Health Management*, vol. 17, no. 3, 339–355.

Nath, G. B. and K. S. Agrawal. (1987). *Politics of Agitation Against Rengali Dam Project: A Case Study*. ISSC Seminar. Orissa: Sambalpur University.

National Mineral Policy 2008 (For non – fuel and non – coal minerals) Government of India, Ministry of Mines. http://mines.nic.in/writereaddata/Content/88753b05_NMP2008[1].pdf. Accessed 15 August 2015.

Ota, A. B. (1996). Countering the Impoverishment Risk: The case of Rengali Dam Project. In A. B. Ota and A. Agnihotri (Eds.), *Involuntary Displacement in Dam Projects*. New Delhi: Prachi Prakashan.

Oza, N. (1997). Marginalisation, Protests and Political Action- Tribal and Sardar Sarovar Project. *Economic and Political Weekly*, vol. 32, no. 29, pp. 1790–1793.

Ramanathan, U. (2011). Land Acquisition, Eminent Domain and the 2011 Bill. *Economic and Political Weekly*, vol. 46, no. 44–45, pp. 10–14.

Rao, K. N. (2006). Integral to State's Good. In B. Gujja, S. Ramakrishna, V. Goud and Sivaramakrishna (Eds.), *Perspectives on Polavaram A Major Irrigation Project on Godavari*. New Delhi: Academic Foundation.

Reddy, K. M. (1992). *Some Aspect of Rehabilitation Policy of the State Government with Reference to Major Irrigation Projects: A Case Study of Sriramsagar and Srisailam*. Ph. D Thesis, Kakatiya University, India.

Reddy, V. R. and B. Behera. (2006). Impact of Water Pollution on Rural Communities: An Economic Analysis. *Ecological Economics*, vol. 58, pp. 520–537.

Saxena, K. B. (2009). *Swelling Displacement and Elusive Rehabilitation Deficits in Policy Interventions*. New Delhi: Council for Social Development.

Sharma, N. K. (1986). Large Dams: A Necessary Developmental Choice. *Bhagirathi*, vol. 33, no. 2, pp. 55–65.

Singh, Sekhar, R. Meheta, V. Uppal, A. Kabra, B. Taneja and P. Rao. (2000). *Environmental and Social Impacts of Large Dams, the Indian Experience*. New Delhi: Indian Institute of Public Administration.

Supakar, K. (2004). *Itihaasra Parihaas* (Oriya) First Part. Sambalpur, Orissa.

Thukral, E. G. (1988). Dams: For Whose Development. *Social Action*, vol. 38, no. 3, pp. 211–230.

Veiga, M. M., M. Scoble and M. L. McAllister. (2001). Mining with Communities. *Natural Resources Forum*, vol. 25, pp. 191–202.

Wood, C. (2011). *The Environment, Intergenerational Equity and Long-Term Investment*. D. Phil Thesis and Abstract, School Geography and Environment, Worcester College, Oxford.

3 Coal mining-induced displacement and its impact on human development

A study on selected tribal households in Odisha

Sujata Sahu and R.K. Kumbhar

Introduction

Odisha is predominantly an agrarian economy where land and forest plays an indispensable role in providing livelihood and promoting human development[1] of her people, including the 39.9 per cent SCs/STs of the state. Land and forest also serve the purpose of collateral, fallback resources and economic and social power through which citizens can claim their rights (Cernea, 1999). But the advent of the neoliberal strategy[2] of development in the lens of modernisation and industrialisation has opened the door of exploitation for the corporate profit-seeker capitalist to acquire land from the SCs/STs with or against their will, and forest has been destroyed to extract mineral ores for business purposes (Bebbington et al., 2008; Bhaduri and Patkar, 2009; Kumbhar, 2012). In this process, including NGOs, the state also acted as an agent to collect the land and hand over to the capitalist along with free infrastructure and violating the Land Acquisition Act.[3] Neither the compensation received by the displaced households is satisfactory nor did they receive any other type of benefit from the corporate social responsibility. However, this land alienation and deforestation have shown a glimpse of silver lining in the form of raising state domestic product, though unsustainable. But this development process has left the SCs/STs of the state in distress (Kumbhar, 2012). Not only are their sources of livelihood destroyed permanently and created a threat to livelihood, but the achievement of human development[4] now became a far-reaching dream. Hence the development process in Odisha has deviated from an eco-friendly to environmental and human hazardous process, and development-induced displacement,[5] especially mining-induced, became common features.

The magnitude of development-induced displacement in Odisha is one of the highest in the country (Ray and Saini, 2011). Major industries in Odisha have grown in those areas where there is availability of raw materials, water and power based on which the state is divided into 12 industrial zones.[6] Among the major minerals, coal has covered two industrial zones: Talcher area and IB Valley area, which is about 7.6 per cent of total area of the state (2,723 square kilometers). Production of coal in these two zones rose from 0.91 MT and 0.55 MT in 1972–73 to 63.973 MT and 46.467 MT in 2013–14, respectively (www.mcl.gov.in). The IB Valley[7] area is extended in two districts (Jharsuguda and Sundargarh) of the state, covering an area of 1,375 square kilometers where five areas comprise Orient, IB Valley, Lakhanpur, Basundhara and Garjanbahal with five underground and seven open-cast mines operate (Mishra, 2009). But these mineral-based industries and other development projects lead to large-scale displacement of people from their land and source of livelihood which brings costs to the economy. The present study is an attempt to explore the conditions of those displaced households. Mining-led displacement has been chosen for the study, as this is one of the important causes of displacement in recent times. In Lakhanpur block of Jharsuguda districts, 26 villages have been displaced, of which four villages are selected based on their area of land acquisition, and from them randomly, Darlipali[8] village has been finally selected for a survey. The secondary information from Census 2011 shows there are 139 households[9] in Darlipali, but in the survey, we found 102 households, which might be due to some of the households leaving the village in search of better employment. Apart from household surveys with structured questionnaires, case studies of selected persons have been conducted, and institutional surveys were also being carried out.

The main objective of the chapter is to understand what has happened to the villagers in the pre- and post-displacement situations with regards to their land possession, agricultural and livestock production, labour disposition, housing, health, education and other civil rights. Based on observations, the following hypotheses have been proposed for tests in the sample village. There is no difference in livelihood pattern of the villagers in the pre- and post-mining period; impact on human development indicators remains unchanged in the pre- and post-mining period. That is, there is no difference in educational and health facilities across the MCL employee and non-employee group in the post-mining period.

The rest of the chapter is divided into four sections. Section one discusses a brief history of coal mines followed by different issues associated with mining and mining-induced displacement in the state. Section two provides the macro picture of mining-induced displacement in Odisha. Section three picturises the ground reality from human development perspectives using micro-level field data. The last section summarises the chapter.

Background of mining in Odisha

Bagchi and Ghose (1980) discuss the history of mining in India. They have stated in 322 B.C., Chanakya in Arthashastra has given a complete picture of mining[10] and its importance to the economy. In the British period, Summer and Heatly of East India Company started commercial coal mining with open-cast coal mines in Raniganj, West Bengal, of India in 1774. Since then many coal mining companies have existed in India, but it was after the independence of the country that the National Coal Development Corporation was formed in 1956, from which commercial coal mining in modern times was started.

In Odisha the significance of coal for industrial development was initiated by Lieutenant Kittoe in 1839 in the Talcher Coalfields and then by V Ball in 1871 in the IB Coalfields. However, the commercial coal mining was started by M/S Villers Ltd. in Handidhua coal mines near Talcher since 1921. But the National Coal Development Corporation started in the state with the first open-cast mining in South Balanda Colliery in 1960 while IB Coalfields and the Belpahar open-cast mines were started in 1983 which was successfully managed by Mahanadi Coalfields Ltd. since 1992.

Mini Ratna Mahanadi Coalfields, a public-sector enterprise and the second-highest coal-producing and profit-making coal company in India, was established in 1992 with its corporate headquarters at Sambalpur in the state. The share of mineral resources of India in the world and that of Odisha in India has been presented in table 3.1, which depicts that while India is having significant share of mineral resources of world and ranked in top third to sixth position, Odisha possesses the lion's share of the country's mineral reserves (92 per cent of total nickel, 83 per cent chromite, 55 per cent bauxite, etc.), which is a reason why several mineral-based industries have already come up in the state.[11]

Figure 3.1 shows the increasing trend of mineral production in Odisha from 1994–95 to 2008–09, which has also earned revenue from the mineral sector for the state. (The state's mining revenue during 2008–09 amounted to approximately Rs. 1380.59 crores, and that of during 2009–10 was Rs. 2020.71 crores)(Geology and Mineral Resources in Odisha, Odisha Reference Annual, 2011). Among all mineral production, coal production is highest in the state during the period (www.orishaminerals.gov.in). The rising trend in figure 3.2 depicts the annual coal production of mines under MCL's command area. However both in terms of poverty and human development, the rank of the state has been remaining towards the bottom (www.undp.org.in, 2009–10). Rather it has given birth to several other issues.

Table 3.1 Mineral Resources in India, Odisha, 2010

Mineral	*Contribution of India in world in (%)*	*India's rank in world*	*Contribution of Odisha in India in (%)*
Nickel	–	–	92
Chromite	14.2	3rd	83
Bauxite	5.8	6th	55
Iron	8	4th	38
Coal	8	3rd	26

Source: Indian Mineral Industry and National Economy (2011)

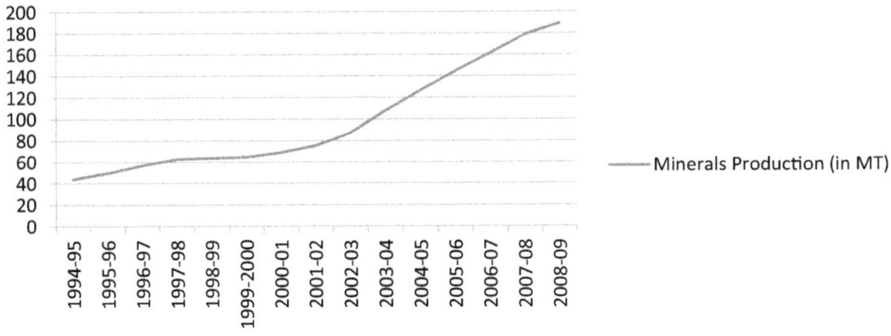

Figure 3.1 Trend of Minerals Production in Odisha from 1994–95 to 2008–09

Source: Based on data from Odisha Minerals, www.odishaminerals.gov.in

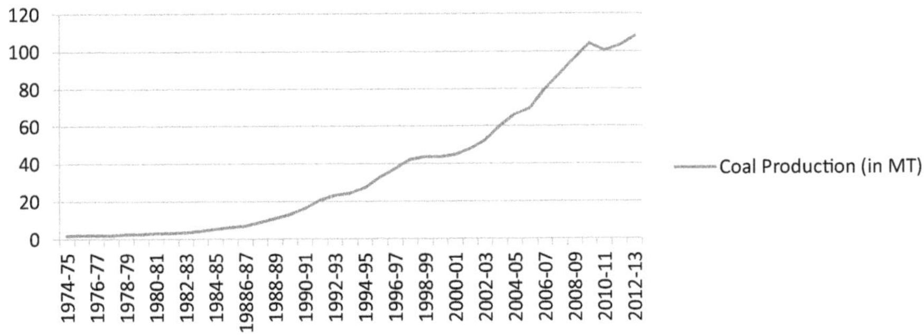

Figure 3.2 Coal Production by MCL

Source: Based on data from MCL, 2014

Issues and mining-induced displacement in Odisha

Mining-led industrialisation may boost the economic growth and employment, but the unsustainable and noneconomic exploitation of these resources may retard economic growth and affect human development adversely by displacing a major share of labour from production processes and by destroying the sources of livelihood. This pattern of development and growth with unequal distribution of wealth-led 'mining' has contentious[12] and ambiguous[13] relationship with 'development' (Bebbington et al., 2008). Bhaduri and Patkar, 2009 stated the present mining-led industrialisation is more displacing, exclusionary (exclusion of labour in lieu of technology) and undemocratic in nature, which produces immediate gainers[14] but permanent losers[15] by violating the constitutional act by weakening the democratic rights of the poor through forceful acquisition of land, habitat, common property resources (water and forest), livelihood sources and socio-cultural milieu; inducing for poverty and human underdevelopment by providing negligible and tardy compensation (rehabilitation and resettlement) and creating scope for people's agitation in democratic/undemocratic ways. Hence, there is increase in corporate profit but human misery as well.

The loss of socio-economic conditions of tribal people through the displacement from their jungle, jamin and livelihood for the development of mining projects has led to high rate of migration and human underdevelopment (Khatua and Stanley, 2006; Kumbhar, 2012; Mishra, 2007, 2010; Naidu, 1976; Sarangi, 2002, Vijay, 2003). The absence of proper rehabilitation and resettlement of displaced people led them to hunger and deprivations where SCs/STs face multiple burdens (Kumbhar, 2012), where the tribals are bound to consume poisonous foods like mango kernels, tamarind seed powder, mushrooms, etc. (Sarangi, 2002). As land of a person is a source of livelihood not only for the current but several generations, the one-time cash compensation is not sufficient for the displaced people (Venkateswaran, 2007). Violation of National Policy of Resettlement and Rehabilitation has led to aggravations, struggles, protests and resistance against mining projects for right to survive in dignity and self-respect, which has further led to death of common people (Banerjee et al., 2007; George, 2005; Mishra, 2006; Mishra, 2007; People's Union for Democratic Rights, 2005; Rao, 1995). All these are ultimately leading to human underdevelopment.

Mining-led industrialisation has destroyed the environment by damaging natural resources like water, land, forest and soil, which affects agricultural productivity through low rainfall and affects human health because of pollution (Basu, 2009; People's Union for Democratic Rights, 2005; Rao 1995; Vijay, 2003). To sum up, mining-induced displacement adversely affects human development.

Mining-induced displacement in Odisha and its impact on human development

Given the availability of mineral resources either on the surface or interior of the earth, both open-cast and underground types of mining[16] have been done in Odisha. These mineral-based industries are associated with large-scale destruction of forests, which the forest dwellers depend on for their livelihood. Table 3.2 states, out of total diverted forest area of 27274.45 hectares in 2003, the diversion in mining projects was the highest, i.e., 34.72 per cent (9469.4384 hectares).

Table 3.3 presents the category-wise displacement of development projects in Odisha, which shows that the mining sector takes second position from the top followed by water resources projects. Table 3.4 gives the picture of mining-induced displacement in tribal-dominated areas in Odisha where Jharsuguda takes the second position in acquiring private land and displacement.

Table 3.2 Sector-wise Diversion of Forest Land to Non-Forest Use (Under Forest Conservation Act, 1980)

Sector name	*Number of projects*	*Forest area diverted (in hectares) as on 31.03.2003*	*Percentage of total area diverted*
Irrigation	59	6092.4829	22.34
Industry	5	2406.086	8.82
Mining	77	9469.4384	34.72
Transmission	44	2723.4265	9.99
Roads and Bridges	25	197.8122	0.73
Railways	5	1965.0287	7.20
Others	32	4420.179	16.21
Total	247	27274.45	100

Source: Kumbhar, 2012

Table 3.3 Number of Displaced Persons/Project-Affected Persons in Odisha (1947–2000)

Category	*Number of DPs/PAPs*	*Percentages*
Water	800000	54.57
Industry	15069	1.03
Mines	300000	20.47
Environment	107840	7.36
Others	100000	6.82
Total	1465909	100

Source: Reference note No. 30/RN/Ref./December/2013, Lok Sabha, Secretariat

Table 3.4 Mining-Induced Displacement in Odisha

Name of the mines	*Private land acquired (in acres)*	*Government land alienated (in acres)*	*No. of families displaced/likely to be displaced*
MCL, Angul	15857.50	7224.69	6760
MCL, Jharsuguda	3934.54	1720.38	725
MCL, Basundhara, Hemagiri, Sundargarh	856.24	19842.00	125
Bhusan Power and Steel Ltd. Hemagiri, Sundargarh	–	–	426
Talbira Mines, Hindalco, Sambalpur	194.69	242.59	144
Total	20842.97	29029.66	8180

Source: Ray and Saini, 2011

Table 3.5 Percentage of Displaced People Who Are Rehabilitated (1951–1991)

Category	*Displaced*	*Resettled*	*Percentage resettled*	*Backlog*	*Percentage unsettled*
Water resource	3,25,000	90,000	27.69	2,35,000	72.31
Industries	71,794	27,300	38.03	44,494	61.97
Mines	1,00,000	60,000	60.00	40,000	40.00
Miscellaneous	50,000	15,540	31.08	34,461	68.92
Total	5,46,794	1,92,840	35.27	3,53,955	64.73

Source: Panda and Sahoo, 2014

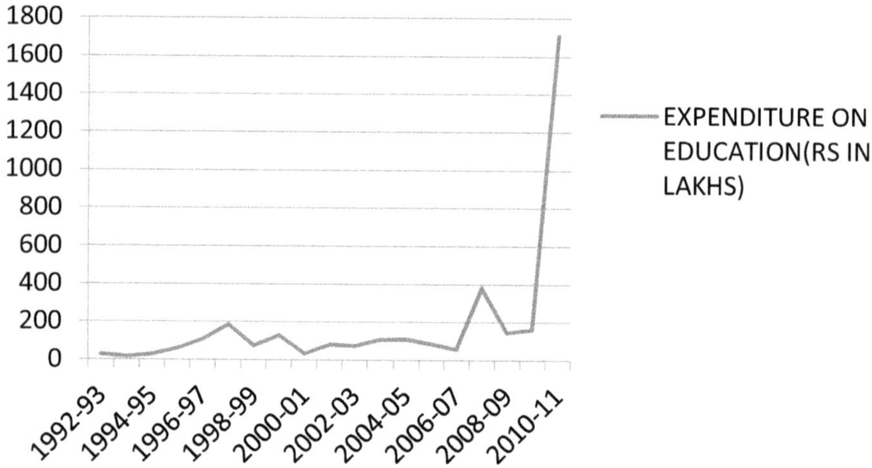

Figure 3.3 Expenditure on Education

Source: Based on MCL, 2014

Table 3.5 presents the percentages of displaced people who are rehabilitated in Odisha from 1951 to 1991, which state, out of total 5,46,794 displaced people, only 1,92,840 people were resettled, which constitute only 35.27 per cent. However, in the mining sector, the percentage of resettled people was highest (60 per cent). The expenditures under CSR by MCL in Odisha also showed an increasing trend in education, health, infrastructure and water supply (see figure 3.3 to 3.6). However, outcomes of such rosy CSR expenditures are absent in the micro level.

Micro study based on field survey

A micro-level survey was conducted in the Lakhanpur area of MCL, which is situated in Lakhanpur Tahasil of Jharsuguda district, where the mining was started on 11 September 1983 with Belpahar open-cast mines. Later

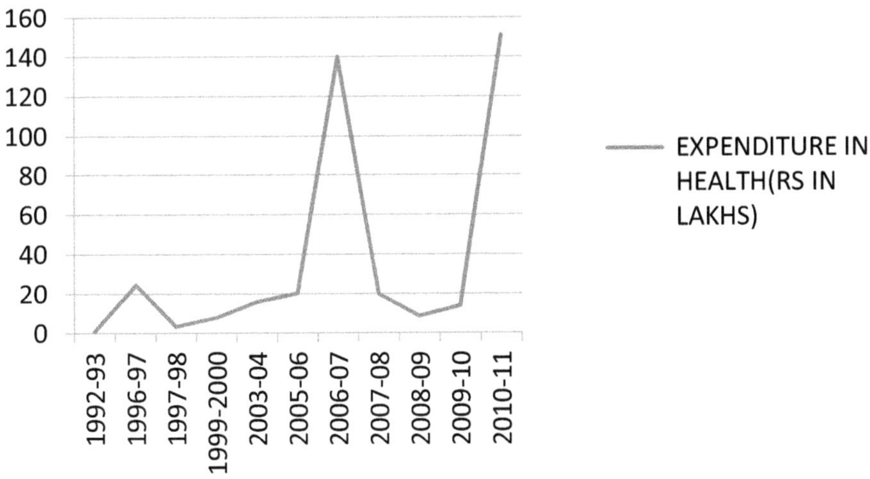

Figure 3.4 Expenditure on Health

Source: Based on MCL, 2014

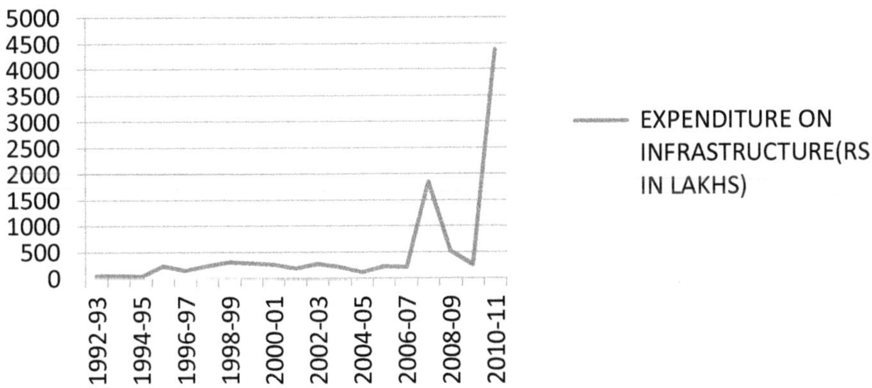

Figure 3.5 Expenditure on Infrastructure

Source: Based on MCL, 2014

on, two mines, namely Lilari and Lakhanpur, came into existence on 10 June 1988 and 3 October 1991, respectively. But the area was named as Lakhanpur area in May 1998 with taking two mines, i.e., Lakhanpur OCP and Belpahar OCP primarily. In October 2002, Lilari OCP was included in this area. Now the three mines are operating with an annual capacity of 15 MTY, 8.0 MTY and 0.8 MTY, respectively. But there are 26 numbers of

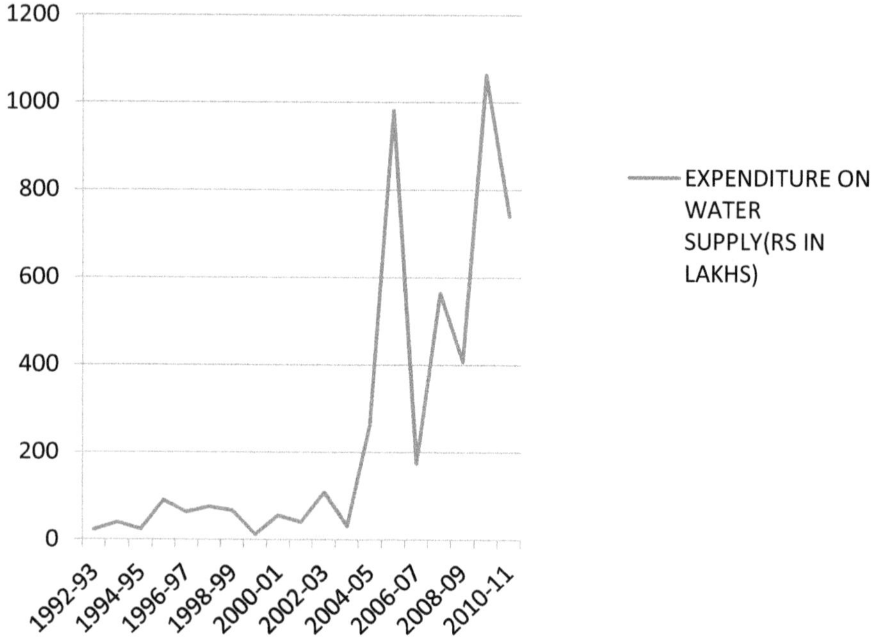

Figure 3.6 Expenditure on Water Supply

Source: Based on MCL, 2014

villages which are affected in the Lakhanpur area. Darlipali, selected as the sample village, was surrounded by these three mines, and all types of land (cultivable land, homestead land, forest land and other government land) of the village are now acquired by MCL for Lakhanpur OCP and Belpahar OCP, though possession was not taken physically. Belpahar OCP has started its extraction in the village on 23 March 1988 on the basis of notification on 20 May 1983 for 257.94-acre land. Before that, the mines have acquired completely the government forest land of 311.85-acre land on 4 September 1981. The second-phase notification was on 7 September 1988 for Lakhanpur OCP for 89.89-acre land, and the land possession was taken place by MCL on 22 March 1991. The third-phase notification was being carried out on 26 October 1991 for both the mines for 17.25-acre land, and physical possession was not completed yet.

But the field survey shows there are 102 households staying in that sample village with possession of 114.92 acres of land (both homestead and cultivable) since MCL has not acquired all the land physically. The socio-economic conditions of the villagers are presented later through tabular analysis and narratives. Table 3.6 presents the demographic profile, which depicts the sex ratio in the households of the village is almost equal, average family sizes

Table 3.6 Demographic Profile of the Sample Village

Sex	Male	213 (49.7)
	Female	216 (50.3)
	Total	429 (100)
Marital status	Married	195 (45.5)
	Unmarried	198 (46.2)
	Widowed	36 (8.4)
	Total	429 (100)
Family size (No. of members)	< 5	65 (63.1)
	= 5	17 (16.5)
	> 5	20 (19.4)
	Total	102 (100)

Source: Field survey

Table 3.7 Social Structure of the Sample Village

Caste (in hh)	ST	78 (76.5)
	SC	21 (20.6)
	OBC	3 (2.9)
	Total	102 (100)
Education	Illiterate	132 (34.38)
	Primary	84 (21.88)
	Secondary	127 (33.07)
	Higher secondary	36 (9.37)
	Graduate and above	5 (1.3)
	Total	384 (100)

Source: Field Survey

are 63 per cent have less than five members and 20 per cent households have more than five members. Table 3.7 states the share of ST, SC and OBC are 78, 21 and 3 percentages, respectively. As per Census 2011, the literacy rate of the state is 72.9 per cent, but the sample village consists of 132 (34.38 per cent) illiterate persons, and 5 (1.3 per cent) graduate persons show low rank in human development indicator.

As the landholding is concerned, 30 per cent of households have one acre or more than one acre of cultivable land, 59 per cent have uncultivable homestead land and the rest, 11 per cent households, are the landless. The housing conditions depict 2.9 per cent villagers have pucca houses, 25.5 per cent have semi-pucca house, and the rest, 71.6 per cent of families, are living either in kutcha or thatched houses. 88.2 per cent of families have their own dwelling unit, and 11.8 per cent have not. All the families have electricity connection, and the common fuel of all villagers is charcoal. While considering the ration card, 61.8 per cent of families have no card, 29.4 per cent have BPL card, and only 8.8 per cent have APL card, which shows the unfair economic status among the households in that village (table 3.8)

Table 3.8 Economic Profile of the Sample Village

Landholding	Have one acre or more cultivated land	30 (30)
	Uncultivable homestead land	61 (59)
	Landless	11 (11)
	Total	102 (100)
House type	Pucca house	3 (2.9)
	Semi-pucca house	26 (25.5)
	Kutcha or thatched house	73 (71.6)
	Total	102 (100)
Dwelling unit	Own dwelling unit	90 (88.2)
	Hired dwelling unit	12 (11.8)
	Total	102 (100)
Ration card	BPL cardholders	30 (29.4)
	APL cardholders	9 (8.8)
	No card	63 (61.8)
	Total	102 (100)

Source: Field survey

Displacement and rehabilitation

All the families in the village are affected by mining in one or other way: 48 per cent have lost cultivable land, 43 per cent lost livelihood and 9 per cent from both land and livelihood. But in the form of compensation, only 14 per cent of the displaced households have received monetary remuneration which was far less than the market value of the land, and 33 per cent have got employment, but the rest have not (Table 3.9)

The complex nature of R&R policy was described through two case studies.

Case 1

While taking interviews of MCL officials, the R&R benefits for the poor displaced were not so harassing since 10 decimals of land in the resettled village was given to each and every adult (more than 18 years) of a household with monetary compensation without considering they had any land in the displaced village.

But the situation was quite different in the survey. The description of the villagers is as follows:

> The cultivable lands were common for two or three or four brothers. But the jobs in the mines were available only to one of the brother. Those people who were got the job in mines, they left the village and living in Bandhbahal colony whose conditions quite well due to high salary. Some of them are living in the village for creating jobs to their children also. The brothers are got land of 10 decimal jointly in the neighbouring village, Khadam. But these compensation lands are in

Table 3.9 Rehabilitation and Compensation

Types of entitlement	*Entitlement received*	
	Yes (in no. of hh)	*No (in no. of hh)*
Employment in mines	34 (33.3)	68 (66.7)
Cash compensation	14 (13.7)	88 (86.3)
Livestock compensation	0 (0.0)	102 (100)
Training for self-employment	0 (0.0)	102 (100)
Homestead land	0 (0.0)	102 (100)
House	0 (0.0)	102 (100)
House-building assistance	0(0.0)	102 (100)
Free transport	0 (0.0)	102 (100)
Any other assistance	0 (0.0)	102 (100)

Source: Field survey

the name of the villagers of Khadam. So how they can make houses in other's land? Monetary compensation was also very negligible and so people are not willing to take the amount. Above all, the poor SCs who have no cultivable land and so they are deprived from all that facilities i.e. neither job in mines nor compensation land and money.

Case 2

Mr Netrananda Mallik said he had been living in Darlipali for the last 25 years with his wife, Anjana Mallik, and father-in-law, Manual Bag. Since Manual Bag has no son, both couples have been taking care of their father. MCL has already acquired 1.5 acres of land of Manual Bag. As per MCL's R&R policy, Manual Bag was unfit to get employment in the company due to old age, and the only eligible member of the household to get employment is Mrs Anjana Mallik. Manual Bag and other neighbouring households were also supporting Mr Mallik. But there is no employment to any member of the household. Moreover, they were supplied 10 decimals of compensated land at Khadam village and Rs. 50000 as compensated money to make house in the resettled village, which is insufficient. Their present housing condition in the village is kutcha, but its market value would be more than Rs. 100000. So the family has refused to accept the benefit and waits for justice.

Comparison of assets holding before and after displacement

There is positive impact on assets after displacement due to electrification and modernisation; hence the number of assets in terms of fans, coolers, refrigerators and two- and four-wheelers have been increased in the sample village. But in case of other factors, the situation has deteriorated.

Comparison of livestock before and after displacement

Livestock, which plays a major role in tribal life, has declined significantly (table 3.10). In the post-displacement period, the number of bullocks has been tremendously decreased to 16 from 192 in the pre-displacement period. This results in overburden to the bullocks in the absence of mechanisation in agriculture or use of tractors in the displaced village.

The total number of cows in the village also reduced to 11 from 60, that of goats to 104 from 609 and hens to 173 from 650. The reduction of milk lessens the protein intake of the villagers (badly affecting human development) where the reduction of waste of the livestock decreases the soil fertility of the village. Moreover, there is absence of livestock compensation.

Comparison of source of livelihood before and after displacement

Land is an asset for future generations where compensation in lieu of land in terms of employment is provided to the present generation only. There is no such guarantee provided by the company to give employment for the successive generation. Before mining, the important source of livelihood was cultivation (58 per cent), but now it is reduced to only 15 per cent resulting decline in agricultural production and productivity. Employment in service sector (i.e., in mining) has increased from 4 per cent to 37 per cent after mining, but the earnings of 90 per cent of the total households have decreased. This has reduced the per capita income and hence endanger human development.

Comparison of education and health facilities, drinking water and environment before and after displacement

MCL was established with the objectives of conducting mining, preventing pollutions in the surrounding habitations, conserving natural resources through recycling of wastes and creating environmental awareness and has also received the Corporate Social Responsibility Corporate Governance Award due to its contribution in making a difference to the people and

Table 3.10 Comparison of Livestock

Livestock	*Before displacement*	*After displacement*
Bullock	192	16
Cow	60	11
Goat	609	104
Hen	650	173

Source: Field survey

Table 3.11 Expenditure on CSR

Year	*Total CSR (in lakhs)*	*Year*	*Total CSR (in lakhs)*
1992–93	99.15	2002–03	431.34
1993–94	99.08	2003–04	455.84
1994–95	89.58	2004–05	480.40
1995–96	380.17	2005–06	1218.46
1996–97	337.55	2006–07	595.31
1997–98	502.01	2007–08	2813.09
1998–99	393.55	2008–09	1084.48
1999–2000	423.36	2009–10	1491.75
2000–01	354.43	2010–11	5345.00
2001–02	270.38	2011–12	2833.00

Source: MCL Presentation, 2014

community as a responsible citizen. The expenditure made by MCL on CSR is shown in table 3.11. But the reality is far below expectations.

The most significant adverse effect of mining-induced displacement is the scarcity of water in that village because the river and well water are being polluted after mining. The tube wells are out of order where the water levels of the open wells have gone down. The people have to wait for a supply of tank water in alternative of four days, which is insufficient for use. The environment is also polluted with heavy amount of dust, endangering chronic health diseases like fevers, gastritis, skin diseases, joint pain, TB and bone TB, etc. This type of chronic problem was absent in the pre-displacement period.

The sample village was covered by dense forest, large cultivable land and a natural water reservoir before mining. The natural reservoir and the common wells in the village were the sources of drinking water. The forest is completely destroyed and directly affected the livelihood of the people after extraction of coal from this area. The people have also lost the natural water reservoir. Due to mines, the water level of the wells and tube wells goes down and also polluted. Mostly the people suffer from acute shortage of water (both drinking and for all purposes). There is a supply of tank water, but that is coming with intervals of four days, which is not sufficient for the people. The people are using chua water for drinking and black, polluted water for all other purposes. This will be clear from photo 3.1.

Table 3.12 presents some of the other amenities in the pre- and post-displacement period. It was observed that the public distribution system, which was in the village, has been moved to five kilometers away from the village. Now the villagers need more time and travel expenses to have access to PDS.

Daily market in the pre-mining period was in the village, but in post-mining period, the villagers have to go three kilometers for daily market for their basic needs, with no facility of transportation and communication.

There was a bus stop in the village in the pre-mining period for easy convenience of the villagers. But the road was damaged after mining so the

Photo 3.1 Sample Village

Source: Author

Table 3.12 Assessment of Education, Health and Other Facilities

Facility type	*Before displacement*	*After resettled*	*If yes, mention distance from the village (in kilometers)*	
	Yes-1, No-2	*Yes-1, No-2*	*Before displacement*	*After resettled*
ICDS Center	1	1	0	0
U P school	1	1	0	0
High school	2	2	7	7
College	2	2	7	7
Post office	2	2	7	1.5
Police station	2	2	7	3
Bank	2	2	7	3
Hospital	2	2	7	3
Bus stop	1	2	0	2.5
Daily market	1	2	0	3
PDS distribution point	2	2	5	5
Drinking water	1	2	0	Tank Water

Source: Field Survey

people have to go to the nearest bus stop, which was two-and-a-half kilometers away from the village.

There is only one primary school in the sample village and also no possibility of a new school with higher class. Therefore, nobody in the village is satisfied with prevailing education facility of the village because there is no better communication facility to go to nearby villages for higher study after class V. However, the children of MCL employees have the opportunity for free education in English medium schools for primary education as well as for higher study, and these families are also financially sound for sending their children by their own vehicles to distant places for higher study. Similarly, only 18 per cent of the households who got MCL regular service are satisfied with the free hospital facility, whereas the rest, 82 per cent, poor displaced are excluded.

Above all, it is impossible to sustain life in such environment, but people are waiting for justice and struggling for existence of their life in that village which is showing a clear picture of a hostile effect of mining-induced displacement on human development and hence responsible for accentuating marginalisation and social exclusion in the state.

Conclusion

The study attempted to examine the human development aspects of mining. It found mining has been destroying the traditional livelihood sources of the inhabitants. The poor tribals are living in a polluted environment with scarcity of water. They are deprived from the basic amenities, which were available for them before mining. The MCL employee groups are somehow satisfied with the prevailing health facility, but all the villagers are displeased with the education facility for their children.

Since benefits from mining are short term in nature, what will happen to these poor displaced after the complete extraction of mines, who have neither their jobs nor their cultivable land in uncultivable condition? Therefore, the state should take care of the interests of the displaced. Moreover, MCL should also try to distribute the benefits in an equitable manner so there is a positive effect on the livelihoods of the poor displaced. The expenditure on CSR should not be only for receiving Corporate Governance Award but should be for the benefits of these affected persons who are living hazardous lives. More emphasis should be given on education facilities for the poor displaced so they have better understanding for decision-making.

Notes

1 Human development is an alternative way of assessing development. Traditionally, development has been measured unidimensionally, that is, through increase in wealth or output of a nation but based on human development, the 'development' of an economy has been expressed with a composite index of wealth, health and knowledge (Human Development Report, 1990).

2 Neoliberalism is the periodical change in political economy from welfare-based government to competitive-driven government, which may be captured through four numbers of principles: (i) markets are the only efficient means to allocate scarce resources; (ii) international free trade is desirable; (iii) state intervention is not desirable and (iv) labour market flexibility is necessary. Neoliberalism is a state-led project signifying as mobilising the state power in the contradictory extension and reproduction of market rule (Birch, 2008). Therefore mines led industrialisation through private corporate sectors such as by Vedanta, POSCO, BHUSAN, TATA and many others can be considered as part of neoliberal policies followed by the government of Odisha.

3 All the three laws (Land Acquisition Act, 1894; Coal-Bearing Areas Act, 1957; and Atomic Energy Act, 1962) of acquisition of land are malfunctioning to safeguard the mining activity as no information is given to the poor tribals about the acquisition of land, but as per government rule, detailed information should be available for the public. The role of gram sabha has been controlled by the mining officers. (Gram sabha has no chance to speak, or their objections are not considered.) Public hearing has also been prevented for the affected persons (George, 2005).

4 Human development here is understood as per the UNDP (1990) reports, where income, health and education have been the prime factors of development.

5 Displacement means forced dislocation of people from their home or home region due to their own government's order for development projects or due to occurrence of natural disasters, and mining-induced displacement is that which leads to vulnerability of the displaced persons to various dimensions due to establishment of mining projects (Kumbhar, 2012).

6 Rajgangpur area (iron and steel, sponge iron, cement and secondary steel, melting and rolling mills, refractories and chemicals), Ib Valley area (thermal power, sponge iron, refractories and coal mines), Hirakud area (aluminum and rolling mills), Talcher Angularea (thermal power, aluminum, coal washeries, ferro alloys and coal mines), Choudwar area (ferro alloys, thermal power, pulp and paper and coke ovens), Balasore area (pulp and paper, ferro alloys and rubber industries), Chandikhol (stone crusher and coke oven), Duburi (integrated steel, ferro alloys and rubber industries), Paradeep area (fertilizer, sea food processing and petroleum coke), KhurdaTapang area (stone crusher), JodaBarbil area (iron, sponge iron, ferro alloys, iron ore crusher and mineral processing) and Rayagada area (pulp and paper and ferro alloys).

7 The IB Valley coalfield (a part of Mahanadi Coalfields Ltd. and Coal India Ltd.) is named after the river IB, a tributary of the river Mahanadi (Mishra, 2009).

8 Darlipali is one of the most affected villages in Lakhanpur block in Jharsuguda district of Odisha surrounded by three mines: Lakhnpur coal mines, Lilari coal mines and Belpahar Open-Cast Mines (B.O.C.M). Jharsuguda is one of the districts of Odisha where there is large-scale mining-led displacement occurred of which a large proportion belonged to SCs/STs. In Jharsuguda district, Lakhanpur is one of the blocks, where 26 villages are displaced for mining (Mahanadi Coalfields Ltd).

9 As per Census 1981, 1991 and 2001, the number of household in the village was 104, 172 and 155 respectively.

10 Mining is the extraction of valuable minerals or other geological materials from the earth. Hence, in mining-led industrialisation, minerals consist of the major share of raw materials.

11 The major ones include Rourkela Steel Plant, Alumina Refinery and smelter of Nalco at Damanjodi and Angul; charge chrome plants at Baminipal, Bhadrak, Choudwar and Theruvali by OMC, FACOR, ICCL and IMFA, respectively; and mineral sand separation unit at Chhatrapur by IRE. Many cement and sponge

iron plants have been set up. Coal-based thermal power plants have been set up at Talcher, Kanihan and Banaharpali. Captive thermal power plants have also been set up by NALCO, RSP, ICCL, INDAL, etc., and many more are in the pipeline (Geology and mineral resources in Odisha, Odisha reference annual, 2011).

12 The relationship between mining and development is termed as contentious due to more adverse effects and less positive effect of mining on society, environment and economy.

13 The previous relationship is termed as ambiguous due to hope for a possibility of mining contribution.

14 Immediate gainers in this chapter refer to the foreign investors, the World Bank and the International Monetary Fund.

15 Here, permanent losers are the poor (the inhabitant) working in the unorganized agricultural sector, losing their land, livelihood and home in the process of industrialisation. They never get back the resources they have lost, and hence their forthcoming generations also became losers.

16 Open-cast mining refers to method of extracting rock or minerals from the earth by their removal from an open borrow. These are used when deposits of commercially useful minerals or rock are found near the surface. Underground mining refers to various underground mining techniques used to excavate hard minerals mainly containing gold, silver, iron, cupper, zinc, nickel, tin and lead. These are used where the overburden is thick as minerals occur deep below the surface.

Reference

Bagchi, S. and A. K. Ghose. (1980). History of Mining in India-Circa 1400–1800 and Technology Status. *Indian Journal of History of Science*, vol. 15, no. 1, pp. 25–29.

Banerjee, A. V., Pranab Bardhan, Kaushik Basu, Mrinal Datta Chaudhury, Maitreesh Ghatak, Ashok Sanjay Guha, Mukul Majumdar, Dilip Mookherjee and Debraj Ray. (2007). Beyond Nandigram: Industrialisation in West Bengal. *Economic and Political Weekly*, pp. 1487–1489, 28 April.

Basu, Moushumi. (2009). Who Pays the Price for Uranium Mining. *Economic and Political Weekly*, vol. XLIV, no. 49, pp. 15–16.

Bebbington, A., Leonith Hinojosa, Denise Humphreys Bebbington, Maria Luisa Burneo and Ximena Warnaars. (2008). Contention and Ambiguity: Mining and the Possibilities of Development. *Development and Change*, vol. 39, no. 6, pp. 887–914. Institute of Social Studies. Published by Blackwell Publishing, 9600 Garsington Road, Oxford OX4 2DQ, UK and 350 Main St., Malden, MA 02148, USA.

Bhaduri, A. and Medha Patkar. (2009). Industrialisation for the People, by the People, of the People. *Economic and Political Weekly*, 10–13, 3 January.

Birch, K. (2008). Neoliberalising Bioethics: Bias, Enhancement and Economistic Ethics. *Life Sciences, Society and Policy*, vol. 4.2, no. 1.

Cernea, M. (1999). The Need for Economic Analysis of Resettlement: A Sociologist's View. In M. M. Cernea (Ed.), *The Economics of Involuntary Resettlement: Questions and Challenges*. Washington, DC: The World Bank.

Geology and Mineral Resources in Odisha, Odisha Reference Annual. (2011). *Information and Public Relations Department*. Bhubaneswar: Government of Odisha, 7th Publication, September, 2014.

George, Ajitha Susan. (2005). Laws Related to Mining in Jharkhand. *Economic and Political Weekly*, pp. 4455–4458, 8 October.

Indian Mineral Industry and National Economy; Indian Minerals Yearbook 2011 (Part-I), Government of India, Ministry of Mines, Indian Bureau of Mines, Nagpur.

Khatua, S. and William Stanley. (2006). Ecological Debt: A Case Study from Orissa, India. In *Ecological Debt: The Peoples of the South are the Creditors: Cases from Ecuador, Mozambique, Brazil and India*. Geneva: World Council of Churches, pp. 125–168.

Kumbhar, R. K. (2012). *Structural Inequality and Displacement: The Multiple Burdens Among the SCs/STs of Orissa*. Samla Hills, Bhopal: Indira Gandhi Rashtriya Manav Sangrahalaya (Published in the book *Displacement and Rehabilitation-Solution for the Future*, by N. R. Mishra and K. K. Mishra).

Mishra, Banikanta. (2006). People's Movement at Kalinga Nagar: An Epitaph or an Epitome. *Economic and Political Weekly*, pp. 551–554, 18 February.

Mishra, Banikanta. (2010). Agriculture, Industry and Mining in Orissa in the Post-Liberalisation Era: An Inter-District and Inter-State Panel Analysis. *Economic and Political Weekly*, vol. XLV, no. 20, pp. 49–68.

Mishra, Ish. (2007). Heat and Dust of Highway at Kalinganagar. *Economic and Political Weekly*, pp. 822–825, 10 March.

Mishra, Prajna Paramita. (2009). Coal Mining and Rural Livelihoods: Case of the IB Valley Coalfield, Orissa. *Economic and Political Weekly*, vol. XLIV, no. 44, pp. 117–123, 31 October.

Naidu, N. Y. (1976). Pains of Industrialisation. *Economic and Political Weekly*, vol. 11, no. 23, pp. 830–831.

Panda, S., N. C. Sahu, and D. Sahoo. (2014). CSR in India: Issues and Challenges. In M. K. Barua and Z. Rahman (Eds.), *Research and Sustainable Business*. New Delhi: Excell India Publisher, pp. 191–196.

People's Union for Democratic Rights, Delhi. (2005). Alumina Projects in South Orissa. *Economic and Political Weekly*, pp. 1794, 1920, 30 April.

Pradhan, JayaPrakash. (2007). *Tata Steel's Romance with Orissa–Minerals-based Underdevelopment and Federal Politics in India*, ISID Working Paper No. 3, New Delhi.

Rao, R. S. (1995). *Towards Understanding Semi Feudal Semi Colonial Society*. Studies in Political Economy. Hyderabad: Perspective.

Ray, S. and Saini Shashi. (2011). Development and Displacement: The Case of an Opencast Coal Mining Project in Orissa. *Sociological Bulletin*, vol. 60, no. 1, pp. 45–64, January–April.

Sarangi, Deba Ranjan. (2002). Surviving Against Odds: Case of Kashipur. *Economic and Political Weekly*, pp. 3239–3241, 3 August.

UNDP. (1990). *Human Development Report 1990*. New York: Oxford University Press.

Venkateswaran, Shankar. (2007). Industrial Displacement: Looking Beyond Cash Compensation. *Economic and Political Weekly*, pp. 2050–2051, 2 June.

Vijay, G. (2003). 'Other Side' of New Industrialisation. *Economic and Political Weekly*, pp. 5026–5030, 29 November.

4 Problems of displacement and deprivation of tribes due to mining industrialisation in Eastern India (Orissa)

S.N. Tripathy

Introduction

Development projects led to the displacement of people from their original habitat, and those displaced are mostly the tribes who have been forced to migrate to new areas. Causes or categories of development-induced displacement comprised of water supply (dams, reservoirs and irrigation); urban infrastructure; transportation (roads, highways and canals); energy (mining, power plants, oil exploration and extraction and pipelines); agricultural expansion; parks and forest reserves and population redistribution schemes. Construction of roads, establishment of industries and mining activities disrupted the settled tribal properties leading to landlessness, homelessness, joblessness, food insecurity, loss of access to common property resources and social disruption. Thousands of families have been involuntarily displaced from their age-old traditional habitat, and tribes constitute about 40 per cent of the total project displaced population (Fernades, 1994). This involuntary displacement of people from their productive assets (particularly land) and homes, due to industrial or infrastructure projects, has been one of the social issues that has caused intense debate among academics, social activists and planners.

The scheduled tribes constituted about 8.6 per cent of the total population of the country according to the 2011 Census, but they also constituted 55.16 per cent of total displaced people which indicates victimisation of the tribes. The development-induced involuntary displacement of tribes takes place in most of the states, mainly in the tribal concentrated regions of Bihar, Orissa, Andhra Pradesh, Madhya Pradesh, Gujarat and Maharashtra. (Please refer to tables 1 and 2.) In the context of Orissa, it has the highest concentration of tribal population in India next to undivided Madhya Pradesh. In Orissa, there are 62 tribes constituting about 23 per cent of the total population of the state, as against 8.6 per cent of India's population as of 2011 Census. The tribes in Orissa continued to remain socially, economically and educationally backward and are languishing at the bottom of the socio-economic ladder. Their geographical isolation and improvised economy have made them objects of exploitation by the non-tribes. The powerful external forces of moneylenders, contractors and officials having their link with political personnel and police could exert dominant control over the tribes. The poverty-stricken, illiterate, innocent tribes fail to withstand the forces and become prey to all types of exploitation.

In the light of the previous illustrations, it can be inferred that development, which has entailed many large-scale forced evictions of vulnerable populations, without the countervailing presence of policies to assist them to rebuild their lives, has only accentuated the negative aspects of displacement, such as lack of information, failure to prepare in advance a comprehensive plan for rehabilitation, the undervaluation of compensation and its payment in cash, failure to restore lost assets or livelihoods, traumatic and delayed relocation, problems at relocation sites, multiple displacement and neglect of the special vulnerabilities of the most disadvantaged groups.

Involuntary resettlement under development projects, if unmitigated, often germinates to severe economic, social and environmental risks: productive systems are dismantled; people face impoverishment when their productive assets or income sources are lost; people are relocated to environments where their productive skills may be less applicable and the competition for resources greater; community institutions and social networks are weakened; kin groups are dispersed; and cultural identity, traditional authority and the potential for mutual help are diminished or lost, a violation of human rights.

Objectives and methodology

In the previous backdrop, the present study has the following important objectives:

i) The study intends to examine briefly the historical processes as well as the contemporary situation of displaced people in various states of India. It is imperative to focus the existent conditions of tribal communities of the uprooted villages and their underlying socio-, psycho-, political and economic factors (to be accumulated mainly from the secondary sources of abundantly available literature) as problems of R&R being multifaceted. Their analyses and solutions require inputs from a broad array of disciplines and perspectives.
ii) The study will evaluate the position of uprooted people through field exploration, particularly the marginalised tribes who have been excluded in the development planning, mainly their compensation packages, status of landholding after the rehabilitation and opinion of the family after rehabilitation.
iii) The study aims at facilitating the reorientation of the policy measures in the context of government's initiative for effective rehabilitation policy and also suggests policy paradigms.

Secondary sources of data accumulated through literature, facts from official records, books and journals, etc. have been used in this chapter for making a comprehensive analysis of the problem under review. Besides, observation method has been followed to infer conclusions on the impact of mining industrialisation on the tribes of eastern India (Orissa).

Mining industrialisation in eastern India

Already in Orissa, Jharkhand and Chhattisgarh, the setting up of new projects to mine bauxite and other minerals has led to tribal people losing their lands. Their protests are met with brutal police repression. The trend of displacing the Adivasi people for industrial projects is getting heightened. All development projects in tribal areas were considered 'public purpose' even for private mining industries. This is the biggest misconception of our development paradigms in tribal areas. Much of what is being called 'development' is essentially destructive: the removal of nonrenewable resources (in the case of Orissa's minerals) and dangerous overuse of water, as well as destruction of communities living basically in harmony with nature. And much of this 'development' promotes *overconsumption*: 'while economists look with pride on the fact that the world economy expanded sevenfold between 1950 and 2000, and world trade is expanding more rapidly, ecologists see that these are based on extravagant use of Earth's "natural capital"' (Cullinan, 2002: 38). Cullinan calls for a swift change in countries' legal systems to protect the fabric of life in a world which most scientists see as entering a period of severe environmental crisis caused by economic growth gone out of control. The irony of displacement in Orissa is that the very tribal people being displaced have been at the forefront of protecting the environment, living sustainably in the true sense of the word.

The threat of accelerating climate change is a case in point. Orissa is a frontline region in climate change causes as well as effects. As it builds new metal factories, deforests its mountains and valleys for mines, depletes its water and food sources and accepts a virtually uncontrolled increase in pollution in order to service foreign investors, it is heating up its own climate as well as making a major contribution towards pushing the whole planet towards the tipping point of inevitable runaway global heating. Economic development not sensitive to the ecologies of their habitations and their special ties with the environment has alienated these people from mainstream development.

Though the development activities in Orissa surged as early as 1950s, there were about 8,117 displaced families from 1,446 villages because of development projects during the period of 1950 to 1993. The UNDP estimates that until that date, more than one lakh people in Orissa has been displaced while 20 lakhs have been affected by development projects. Industrial projects like Rourkella Steel Plant (RSP), the Hindustan Aeronautics (HAL) and the National Aluminum Company (NALCO) have displaced people, mainly the tribes (Fernades, 1994; Tripathy, 2003). A couple of anthropologists have made their investigation into the issues related to displacement,

Table 4.1 Dams and the Displacement of Tribal People

Project name	*State*	*Population facing displacement*	*Tribal people as percentage of displaced*
Karjan	Gujarat	11,600	100
Sardar Sarovar	Gujarat	200,000	57.6
Maheshwar	Madhya Pradesh	20,000	60
Bodhghat	Madhya Pradesh	12,700	73.91
Icha	Bihar	30,800	80
Chandil	Bihar	37,600	87.92
KoelKaro	Bihar	66,000	88
Mahi Bajaj Sagar	Rajasthan	38,400	76.28
Polavaram	Andhra Pradesh	150,000	52.90
Maithon and Panchet	Bihar	93,874	56.46
Upper Indravati	Orissa	18,500	89.20
Pong	Himanchal Pradesh	80,000	56.25
Inchampalli	Andhra Pradesh–Maharashtra	38,100	76.28
Tultuli	Maharashtra	13,600	51.61
Daman Ganga	Gujarat	8,700	48.70
Bhakra	Himanchal Pradesh	36,000	34.76
Masan Reservoir	Bihar	3,700	31.00

Source: Satyajit Singh, Taming the Waters, OUP, 1997, and government figures

rehabilitation and resettlement, particularly in the context of tribal society (Mohapatra, 1998, 1999; Behura, 1990, 1996; Patnaik, 1996; Ota, 1998; Panda and Panigrahi, 1989).

A significant number of tribal people, who are generally dependent on the natural and common resources, are displaced, and their ethos and lifestyle are dismantled and denigrated for the sake of developmental projects. Apart from the loss of land, living and lifestyle (of generations) displacement causes other traumatic, psychological and socio-cultural consequences, making their life more miserable and impoverished (Mohanty, 2005).

Table 4.2 reflects the extent of land acquired, the number of project-affected villages, the magnitude of affected families and the number of people displaced in western Odisha.

Mineral resources of Orissa

Western Orissa forms a continuum with the Northern Andhra and Jharkhand bauxite belt, most of it in its tribal areas. Major and minor metal deposits exist in 20 of the state's 30 districts, but two thirds of them are in the tribal-majority Keonjhar, Sundergarh, Koraput, Jajpur and Mayurbanj districts and the nontribal majority Jharsuguda and Angul districts. So mining can result in a cultural genocide if preventive steps are not taken to ensure their development. In reality MOUs are signed with various companies, including

Table 4.2 Displacement Due to Dam and Industrial Projects in Western Odisha

Project name	*Total land acquired (in acres)*	*No. of villages affected*	*No. of families affected*	*No. of people displaced*
Hirakud Dam	167,377	249	22,144	160,000
Upper Indravati Dam	32,477	105	5,301	18,500
Rengali Dam	102,672	263	11,289	46,570
Rourkela Steel Plant	19,277	30	4,251	23,400
Bhusan Steel	1,315	13	164	854
IB Thermal Power Station	487	03	147	748
Ib Valley Open Coal mine	4,500	18	110	495
OCL India, Rajgangpur	1,133	–	13	105
VAL, Lanjigarh	1,516	–	1,248	600
Upper Kolab Dam	2,8375	49	3,179	15,890

Sources: Bag, 2015: 79

one of the biggest with POSCO of South Korea for mineral exploitation and industries. In 1995, the state had 579 leases on 281,187.27 acres (113,840.99 hectares) of which 82,848.74 acres (33,542 hectares) in 113 leases in Keonjhar, 135 for 62,708.36 acres (25,388 hectares) in Sundergarh and 11 for 22,220.12 acres (8,996 ha) in Koraput, all three of them tribal majority districts. The metallic ores for which leases have been granted are bauxite, chromite, iron, lead and manganese ore. The nonmetallic minerals include asbestos, dolomite, graphite, kyanite, pyrophillite, quarts, and various clays and sands, both industrial and nonindustrial (Directorate of Mining and Geology, 1996: 36–43).

Not all the land of the operational mines could be identified. For example, data could be obtained for only 2,334.83 acres (945.28 hectares) that Mahanadi Coalfields (MCL) owned in 1995. But MCL was going to acquire 8,636.91 acres in the mid-1990s and more during the following years. Much of the land acquired in the past as well as what was proposed to be acquired is common or forest. For example, of the 8,636.91 acres mentioned previously, 4,095.09 acres (51.7 per cent) were private against 2,499.61 acres (31.56 per cent) revenue commons and 1,326.21 acres (16.74 per cent) forest (MCL, 1995: 3–12). Almost all the land that has been handed over to Utkal Aluminium near Kashipur, Rayagada district for bauxite mining is tribal commons; so is the land used by the NALCO mines near Damanjodi in Koraput district (Fernandes and Asif, 1997: 76). Of the 410,137.24 acres (166,047.47 hectares) used by mining until 1995, only 68,328.86 acres (16.66 per cent) were private, the rest being predominantly tribal commons and forest land (Fernandes and Asif, 1997: 84).

In other states too, limited data on displacement and deprivation could be got only from the 1980s. The initial figure of 2.55 million 1951–1900 arrived at from secondary sources (Fernandes, 1998: 231) is an underestimate. Table 4.3, based on primary data-based studies, gives a little over

Table 4.3 Conservative Estimate of Mining-Induced Displacement

State	*Years*	*Tribals*	*Dalits*	*Others*	*N/A*	*Total*	*Source*
Andhra	1980–1995	NA	NA	NA	100541	100541	Fernandes et al., 2001
Assam	1980–2000	NA	NA	NA	41200	41200	Fernandes and Bharali
Goa	1980s	NA	NA	NA	4740	4740	Fernandes and Naik, Forthcoming
Gujarat	1980–2000	NA	NA	NA	4128	4128	Lobo and Kumar, 2009
Jharkhand	1980–1995	83543	63352	220076	00	402882	Ekka and Asif 2000
Orissa	1960–1995	150000	45000	105000	00	300000	Fernandes&Asif 97
Kerala	1990s	NA	NA	NA	78	78	Murickan et al., 2003
W. Bengal	1960–2000	2459	99244	4373	311579	418061	Fernandes et al., 2006
Total		236002	207596	329449	462266	1571630	

Source: Compiled by the authors

1.5 million mining DP/PAPs in the 1980s and 1990s in a total of 60 million DP/PAPs of all the projects 1947–2000 (Fernandes, 2007: 204). It does not include Maharashtra, MP and Chhattisgarh, which have high deposits. Many others are up to 1995. When these states are studied and data on the others updated, one can expect the number 1947–2000 to be 5 million.

Landlessness takes the form of downward mobility from large to medium landholders, from medium or small to marginal and small and marginal farmers to landless. It has a caste tribe as well as a gender dimension. In Orissa, for example, among the mining-displaced families, 16.7 per cent of the tribal and 13 per cent of the Dalit DPs became landless against 3.6 per cent of the general castes (Pandey, 1995: 180).

Data from MCL also shows that the state had by then issued notifications for private land but took a long time to part with common land even after allotting it to MCL. For example, in 1995, 51.43 per cent of the private land that MCL had applied for was in its possession against only 19.87 per cent of the revenue commons and 17.64 per cent of the forest land (MCL, 1995: 13). The state speaks of development as a public purpose but seems to take its own precepts seriously only when it comes to people's sustenance, not to what it owns.

The state of Orissa has been confronting an enormous menace from the onslaught of projects for mining of bauxite, alumina refinery, sponge iron plants, etc. The environment, forest and other legislations that have been promulgated to protect the rights of the local communities, their natural resource-based livelihoods and the environment seem to appear too weak to achieve this objective in the face of the massive thrust for economic development from the state government (Tripathy, 2012: 114).

The project proposal of M/s Utkal Alumina International Ltd (UAIL) in Kashipur Tehsil, District Rayagada and Orissa (called the Utkal project here) was presented in such a manner that it ensured environment, forest and pollution laws have been implemented properly. As many as five bauxite mining and alumina projects are in the pipeline, covering five blocks of three districts: Kashipur (Rayagada district), Luxmipur and Dasamantpur (Koraput), Lanjigada and Thuamulrampur (Kalahandi). Sterlite is proposed to source bauxite from Sasubohumali of Kashipur block, Larson and Tubro from Sijimali and Kutrumali (Kashipur block), Birla from Kodinga Mali (Luxmipur block) and Vedanta from Niyamgiri and Khandualmali of Kalahandi district (Tripathy, 2012, op. cit.).

It has been estimated that the total investment in the Orissa bauxite projects is to the tune of Rs. 20,000 crores. Taking into consideration the present price of even just UAIL, the joint venture will reap a profit of at least Rs. 2,88,000 crores during the 22 to 23 years of the project life, whereas the government will get Rs. 1,300–1,400 crores as royalty during that period, whereas the tribes and Dalits of these villages will get state repression and a lifetime of misery and slum life.

Orissa has 90 per cent of India's chrome ore and nickel reserves, 70 per cent of bauxite and 24 per cent of coal reserves. With no other state having such abundance of natural resources, the big business houses have no option but to set up steel, alumina and coal-based power projects in Orissa only. Orissa's post-reform ability to attract both private and foreign investment makes it plausible that its pre-reform failure was due primarily to ineffective or nonexistent industrial policy to exploit its mineral wealth.

In recent years, Orissa grew somewhat more rapidly than in its pre-reform phase, 2.53 per cent per annum, but was still near the bottom of the states in growth performance (twelfth during 1991–98 as opposed to fourteenth during 1980–90). In some ways, moreover, Orissa became an innovator in economic reforms. It was the first state to reform its power sector, and it has strongly set out industrial policy (Tripathy, 2012: 115).

In recent years, Orissa has emerged on the investment map of India with a long list of investment proposals, largely backed by foreign investors. Apart from its new industrial policy, Orissa has also announced its agricultural and tourism policies. In the post-liberalisation period, Orissa ranks sixth in foreign investment and received the largest amount of private investments in India, both foreign and domestic, followed by Gujarat, Karnataka and Maharashtra. With the state government declaring heavy industry, infrastructure and aquaculture as thrust areas, the majority of new investments are in heavy industries consisting of steel, alumina and power projects. The abundance of cheap labour further makes it an investor-friendly state. Moreover, the state government has been offering exceptionally huge subsidies to investors, in the form of guarantees, tax concessions and investment subsidy Orissa.

Bauxite mining and ecological profile of the Niyamgiri hills

In 2003, Vedanta Resources signed a memorandum of understanding with the state government of Orissa for construction of a refinery for aluminium production, a power plant and related mining development at Lanjigarh in Kalahandi district. M/s Sterlite Industries (India) Limited (SIIL), fully owned and controlled by Vedanta Resources, proposed to set up a refinery with a capacity of 1 million tonnes per annum (tpa) for processing aluminium for export. It also proposed to extract bauxite from the area adjoining the refinery, which is estimated to have approximately 73 million tonnes of mineable ore. The location of the proposed mine lease (PML) site is between 190 38" to 190 48" North latitude and 830 22' to 830 25' East longitude. The mining is proposed to be undertaken on the top of the Niyamgiri hills in Kalahandi and Rayagada districts in Orissa, with the PML site between 900 to 1000 meters above mean sea level. The site will be spread over an area of seven square kilometers. As per the proposal, the PML site contains 72.897 million tonnes of bauxite and 17.9 million tonnes of overburden. When justifying the choice of Lanjigarh, district Kalahandi, as the site for the refinery, the proposal cited the proximity of the bauxite reserve to Lanjigarh, as well as the fact that SIIL had a lease agreement with the Orissa Mining Corporation (OMC).

The total PML area involves 721.323 hectares of land, including 672.018 hectares of forest land in the Niyamgiri hills, which are a part of the northern Eastern Ghats hill ranges and form Biotic Province 6C of the Deccan Plateau Zone 6 of the biogeography classification of the Wildlife Institute of India (WII). The PML area, which lies on the upper reaches of the Niyamgiri hills, Lanjigarh in Kalahandi district (Orissa), is surrounded by dense forests and is the habitat for diverse species of plant and animal life. The forest cover in the general area is very dense and consists of a number of ecological communities such as tropical evergreen forests, tropical moist deciduous forests, dry deciduous mixed forests, moist peninsular sal forests, dense bamboo forests, scrub woodlands and open grasslands. In addition, tropical semi-evergreen forests are also found along the stream courses.

The PML site, largely grassland surrounded by Sal forests, is an ecosystem inhabited by the DongariaKondh. The area covered under the PML falls under four different administrative blocks of forests representing three distinct legal categories of reserve forests, proposed reserve forests and unclassed protected forests, namely (1) Niyamgiri Reserve Forests, Kalahandi; (2) Khambesi Proposed Reserve Forests, Rayagada; (3) Niyamgiri Proposed Reserve Forests, Rayagada and (4) Jungle Block Unclassed Protected Forests, Rayagada. Recognising the wealth of biodiversity in the region, two plans were proposed by the government: the Niyamgiri Wildlife Sanctuary and the South Orissa Elephant Reserve.

The PML area is used by both Dongaria and KutiaKondh, which have been a part of their community reserved forests as well as their habitat since they depend on it for their livelihoods as well as socio-cultural practices. Their reverence for the hills is rooted in their strong dependence on the natural resources that the mountains provide.

Ecological impact of mining on the site

The mining site extends over more than seven square kilometers. Besides this area of excavation, the surrounding habitats would be severely disrupted by hundreds of people working continuously as part of the mining operations and living there, including those employed to protect the mining area and equipment from theft, etc. The consumption demands of this large human population would place an enormous burden on the surrounding biodiverse forests and wildlife; extraction for firewood and other minor forest produce including rare medicinal plants would increase several-fold. The increased presence of humans would disturb the wildlife population while simultaneously giving more people an opportunity to poach them. Even assuming best intentions on the part of the company to conserve these habitats, a higher incidence of wildlife poaching would be unavoidable.

The apprehension of environmental degradation of the Niyamgiri hills ecosystem by land degradation, geo-hydrological drainage change, air and water quality reduction and public health hazard caused by mining is based on extensive documentation by the Wildlife Institute of India (WII).8 The WII study stated,

> the threats posed by the proposed project to this important ecosystem will lead to irreversible changes in the ecological characteristics of the area.

Emphasizing the importance of ecosystem services, the WII report further stated,

> This cost benefit value should not only take into account the material benefits of the bauxite ore mining over a period of 26 years but should take into account the perpetuity of the resources and ecosystem services that would be provided by these forest in the future.

The Wildlife Institute of India concluded,

> Bauxite mining in Niyamgiri plateau will destroy a specialized kind of wildlife habitat, dominated by grasslands and sparse tree communities. These kinds of sites are breeding habitats of many herbivores such as barking deer and four-horned antelopes.

According to the previously mentioned WII study, as many as 1,21,337 trees will have to be cut if the mining lease is granted. Of these, 40 per cent will be in the PML area, and the remaining 60 per cent will be outside the PML site. The trees in the latter area would have to be removed to construct the access road and conveyor belt and other planned activities. This count of trees only accounts for planned felling of trees and does not include the illegal tree felling that invariably takes place once a large number of workers are able to access interior forest areas. Further, this number of 1.21 lakh includes only trees and not shrubs and herbs. Since the number of shrubs and large herbs in a rich tropical forest is at least three times the number of trees, it is reasonable to conclude that more than 3.63 lakh shrub and ground-level flora would also be removed under the project. This is a massive ecological cost of the project.

The mining operation of the kind and intensity proposed in the project would cause immense disturbance to the wildlife in this region. Mining operations such as blasting and excavation are accompanied by tremendous noise. Further disturbance is generated by the constant vehicular movement of large trucks transporting labourers and material connected to the mine. Hence, elephants and other wildlife populations would be perpetually disturbed. The road and the conveyor belt connecting the mining site to the refinery would cut through a large part of the habitat, particularly the elephant corridors, leaving it all but useless for them. If mining at this large-scale is permitted in this habitat, it would be a severe blow to the important task of elephant conservation in south Orissa.

As is well known, Kalahandi is one of the most drought-prone districts in the country, and thus water in streams and rivers in this district is a precious commodity. The bauxite-bearing soils have a highly porous structure that gives them an increased capacity for water retention. These hilltop bauxite-containing soils are sources of perennial water and are crucial for ensuring a continuous water supply in low rainfall seasons. The PML area is known for its ability to absorb rainwater and release it slowly, thereby making it an important contributor to the water that flows in rivers downstream. Several perennial springs appear to flow from below the top PML plateau. The hills form part of the catchment of two perennial rivers, the Vamsadhara and Nagavalli, with the PML as one of the main sources of the Vamsadhara. Similarly, Nagavalli, another important river, also originates from the Niyamgiri hills as well as the Bijipur Hills of the Eastern Ghats near Lanjigarh. Any negative impacts on the streams, through changes in recharging and drainage patterns, pollution or any other effect which changes the quantity and quality of water could have disastrous consequences for these communities. Mango and champa (*Michaeliachampaca*) trees are found just below the plateau on the hillsides. Given that these trees usually grow along water courses, their presence suggests that they are able to access perennial sources of water just below the surface. The loss of vegetation and topsoil can cause flooding, and the water emerging from the debris contains toxic solutes including selenium, metals and sulphates. The mining project would cause soil erosion and pollution of the water systems, which in turn would result in deteriorated water quality and damage to riverine habitats, and the consequent changes in the hydrological regime would also adversely affect the flora and fauna in the entire region. The potential impacts of the mining project on perennial streams that form the catchments of two important rivers extend beyond local human and wildlife populations to a far wider area, indicating that great caution must be exercised in this regard. These concerns become even more significant in the context of climate change-induced fluctuations in rainfall and weather patterns.

Lacunae in the rehabilitation policy

In the context of rehabilitation of displaced people in tribal regions of Orissa, it has been observed that on the part of government and its agents of development, cash compensation seems to be the only panacea for the problems induced by displacement and only policy for rehabilitation, whereas in practice it is the most inadequate means for rehabilitation. No procedure and principles are laid down to estimate the costs, showing the arbitrariness of compensation.

Apart from loss of land, the villager suffers loss from common property resources forest produce, village grazing land, community centre, social security and so on. The problem is more acute with the artisans. Some of them may own land, but their major income is from their profession within the known community. There seems no provision with regard to their rehabilitation. Besides, the landless and the tribes are probably the worst sufferers.

The situation of the tribal people is all the thornier since the compensation is paid on the basis of land owned; the tribes who have no inclination to own land but use it as a common property fail to claim compensation on the basis of the lost common land. It's difficult to estimate how land, natural resources, means of livelihood and social and cultural loss resulting from displacement can be quantified and compensated in monetary terms. And the non-quantifiable nature of numerous human and ecological costs are not quantified nor even acknowledged.

The government acknowledges the problem that in tribal areas, where the displaced persons are given only cash compensation, the tendencies to spend the compensation amount by buying consumer goods/unproductive investments and finally becoming destitute.

The benefits of this paradigm of development have been disproportionately cornered by the dominant sections at the expense of the poor, who have borne most of the costs. Development which is insensitive to the needs of these communities has invariably caused displacement and reduced them to a subhuman existence. In the case of tribes in particular, it has ended up destroying their social organisation, cultural identity and resource base and generated multiple conflicts, undermining their communal solidarity, which cumulatively makes them increasingly vulnerable to exploitation.

Displacement deprives the vital sustenance of the tribal people who are dependent on the land, forests and common property resources (CPR) for their livelihood, and finally their long-term sustainability is also endangered. As has been outlined previously, whereas the tribes constitute 8.08 per cent of country's population, they are 40 per cent of the total displaced/affected persons by the projects (GoI, 2008: 22).

Concluding remarks and policy implications

In light of the previously stated discussion, we can suggest that:

1) In order to achieve the goals of sustainable development and for the development itself to sustain, it must come from the bottom, which is possible only when the third tier of the governance (functional in its real sense) has determinative rights of participation in policy framing and decision-making when it proposes to affect their interests. Though the structural arrangements in this regard are ensured through the 73rd and 74th amendments of the constitution and numerous Panchayat Acts in the states, the irony (all too commonplace now) is that the provisions are seldom upheld in practice.
2) A functional grassroots democracy and people's participation in decision-making that benefits and harmonizes all interests is probably the best possible way to complete the projects on time and keep the costs from

escalating and minimizing the miseries of affected. '"Development which cannot provide the basic necessities of life should be shunned" and attempts be made for an alternate mode of development which should aim at providing roads in villages instead of flyovers in cities, schools in all places instead of five star hotels'. Protagonists of development should understand that it is not possible for the multinational companies to ameliorate the plight of the starving millions in the country.

3) We can also suggest that our legal frame should be restructured with the right to life of the common man, particularly the poverty-stricken marginalised tribes as the central point. First of all, all unconstitutional elements should be identified and eliminated from all the laws, particularly those concerning the command over resources, ownership of means of production and existence of labour (Sharma, 2010).
4) The Panchayat Extension to Scheduled Areas (PESA) Act, 1996, has made it mandatory for the states to have scheduled areas to make specific provisions for providing a wide range of powers to the tribes for their development. The act recognizes traditional customary rights over local natural resources. It accepts the validity of customary law and social and religious practices of community resources. It empowered villages to protect community resources, control social sector functionaries, own minor forest produce, manage water bodies, give recommendations for mining leases, be consulted for land acquisition, identify beneficiaries for poverty alleviation and other government programs and have a decisive say in all development projects in the villages (Das, 2005).

Section 4 (M) of PESA authorizes the gram sabha to act in all areas where the tribes face threat to their survival and welfare because of their continued exploitation. The PESA creates legal space for direct community action; therefore PESA directly confers ownership to the gram sabha on minor forest produce (MFP) which has been a support for their survival. But it has been observed that this right has been neglected or violated rather than adhered to. The commercial value of MFP has been appreciated, resulting in the nationalisation of MFP and thereby optimizing the state's revenue (Tripathy, 2013).

Thus, despite PESA, as well as several other protective legislations in the tribal regions of our country, there has been extensive violations of fundamental rights and human rights of the tribal people. The second hindrance lies in the inability of the poor peasants to make their voice heard in the face of elite domination of the traditional power structures. The ingrained problem of elite domination can hardly be resolved unless the tribal poor themselves can exercise enough bargaining power and be organized so their collective voice can be audible to the irrigation executives and bureaucrats. It is lamentable fact that the purpose of the PESA Act has not been completely understood either by the political leaders or by the bureaucracy. People at large are also not aware of the provisions of PESA Act, except in those areas where the NGOs are seriously working with the people (Tripathy, op. cit.).

Thus, PESA aims at ensuring significant protection against any arbitrary, discriminatory and motivated action of the state relating to land acquisition and resettlement and rehabilitation (R&R) in tribal regions. It has been revealed that the local administration in league with the company officials was indulging in deliberate falsehood. In the consultation of 'gram sabha', the method adopted is dubious as the consent was obtained through coercion and brutal force (Das, op. cit.).

5) It is therefore suggested that the Land Acquisition Act should be amended in consonance with the PESA Act so that rights of the people are protected in fifth schedule areas. No act of force should be used when there is conflict over resources, and as per the recommendation of the 28th Report of the scheduled castes and scheduled tribes commissioner, laws should be passed prohibiting the use of force in case of disputes over resources in the tribal areas. There should be tribal development plan in collaboration and coordination with the department of forest whose involvement is critical for the promotion and implementation of legal provisions pertaining to tribal land and resource entitlements.
6) An appropriate development strategy calls for a reorientation of economic policy where priority to the protection of existing livelihood, generation of usual employment, production for people's needs and ecologically sustainable harnessing and use of natural resources are ensured. The local population in all its diversity must be empowered to control natural resources and decide their utilisation and replenishment to ensure fulfilment of basic needs. Such an approach will safeguard the cultural values and ensure biodiversity, allowing space for participation of women and marginalised peoples in all decision-making processes of the village community. Committed to a people-oriented and ecologically sound economic policy approach requires the development of a people's democracy based on people's control over resources. This should be inbuilt in the local community following the basic principle that the first claim on the use of resources should be the satisfaction of basic needs and the protection of livelihood.
7) Investment in social forestry, reclamation of agricultural land, provision of free and compulsory education, health services and guaranteed employment or source of employment with multiple livelihood options, equitable sharing of resources with utmost priority for tribes and immediate implementation of PESA in the fifth schedule areas will certainly ameliorate the situation of the marginalised section.
8) We can conclude that environmental problems are those which arise out of the misuse of the natural resource base: the soils, forests and water resources. These problems are created to a great extent because of the pressure to produce raw materials for modern industry. Therefore,

what we need is a fundamental shift of consciousness. We should be learning from Orissa's indigenous people, not dispossessing them of the land they have safeguarded over centuries.

9) There is a need to maintain ecological balance, to prevent further ecological destruction while increasing the productivity of land, water and forest resources and to identify and implement a development process that will lead to greater equity, growth and sustainability. Development without concern for the environment can only be short-term development. In the long term, it can only be anti-development and can go on only at the cost of enormous human suffering, increasing poverty in mobilizing people.
10) In view of the skewed distribution of income and wealth in the society and concentration of poverty, we need to provide a suitable rehabilitation strategy for the benefit of tribes which can ensure a strategy for their livelihood. As such, we need to rethink and reformulate our policy so as to percolate the benefits our resources on a sustainable basis for the greater interest of public, especially for employment and income generating through linkage effect on industry and other service sectors.
11) Overexploitation of natural resources like land, forests, water, etc. have often been held responsible for environmental degradation. In order to reduce the exploitation of natural forests, scientific management of forest resources is the imperative need of the hour which would require plantations of mixed species and recycling of forest products.
12) The most crucial issue is that despite the development of mining industries, the inequality in the distribution of income and wealth widens and results in concentration of poverty among the tribes in Orissa. In view of the skewed distribution of income and wealth in the society and concentration of poverty, we need to provide a suitable rehabilitation strategy for the benefit of tribes which can ensure a strategy for their livelihood.
13) The resettlement and rehabilitation policy should recognise the traditionally established rights of the tribal and rural communities over natural resources and their sustenance. Full compensation and prior consent are indispensable ingredients which must be applied to the common property resources (CPR) with a prudent cost-benefit analysis emphasizing the distribution patterns. Even if the principle is acknowledged that displacement projects/project-affected peoples should receive a share in the benefits of projects that displace them, monetary payments are inadequate for the CPR dependants since they are not sufficiently in contact with the monetary economy. Therefore, an alternative paradigm needs to be evolved to ensure that they get permanent income from the project, for instance, through becoming shareholders in it.
14) The displaced tribes should be resettled in a safe habitat wherein they can start their life afresh. However, this would require more than mere allocation of certain piece of land for resettlement or mere construction

of makeshift camps for temporary settlement. What is needed is the 'rehabilitation' of the persons affected by the projects; rehabilitation means to 'restore to the former condition', and thus, all that was lost by displacement and the emotional, cultural, social, political and economic losses must be restored at a priority basis than to the project itself, which is the cause of the impoverishment.

As such, we need to rethink and reformulate our policy so as to percolate the benefits of our resources on a sustainable basis for the greater interest of public, especially for creation of employment and income generation through linkage effect on industries and other service sectors.

References

BAGH, G. (2015). The Drive for Industrialisation: Displacement and Misery of Tribal at Large (With Reference to Odisha State). *IUN Journal of Social Sciences*, vol. 1, no. 2, 69–83.

Behura, N. K. (1990). Socio-Economic Problems and Social Change. In V. Sundersen and M. A. Kalam (Eds.), *The Uprooted*. New Delhi: Gian Publishing House.

Behura, N. K. (1996). Environment, Displacement and Development: Case Study from Orissa. *Journal of Indian Anthropology Society*, vol. 31, pp. 149–159.

Biswaranjan, Mohanty. (2005). Displacement and Rehabilitation of Tribals. *Economic and Political Weekly*, pp. 1318–1320, 26 March.

Cullinan, Cormac. (2002). *Wild Law: A Manifesto for Earth Justice*. Totnes: Green Books, with the Gaia Foundation 38.

Das, Achut. (2005). *Governance in Tribal Arrears: Myths and Realities*. Rayagada, Orissa: Agragamee.

Directorate of Mining and Geology. (1996). *Mineral Statistics of Orissa 1994–95*. Bhubaneshwar: Department of Steel and Mines.

Ekka, Alexius and Mohammed Asif. (2000). *Development-Induced Displacement and Rehabilitation in Jharkhand: A Database on Its Extent and Nature*. New Delhi: Indian Social Institute.

Fernades, Walter. (1994). *Development Induced Displacement in Tribal Areas of Eastern India*. New Delhi: Indian Social Institute (mimeo).

Fernandes, Walter. (1998). Development Induced Displacement in Eastern India. In S. C. Dube (Ed.), *Antiquity to Modernity in Tribal India*, vol. I. New Delhi: Sage Publications.

Fernandes, Walter. (2007). Singur and the Displacement Scenario. *Economic and Political Weekly*, pp. 203–206, 20–26 January.

Fernandes, Walter and Mohammed Asif. (1997). *Development- Induced Displacement in Orissa 1951 to 1995: A Database on Its Extent and Nature*. New Delhi: Indian Social Institute.

Fernandes, Walter and Gita Bharali. (2006). *Development-Induced Displacement in Assam 1947–2000: A Quantitative and Qualitative Study of Its Extent and Nature*. Guwahati: North Eastern Social Research Centre (mimeo).

Fernandes, Walter, Shanti Chhetri, Sherry Joseph and Satyen Lama. (2006). *Development-Induced Displacement and Deprivation in West Bengal 1947–2000: A Quantitative and Qualitative Database on Its Extent and Impact*. Guwahati: North Eastern Social Research Centre (mimeo).

Fernandes, Walter, Nafisa Goga D' Souza, Arundhuti Roy Choudhury and Mohammed Asif. (2001). *Development-Induced Displacement, Deprivation and Rehabilitation in Andhra Pradesh 1951–1995: A Quantitative and Quantitative Study of Its Extent and Nature.* New Delhi: Indian Social Institute and Guwahati, North Eastern Social Research Centre.

Fernandes, Walter and Niraj Naik. (Forthcoming). *Development-Induced Displacement in Goa 1965.1995: A Study on Its Extent and Nature.* Guwahati: North Eastern Social Research Centre.

Government of India. (2008). *Development Challenges in Extremists Affected Areas.* Report of an Expert Group to Planning Commission, New Delhi.

Lobo, L. and S. Kumar. (2009). *Land Acquisition, Displacement and Resettlement in Gujarat: 1947–2004.* New Delhi: Sage.

MCL. (1995). *Status of Land Acquisition in 1995.* Sambalpur: RR and LA Department, Mahanadi Coalfields Limited.

Mohapatra, L. K. (1998). *Participatory Approach in Resettlement and Rehabilitation, Implementation.* Paper presented at Gopabandhu Academy of Administration, in the seminar of Resettlement and Rehabilitation.

Mohapatra, L. K. (1999). *Impoverishment and Reconstruction in India: Development for the Deprived.* New Delhi: Vikash Publishing House.

Murickan, Jose, M. K. George, K. A. Emmanuel, Jose Boban and Prakash Pillai R. (2003). *Development-Induced Displacement: Case of Kerala.* New Delhi: Rawat Publications.

Ota, A. B. (1998). Countering Impoverishment Risks: The Case of Rengali Dam Project. In H. M. Mathur and David Marsden (Eds.), *Development Projects and Impoverishment Risks.* New Delhi: Oxford University Press.

Panda, P. and N. Panigrahi. (1989). The Problem of Displaced People: A Study in the Coal Mines of Brajarajnagar, Sambalpur, Orissa. In R. N. Pati and B. Jena (Ed.), *Tribal Studies in India.* New Delhi: Ashish Publication House.

Pandey, Balaji. (1995). Impoverishing Effects of Coal Mining Projects: A Case Study of five Villages in Orissa. In Hari Mohan Mathur and David Marsden (Eds.), *Development Projects & Impoverishment Risks: Resettling Project-Affected People in India.* New Delhi: Oxford University Press, pp. 174–192.

Pandey, Balaji. (1998). *Depriving the Underprivileged by Development.* Bhubaneswar: Institute of Socio-Economic Development.

Patnaik, S. M. (1996). *Displacement, Rehabilitation and Social Change.* New Delhi: Inter-India Publication.

Sharma, B. D. (2010). *Unbroken History of Broken Promises- Indian State and Tribal People.* New Delhi: Sahyog Pustak Kuteer.

Tripathy, S. N. (2003). Problems of Displacement and Development. In *Economic Development and Problem of Displacement.* New Delhi: Anmol Publication (self-edited).

Tripathy, S. N. (2012). Mining and Displacement Problems in Orissa. In NiharRanjan Mishra and Kamal K. Misra (Eds.), *Displacement and Rehabilitation.* New Delhi: Gyan Publishing House.

Tripathy, S. N. (2013). *Tribal Development: Issues and Policy Options.* New Delhi: Abhijeet Publications.

Wildlife Institute of India Report, Commissioned by the MoEF. Studies on Impact of Proposed Lanjigarh Bauxite Mining on Biodiversity Including Wildlife and Its Habitat, 2006–2007.

5 Land grabbing in tribal mineral belt of Odisha

Implications for livelihood and environment

Ramya Ranjan Patel

Introduction

The standard economic theory says natural resources (i.e., minerals and forests) play an important role in the development of an economy. If a country is abundant with natural resources, it enhances higher economic growth, development and general prosperity. In other words, development of region depends on how richly it is endowed with natural resources. It has been a popular belief that resource-rich regions, states or countries are less likely to be poor and underdeveloped.

However, it has not happened with most of the resource-rich regions; rather poverty and underdevelopment are more closely associated with them. The experience of many developing countries and particularly the mineral-rich states or regions show the reverse. The proposition that 'resource-rich regions are more developed' is quite contradictory (since the regions with plenty of natural resources are poorer and underdeveloped). Resources have failed to play a positive role in the development of many states or regions.

Nonetheless, the same has contributed immensely in the development of other countries, states or regions. England, France, Spain or Portugal gained, at the cost of extraction and transfer of raw material at cheapest price or with no price from their colonies in Asia, Africa and Latin America. The colonial exploitations in the forms of slave trade, transfer of revenue, transfer of resources (raw material) and, more importantly, 'export of unemployment'[1] to their colonies made the present developed countries at the cost of their resource-rich colonies.

In many cases, natural resources seem to have been a *curse* for those regions and people. Instead of making the regions develop and prosperous, it has led to large-scale land grabbing, displacement and forceful eviction of people, particularly indigenous-tribal and destruction of their livelihoods, further depriving them of their own culture and society. There is underdevelopment along with environmental destruction. A.G. Frank (1970: 1179–1180) explained the previous contradiction as:

> If we examine the historical evidence honestly, we must come to the conclusion that if Europeans went to New England in order to work,

> it is not because they wanted to, but because in New England they could not do anything else. There was nobody and nothing to exploit, whereas it was possible to build an exploitative colonial economy in the South of the United States, in the Caribbean and in most of Latin America, although for a long time it was not possible to do so in Argentina because the land there was not suitable for export production until wool, meat and wheat could be profitably transported to Europe in the fourteenth century. So we must come to the apparently paradoxical, but on reflection "not really so surprising", conclusion that development occurred where there was poverty and, underdevelopment occurred where there was wealth. That is to say, in the "rich" colonies, rich in silver, rich in climate and rich in native or imported but exploited labour, underdevelopment developed; and in the "poor" regions, where it was not then possible to exploit anybody, development developed.

There are many instances of such contradiction (between resources and development) prevailed in India, particularly in the mineral-tribal belt of Odisha, Chhattisgarh and Jharkhand. The three states are famously known for their abundance of resources as well as abundance in poverty. Their land is rich, but people are poor. Poverty, backwardness and underdevelopment have been persisting in those states for decades despite their rich resource base. It has happened even after 65 years of independence (without colonial plunder) of a Socialist Democratic Republic that says 'the state to strive to promote the socio-economic and political welfare of the people' (Art 38).

The high growth rate realised in India is mainly because of these mineral-rich states (like Odisha, Jharkhand or Chhattisgarh) which provides raw material to the core industries, vital for the growth of rest of the economy. Moreover, the regions are highly industrialized (with mineral-based heavy industries) and experienced the first phase of industrialisation in India after independence. On the other hand, the 'temples of modern India' (the steel industries established in Rourkela, Bokaro and Bhilai) have not transformed these states to the path of development even after more than 50 years of such may be establishments. The rich lands and the industries based on it have failed to lift its population out of poverty. At a micro level, the contradiction between resources and development or 'resource curse' is more clearly visible, particularly in the districts or regions like *Joda-Barbil (iron ore/Keonjhar), Damanjodi (bauxite/Koraput), Gopalpur (Vasundhara coal mines, Sundergarh) or the famous Niyamgiri* where mineral resources are found in abundance.

It surprises many why the state (Odisha) is poor despite its rich natural resource base. It is a common perception: a state abundant with natural resources should not remain poor. Haan and Dubey (2005: 2328) remark poverty persists in Odisha 'despite significant mineral wealth', no absolute food shortage and democracy with a free press. According to M. Govind Rao (2009), though Odisha, Rajasthan and undivided states of Bihar and Madhya Pradesh are rich in minerals, yet these are the poorest states. The title of the book *Rich Lands and Poor* by Gunar Myrdal (1958) and the title of one of the reports *Rich Lands, Poor People: Is Sustainable Mining Possible* (2009) by Centre for Science and Environment indicate somewhat such relationship. All these imply a state (or region) endowed with plenty of natural resources is less likely to be poor or there should exist an inverse relationship between the richness of resources and poverty of a region.

In this context, this chapter broadly answers if the resource and industries based on those resource benefits the state or its people, particularly living in the regions where those resources are found and the industries are established. In other words, it probes if those resources have become a win-win for the state or a 'pyrrhic victory'. The objectives of the chapter are to study the impact of land acquisition on the livelihood of people, particularly the scheduled tribe of Odisha on the one hand and its environmental implications on the other. It also studies the politics behind governments' motivation of large-scale *land grabbing* in promoting such extraction-based industries.

This chapter begins with the analyses of the paradox between resources and development in the context of Odisha. This is followed by the impact of land grabbing on the livelihood and employment of the people, particularly the tribal. The next section discusses the impact of such activity (mining, extraction industries and land grabbing) on the environment. Lastly it highlights the political economy of such a pattern of development model.

Data sources and methodology

This is an interdisciplinary study that primarily deals with economics, politics and environment. To answer the questions, secondary data at a district level are collected from various sources of the state department and census of India, NSSO (district-wise poverty from unit-level data) and Association of Democratic Reforms (ADR). The other sources of data are RBI, Indian Bureau of Mines, Economic Survey and Odisha Pollution Control Board. The study critically analyses the government's policy towards the mining-based industrialisation model of development. It is an attempt of intellectual analysis of studying ethics and related obligations, particularly of the state machinery towards its citizen.

Odisha: abundance of poverty and abundance of mineral resources

Odisha is the poorest state in India (see table 5.1), and it is even worse in terms of some of the African and sub-Saharan countries (see table 5.2).

The poverty and backwardness are not equally found in all the regions of the state; in some regions of the state, the incidence of poverty is much

Table 5.1 Poverty and HDI in Indian States

States	*Poverty (Rural, 2004–05)*	*HDI Value (2011)*
Andhra Pradesh	10.5	0.485
Assam	22.1	0.474
Bihar	42.6	0.447
Chhattisgarh	40.8	0.449
Gujrat	18.9	0.514
Haryana	13.3	0.545
Himachal Pradesh	10.5	0.558
Jammu and Kashmir	4.3	
Jharkhand	46.2	0.464
Karnataka	20.7	0.508
Kerala	13.2	0.625
Madhya Pradesh	36.8	0.454
Maharashtra	29.6	0.549
Odisha	46.9	0.442
Punjab	9	0.569
Rajasthan	18.3	0.468
Tamil Nadu	23	0.544
Uttarakhand	33.3	0.515
Uttar Pradesh	40.7	0.468
West Bengal	28.4	0.509
India	28.3	0.519

Source: Col 2. (NSSO 61st round), Col 3. UNDP India 2011 (Inequality Adjusted Human Development Index for India's States)

Table 5.2 HDI Value of Odisha and Some African Countries

Countries	*HDI value (2011)*
Eq. Guinea	0.538
Swaziland	0.498
Congo	0.489
Ghana	0.467
Cameroon	0.46
Odisha	0.442

Source: UNDP India 2011

higher in comparison to the other. For example, poverty in the Southern region is as high as 72.7 per cent in comparison to 59.1 per cent in Northern and only 27.4 per cent in the Coastal region (table 5.3). Secondly it is important to note that poverty in the Southern and Northern regions are increasing during the period 1993–94 to 2004–05. The incidence of poverty among the tribal is even highest in all the regions of the state.

Abundance of resources and industrialisation

The state is poorest in India though enriched with plenty of natural mineral resources (see table 5.4). To move people out of poverty, the government of

Table 5.3 Incidences of Poverty Across Regions and Social Groups

Region	*Poverty (HCR), 93–94*	*Poverty (HCR), 04–05*	*Poverty by social groups (1999–00)*			
			ST	*SC*	*Other*	*All*
Coastal	45.3	27.4	66.63	42.18	24.32	31.74
Southern	68.8	72.7	92.42	88.9	77.65	87.05
Northern	45.9	59.1	61.69	57.22	34.67	49.81
Total	49.8	46.9	73.08	52.3	33.29	48.04

Source: Col. 2 and 3, Manoj Panda (Economic Development of Orissa: Growth without Inclusion? IGIDR, 2008) *Col. 3*, Haan and Dubey (EPW, May 28–June 4, 2005)

Table 5.4 Mineral Deposits in Odisha (2004–05), in Million Tonnes

Mineral deposits	*India*	*Odisha*	*Percentage of deposits in Odisha*
Bauxite	3289.82	1808.27	54.97
Coal*	253301.66	61999.26	24.48
Chromite	213.06	202.96	95.26
Manganese Ore	378.57	152.96	40.4
Fireclay	704.76	175.49	24.9

Sources: (1)*mineral deposits by the end of 2005–06, from Indian Mineral Year Book, 2006; (2) Indian Bureau of Mines, New Delhi

Odisha primarily relies on mineral-based industrialisation policy as a panacea for all economic problems looking at its abundance.[2] In the last decade, it has speeded up the process of industrialisation and signed 89 MOUs (Memorandum of Understandings) until 2011 to establish such mineral-based extractive industries; 49 (MOUs) are for setting up steel plants, more than 20 coal-based power plants and a few alumina refineries.[3]

The motivation of Pandit Nehru and the planning commission (existing earlier) is equally reflected in the case of the government of Odisha, the way it pursues the present industrialisation (mining-based, capital-intensive industries) model of development, simply on the basis of the belief that only industry will move Odisha out of poverty and backwardness. It presupposes that it creates employment opportunities for the people, including the tribal.

Do resources and mineral-based industries lead to development?

Resources and industries based on those resources have been a contributing factor for escape from poverty, but its contribution has been much less than its expectations. Table 5.5 shows that the regions (Northern and Southern) have the highest and second highest numbers of mines (30.67 and 6.67) respectively, and area-covered mines (7910 and 1045 respectively) are also positively related to percentage of government forests (32 and 44) and ST population (36 and 56). It also indicates that a majority of mineral-based

Table 5.5 Resources (Minerals and Forests) and Development Indicators of Odisha

Regions	*No. of mines (2010–11)*	*Area covered under mines, 2010–11 (hect.)*	*% of govt. forest (05–06)*	*% of ST population*	*Percentage of poor, (URP), NSSO- 61, 04–05*	*Malnourished children (grade 1–4) 2010*	*Per capita NDDP, 2010–11 (2004–05 price), RS*	*MPCE (NSSO, 2004–05)*
Northern	30.67	7910.00	32.43	36.38	61.29	55.05	28295.22	256.33
Southern	6.67	1045.83	44.75	56.43	65.84	56.23	22002.67	241.50
Coastal	3.22	850.00	26.81	7.17	30.74	43.92	22352.33	353.44
Odisha	12.83	91390			46.9	52.31	23968	279.53

Source: Col. 2 and 5, Statistical Abstract of Odisha 2012; Col. 6, URP, NSSO, 61, 04–05; Col. 7, Dept. of Women and Child Development, Orissa; Col. 8, Economic Survey of Odisha 2013–14; Col. 8, Food Security Atlas of Odisha 2008

industries are located in those regions (since such industries are primarily located nearer to the point of origin of its raw materials), but those regions also experience highest percentage of poverty (61 and 65) or lowest monthly per capita consumption expenditure (Rs. 256 and 241 respectively) and higher percentage of malnutrition (55 and 56). On the other hand, the region (Coastal) has the lowest number of mines (3.22) or lowest area under mines (850 hectares), and extraction-based industries experience the lowest percentage of poverty (30.74), malnutrition (43.92) and highest monthly per capita consumption expenditure (Rs. 279).

The problems with mineral resources not only fails to uplift people from its availability but is also associated with various other problems like displacement of people, destruction of their livelihood and large-scale damage to the environment. The benefits are seen only at a macro level; The positive impacts are shown on a national level while the negative impacts are borne at the local level. The mining activities destroy the livelihood of the local communities.

Land grabbing: displacement and livelihood

It is the very nature of mineral resources that are found mostly in the high lands (hilly-plateau-table lands) or forest land,[4] which also has a large indigenous tribal population. Thus, mining and industries based on mining are responsible for the destruction of forests as well as the habitats and livelihood of the tribal population. There has been a historical injustice to forest dwellers who are forced to relocate due to various state developmental projects like mining. In this process, there is large-scale acquisition of land, particularly in the mineral-rich forest land, or there is large-scale 'land grabbing' in those regions. During the period 1980–2012, about 1.1 million hectares were diverted, 40 per cent of which is for mining and power projects.[5] Since 1980, diversion is steadily increasing while the rate of rejection of projects is decreasing.[6] During eleventh Five-Year Plan (2007–2012), over 0.2 million hectares were diverted for these development projects. During January 2013–April 2013, more than 12,000 hectares were diverted, and it is estimated that 135 hectares are being diverted daily.[7] According to CSE (Centre for Science and Environment), in the next ten years, more than 1.1 million hectares of forest land will be diverted for various developmental projects.[8]

In Odisha, 12,186 hectares of forest land has been diverted only for the mining and industrial activities that composed 42 per cent of the total forest diverted for non-forest use during 1982 to 2005 (Directorate of Economics and Statistics, Government of Odisha, 2005). Table 5.6 shows mining only is responsible for the highest area of forest land occupied during the period 1982–2012.

Displacement

The projects, including the mining activities, have led to large-scale displacement of people and more particularly the tribal, primarily residing in

Table 5.6 Project-Wise Forest Area Diverted for Non-Forest Use in Odisha, 1982–2012, in Hectares

Purpose		
Irrigation	Number of projects	83
	Forests area diverted	9712
	Percentage of forest area diverted	24.45
Mining	Number of projects	148
	Forest area diverted	16053
	Percentage of forest area diverted	40.41
Others (energy, roads, bridges, industries, railways and defence, etc.)	Number of projects	153
	Forest area diverted	13955
	Percentage of forest area diverted	35.13
Total	Number of projects	384
	Forest area diverted	39720

Source: Directorate of Economics and Statistics, Government of Odisha, 2012

the forest and hilly regions. They directly or indirectly depend on the forests for food, shelter and livelihood. These people and particularly the primitive tribes *(Kondh, Paharia and Juanga)* know no other economic activities other than cultivation and collection of forest products for their survival. Forest has a vital source of livelihood for them, and if they are displaced from it, there is scarce possibility they would survive practising any other economic activities.[9]

'It is estimated that some 50 million persons have been displaced since 1950 on account of various development projects, of which more than 40 per cent are tribal. Some 3 to 5 million people in Odisha have been displaced since 1950 for various development projects out of which more than fifty percent are tribal'.[10] Mining activity has displaced 1.03 million tribal people, who constitute 52.2 per cent of the total population displaced, over 75 per cent of those displaced remain without proper rehabilitation (Tripathi, 2011). Those who owned and tilled their own land or eked out a living from forests and other natural resources have been reduced to being landless workers, doing odd jobs for a living and leading lives of penury. In these large development projects, tribals lose their land not only to the project authorities, but even to non-tribal outsiders who converge into these areas and corner both the land and the new economic opportunities in commerce and petty industry.

Moreover, the government claims, it is adequately compensating the displaced tribal so they will eke a living out of it. Two questions arise from the monetary compensation of the government. First, the monetary compensation is given only to the people who have legal rights of their land and not the customary rights, and the tribals residing in the forests, for example, in *Niyamgiri* hills, have customary rights and not legal rights. Thus, majority of them are excluded even from monetary compensation. Second, even if monetary compensation is given, what utility does it hold for them? Since M-C-M (Money-Commodity-Money) circuit is missing in their society,[11] the concept of money has not penetrated their life, as it happens in the primitive stage of (development) of any society. Padel et al. (2013: 3) argue that tribal people's understanding of wealth focuses less on money and possessions and more on assured abundance in nature. Once it is spent out, once their habitats have been destroyed, they are left with no options, and their life is at the verge of collapse. Thus, money is less required by them, and what they require is their own natural habitats.

If comparatively developed, economic activity (i.e., mining and mining-based industries) is imposed to a region, practising traditional economic activities (i.e., subsistence agriculture and food gathering), it is very likely that it will ruin the latter and people depending on it. People depending on the latter find it difficult to cop up with a change in socio-economic environment since a 'backward productive' force cannot exist in an 'advanced production relation' (Lange, 1963: 12).

Employment

Many projects worth billions of rupees have been established in the tribal-mineral belt of Odisha, particularly in extraction and extraction-based industries. The governments interested in those projects presuppose that it creates employment opportunities for the people, including the tribal. Questions arise. Are the poor, uneducated, illiterate, unskilled local tribal population getting any employment opportunities in the developed industrial sector? If yes, at what wage rate?

The ability of the poor to participate in the growth process depends on the presence of some enabling conditions like literacy, good health and information about the new opportunities, or popularly known as the 'capabilities'.[12] They are less likely to take part in the opportunities created at their doorsteps or in their locality because of lack of human capital formation or 'capability' deprivation (see tables 5.7 and 5.8). The tables show the educational attainment of scheduled tribes is much lowest in comparison to any other community, both in case of India (table 5.7) as well as in Odisha (table 5.8). Since they are illiterate, unskilled, undernourished or not well informed about the opportunities created in the advanced urban sector, they seldom participate in the growth process. The 'transitional victims' of the present model of industry-led growth are less likely to get absorbed in the modern economy because of two reasons: low absorptive capacity of the capital-intensive modern industries and lack of human capital formation of the rural poor, said Patnaik (2010).

Education is a potentially important determinant of access to employment because it converts individuals into a different kind of labour by imparting skills (Nayyar, 2009: 5). Therefore, more educated people are likely to be employed in the formal sector. The challenges of education, skills and training is a question of level of income, which is low in the rural tribal belt because of the shackles of the 'vicious cycle of poverty'. There is an overlap between poverty and poor quality of employment as well. Levels of education and

Table 5.7 Educational Attainment (Percentage) for Youths (Male), Aged 24–29

Educational attainment	*1999–2000*
Others	
Never enrolled	17.08
Below primary	8.18
Primary completed	11.61
Middle school completed	20.47
Secondary completed	28.25
College graduate	14.41
Dalit (SC)	
Never enrolled	36.75
Below primary	11.21
Primary completed	13.87
Middle school completed	16.76
Secondary completed	16.58
College graduate	4.83
Adivasi (ST)	
Never enrolled	43.94
Below primary	11.52
Primary completed	11.17
Middle school completed	14.22
Secondary completed	14.21
College graduate	4.94

Source: Desai and Kulkarni (2008), Demography. May, 45(2)

Table 5.8 Region-wise Literacy Rate of ST Population in Odisha

Social groups	*Male*	*Female*	*Total*
Odisha (all social groups)	82.0	64.0	73.0
SC	75.2	56.5	66.1
ST	68.5	49.4	59.0

Source: Census, 2011 (Directorate of Economics and Statistics, Government of Odisha, 2012)

professional and vocational skills are extremely low and mostly confined among the rich since acquisition of education and skills is directly related to income. Mobility from the unproductive-casual employment to productive formal employment is low due to differential access to education and training facilities (India Labour and Employment Report, 2010: 8).

Even wage employment to local tribals is rare in those industries. For example, in Chotanagpur area, though the tribals constitute more than 50 per cent of the total population, there are not more than 5 per cent of them in the industrial working force. In some of the large firms like TISCO, Jamshedpur and Bharat Coking Coal Ltd., Dhanbad, the tribals employed are less than 5 per cent.[13] As a result, their chances of earning income from employment in those industries are threatened, and they move further and further into distress. They have been reduced to being landless workers, doing odd jobs for a living and leading lives of penury because of those projects (Tripathi, 2011: 12). They suffer from the cumulative disadvantages of labour market marginalisation, poverty and social exclusion.

Secondly, modern industrial sector requires good contacts, networks, articulateness and mobility to get a job, which people residing in rural areas, particularly the innocent, ignorant tribal population, lack very much. The opportunities created in industrial sectors become the opportunities for few; comparatively some well-to-do and not the one who are displaced and in real need of those opportunities. Lipton (1990: 337–338) in this context said, 'rural sector contains most of the poverty . . . but the urban sector contains most of the articulateness, organisation, and power. So the urban classes have been able to win most of the rounds of struggle with the countryside; but in so doing they have made the development process needlessly slow and unfair'. When no substantial has been made in skill and capacity building of the people through massive spending on human capital formation, people displaced from their livelihood have scarce possibility of getting absorbed in the opportunities created in the industrial sector. The rich lands and the industries based on those rich lands fail to make them rich. All these investment opportunities in the tribal belts, on the other hand, have opened up new employment opportunities for the relatively highly-skilled, better-educated and relatively rich people of other regions. Thus, development for the nation has meant displacement, pauperisation or, at its very best, peonage for the tribals.[14]

Industrial development growth is not equivalent to real development and has massively increased poverty, argues Dreze and Sen (2011). Mining and the industrial projects have widened gaps between haves and haves-not and caused repeated injustice to the poor tribal people of the land they have always lived and safeguarded. They are uprooted from their ancestral lands and unable to adapt to the demands of a modern economy. According to Singh (2010: 5), such model of development is akin to what Marx, in his account of the genesis and development of capitalism in the West, noticed as 'primitive accumulation of capital' which apart from the colonial plunder, slavery, and massacres of indigenous populations, included mass uprooting of peasantry by force and legislation'.

Environmental destruction

Industries in Odisha mostly belong to the energy-intensive and highly polluting category. Being endowed with mineral resources, mining sector continues to form an important part of the state's economy. Many of the mineral resources are found on forest lands which are destroyed in this process. In addition, there are a number of mining companies that do not adopt sustainable practices.

Mining-related industrialisation in forest areas or on agricultural land will not only affect the people who are displaced for the projects. It has a wider environmental impact. Possibly for this reason, mining is one of the economic activities that generate most environmental controversies. The mineral-based industries are energy-intensive, and the acceleration of such industrialisation is closely linked to carbon emission, water pollution and destruction of forests. Out of 58,136-square-kilometer forest area, 28,769 hectares have been diverted for non-forest use, of which mining and industry composed 12,186 hectares (Directorate of Economics and Statistics, Government of Odisha, 2005). The deforestation as well as the release of gas and water without proper treatment have resulted in the rapid increase in atmospheric temperature during summer. Mining activities have severe negative impacts on the land quality and directly contribute to environmental degradation and pollution.

There are frequent incidences of acid rain in the western part of Odisha. Rengali (industrial belt between Jharsuguda and Sambalpur) received acid rain in the year 2009. Similarly just a year before, on 19 June 2009, people experienced acid rain in Bargarh, Balangir, Nuapada and Kalahandi district of Odisha.[15] Arttabandhu Mishra[16] suspects the rain was caused by Odisha's thermal power belts of Angul-Talcher and Ib Valley. 'Odisha's two big coal fields emit over 320 tonnes of sulphur dioxide, 919 tonnes of nitrogen oxide and 33,883 tonnes of carbon dioxide. Acid rain can travel up to 400 km, and surely the rain in the region was acid rain', he said.[17]

Jharsuguda has been identified as one of the critically polluted areas (CPA) out of the 43 CPAs in India in the year 2009.[18] The National Environmental Engineering Research Institution (NEERI), which undertook the 'carrying capacity' survey in Odisha'a new industrial hub of Jharsuguda and Sambalpur, has given a thumbs-down to the quality of air in the area. NEERI reports revealed that emission of sulphur dioxide, nitrogen oxide and fluoride are causing environmental hazards in the area.[19]

In Odisha, particularly four industrial clusters (Angul-Talcher, Jharsuguda-Sambalpur, Joda-Barbil and Sukinda-Jajpur) are highly polluting. Table 5.9 shows the level of air pollution in the Angul-Talcher region. It shows that all parameters are increasing gradually over the period from 2005–2009, both in the industrial as well as in the residential area.

Decades of indiscriminate mining have left many villages highly polluted, rendering the lives of the inhabitant miserable due to widespread pollution levels and ill effects on health and agriculture. The mining and industrial activities have severe negative impacts on the land quality; the dust and the pollutants released by the industrial units and mines make the land no more cultivable. This creates further crises in food supply and worsened the livelihood of the farmers by destroying their land without any compensation paid to them. P.C. Mishra,[20] in his study found, around the MCL coal operations that, coal dust had severely affected plant growth and productivity. Dust on the leaf surface retards plant productivity, he said.[21]

Table 5.9 Status of Ambient Air Quality at Angul, 2005–2009

Location	*Category*	*Parameters* (values expressed in microgram per cubic meter), annual average (24 hourly range)*		
		SPM	*RSPM*	*NOX*
2005				
Regional Office Building, Industrial Estate, Angul	Industrial	214	100	12
NALCO Township, NALCO Nagar	Residential	116	65	20
2008				
Regional Office Building, Industrial Estate, Angul	Industrial	282	130	21.8
NALCO Township, NALCO Nagar	Residential	172	89	18.2
2009				
Regional Office Building, Industrial Estate, Angul	Industrial	326	158	21.9
NALCO Township, NALCO Nagar	Residential	165	80	17.3

Source: Odisha Pollution Control Board

Apart from dust, there is a bigger concern for the ash pond, which causes large-scale damage to the standing crops of the farmers, particularly during monsoon.

In the mining and industrial areas, there are many reported incidences of violation of the forests and Environmental Protection Act. The irrational and haphazard development of mining and industries, as well as the serious violation of forests and environmental norms, has made those regions unlivable for human beings. According to Shah Commission reports, a total of 146 cases of excess mining were registered by Odisha's mining department for violation of environment clearance, mining plan and consent to operate without abiding norms of air and water acts.[22] The report also observes about 55 mining leases directly pollute the Baitrani or river, having its major catchment area in two districts, Keonjhar and Sundargarh, and is a lifeline of the area. Since a substantial portion of India's mineral wealth is located under the country's forests and the watersheds of our major rivers, especially in the central and eastern parts of the country, mining activity is largely responsible for the pollution of those water sources.

Dhenkanal district collector filed two cases against the Bhushan Steel managing director for alleged violation of the Forest and Environment Act. Bhushan Energy, while increasing its capacity from 300 MW to 485 MW, allegedly did not obtain any environmental sanction from the Ministry of Environment.[23] It is alleged in the petition of the collector between 15 July 2010 and 25 February 2014, Bhushan Energy Limited and Bhushan Steel and Strips Limited were engaged in air, water and land pollution, causing great difficulties for the local people. Similarly, according to the Press

Information Bureau, four mines to Mahanadi Coalfields Limited (MCL) were operating in violation to the Environmental Impact Assessment (EIA) Notification 2006. These mines never applied for clearance and were operating on renewal of lease basis.[24]

The lack of effective regulations compounds the problem. Mining is one of the very few sectors where environmental regulations have not been codified in detail. While India has regulations governing waste management, air and water pollution or mine closure, there is enough ambiguity in each of these to prevent them from having sufficient teeth. Regulations on diversion of forests, protected areas and ecologically sensitive regions suffer from a similar fate.[25] The destruction of environment in developing countries in general and mining regions in particular are increasing day by day because the world's most polluting industries are shifting their operations to developing countries with weak environmental regulation.

There is underdevelopment along with environmental destruction. Moreover, it severely undermines the local democratic institutions, like *gram sabhas*, and goes against the will of people, resulting in violation of their democratic rights. It is all done in the name of development that does not seem to happen particularly for the indigenous displaced people. As a consequence, there are many instances of movement and agitations. It has serious implications for democracy and governance.

Politics of land grabbing and industrialisation

Economic growth caused by the resources and industries based on those resources might benefit at the national level, but its costs and destruction are felt certainly at the local levels. The development paradigm has been such that, the benefits are disproportionately cornered by the dominant sections (the ruling class/capitalists) at the expense of the poor (the peasantry and the tribals) who have borne most of the costs. Bhaduri (2014), in this context, says there is growth in industrial sector, but there is destruction of livelihood of people in agriculture and forestry, without being absorbed in the industrial sector.

Questions arise. Why is the state interested in such a model of development despite its many negative externalities? The answer is the search of capital, which has severely forced the Indian state to heavily compromise on land (agriculture), mineral resources, environment and, most importantly, livelihoods and habitats of people, particularly the indigenous tribal. In other words, there is large-scale dispossession of people depending on land (land for cultivation/land for forests) in the process of development (so-called). On the other hand, it opens a road for loot of natural resources for the interest of the capitalist class. The capital-led development model has never made the tribes prosperous from the mineral-rich land on which they live. In fact, the tribes have gradually lost control over community resources such as forests to both settlers and the states (Kurup, 2014: 10). Even in tribal-majority states like Jharkhand, the tribes are worst affected in the population since the state's government mining operations and hydro-electric power projects exploit natural resources in the resource-rich tribal areas, thus making the tribes outsiders in their own land.

In the rising importance of capital, the capitalist class seems to have influenced, dictated, directed or controlled the state machineries. There appears to have nexus between the capitalist class and the state in the formulation of plans and policies. The interest of the capitalist class is to stay in business and expand its base or, in other words, to maximise profit and minimise costs or to amass as much wealth as possible. Kumar (2014) says they want efficient capitalism to multiply their capital rapidly. It is possible only by getting easy land, easy raw material and easy water, with no environmental clearance, exploiting the nature as much as possible without caring for the displaced people. This could happen under the wish of the 'state'. It is well explained by Ganesan (1999: 7) that, for the purpose of getting money from the industrial class, it (political class) uses its administrative power of granting favours through control of imports, exports and other licenses, which becomes very useful for the capitalist class. This is how the owner of power comes under the owner of money, and the latter becomes all-powerful. Thus, Sir William Pitt (2009: 223) said, there is something behind the throne greater than the king himself.

The political class everywhere mostly care about one thing, 'winning elections'. The interest of the political class is their material well-being and to stay in power. All that requires huge amounts of money. The huge and urgent need of money could only come from the owners of it, the capitalists or the big companies. Tables 5.10 and 5.11 show that majority of the donors to two major political parties in India are nothing but the corporate and business houses. According to Association for Democratic Reforms (ADR) 2014, they provided 90 per cent donations to national political parties in 2013–14 (tables 5.10 and 5.11).

Similarly, 'Sesa Goa' admitted to political donations that, the company claimed to have made with a sense of propriety and transparency.[26] Ganesan (1999: 7) explains that 'the ruling party at the Center and to some extent at

Table 5.10 Top Donors from Odisha to INC and BJP, 2003–04 to 2011–12

Parties	*Name*	*Total donations (Rs.)*
Indian National Congress	Jindal Steel and Power Ltd	50,00,000
	Shri Jayadev Jena, President Odisha PCC	51,000
	Rajiv Gandhi Memorial Charitable Trust	30,000
	Shri Chinmaya Sundar Dash	30,000
	Nava Kishore Dash	27,275
	Total	51,38,725
BJP	Jindal Steel and Power Ltd	25,00,000
	Bhawani Construction Pvt. Ltd.	6,51,000

Source: Odisha Election Watch and ADR

Table 5.11 Foreign Funding of Major National Political Parties, 2003–04 to 2011–12

Parties	*Name*	*Total donations (Rs.)*
Indian National Congress	Sterlite Industries India Limited	6,00,00,000
	Sesa Goa Ltd.	2,78,50,000
	Solaris Holdings Ltd.	1,00,00,000
	Hyatt Regency	5,00,000
BJP	Public and Political Awareness Trust	14,50,00,000
	Vedanta The Madras Aluminum Co. Ltd.	3,50,00,000
	Sesa Goa Ltd.	1,41,50,000
	DOW Chemical Int. Pvt. Ltd.	1,00,000

Source: Odisha Election Watch and ADR

the State level is able to coerce any business house at any time to part with large sums of money. The ruling party could intimidate, delay and ruin business, and on the strength of coercive means, collect fat sums from those in charge of management of companies and industries'.

The farmers and the *Adivasis* or the rural class majority of whom are poor are unable to satisfy the previous needs of the political class representing the state. Heston and Kumar (2008: 1254) rightly said the parties' reliance upon individual contribution to fund elections is not practical; they are reluctant or unable to take small collections and resort to short by tapping the fat cats. It is common practice among political parties to approach business houses for donations at different points of time. It shows, there is increasing hold of the corporate sector on political parties.

On the other hand, the capitalist class willing to invest their surplus (capital) in various projects have created many opportunities for the political class and the bureaucracy to seek rents (Heston and Kumar, 2008: 1284). There was no denying of the fact that 'power captures money and money captures power'. In democracies, when the state frames easy norms for land acquisition, environmental clearance, extraction of minerals and flexible labour laws bypassing the interest of majority of the poor, for the interest of small sections of owners of capital, the nexus between capitalists and political classes are well imaginable. Instead of addressing the peoples' aspirations, in reality the state furthers the interest of the capitalists. In this process, democracy is reduced to 'for the capitalists, of the capitalist and by the capitalist'. The MOUs are nothing but a bargain, a bargain between the industrialists and the state, a state which is responsible to the people, but seems the other way round.

In the whole process of bargaining of self-interests between the political class and the capitalists, the former hides the reality, deludes people by spreading propaganda that, through industries there comes employment, there comes revenue, there comes development and there comes general prosperity. The propaganda is so large that people come to believe in it, so much so that those who oppose it are termed as anti-development.

When capitalists provide money to the political class, it is neither an act of charity nor alms; it is a clear case of expectation of getting something in return for giving something. The return comes in the form of such policies and institutions according to the requirement or suitability of the industrial class that could further enhance the scope of amassing wealth by tacitly permitting them not to care for the environment and displaced people. It even undermines the state exchequer. In this process, there arise various scams and corruptions. For example, the Shah Commission reported 59,000 crores of scams due to unlawful extraction of iron and manganese ores for a decade (2000–01 to 2009–10) in only two districts of Odisha (Keonjhar and Sundergarh).[27] Sesa Goa, in 2007–08, paid 28 lakh each to the two national parties, and in the same year, the company got permission to enhance iron ore production from 4 million tonnes to 7 million tonnes from its three mining sites.[28]

Thus, it could at least be concluded in the wider possibilities and evidence of corporate funding of election, rent-seeking attitude of the political class and bureaucracy on the one hand and maximisation of profit of the corporate on the other, it is not denied that, the rent-seekers and the beneficiaries of corporate funding do not benefit the party from whom they are benefitted. After all, they are all guided by 'invisible hands' or self-interest[29] (not charity) of amassing of wealth, but it could only happen at the misery of others.

Conclusions

The study concludes that, mineral-based industries have lesser chances of bringing a backward economy to the path of development. On the other hand, it causes severe environmental damages along with displacing the original inhabitants of the region, without contributing anything on economic development of it. There is absence of any trade-off between development and environment because of such industrialisation policy. Both go simultaneously, i.e., there is destruction of environment without promoting economic development. It seems, resources have become a *curse* rather than blessings particularly for the people, regions and district where it is available. The outcome of such models has become a pyrrhic victory for the states.

The state, despite knowing the outcome, is keen in such policy because it knows money buys power and it also knows where money comes from. The MOUs are nothing but a bargain, a bargain of self-interest between the industrialists and the state, a state responsible to people, but seems the other way round.

Notes

1 Patnaik, P. (2010). *Globalisation and Social Progress*. Annual Convention of NAOP and International Conference on Mind, Culture and Human Activities, Jawaharlal Nehru University, New Delhi.

2 The nature of industries in Odisha is primarily mineral-based heavy industries depending on the availability of its resources (raw material).

3 *The Frontline*, vol 27, no. 14, 16 March 2010.
4 India's mineral deposits are largely found in the forests area, which is also the inhabitant of the majority of the tribal population. (See the map of *Rich Land Poor People: Is Sustaining Mining Possible*. CSE, 2009. P-8. CSE, New Delhi).
5 http://articles.timesofindia.indiatimes.com/2013-06-11/developmental-issues/39897960_1_forest-land-forest-cover-total-forest. Accessed 11 December 2014.
6 Gopalkrishanan, S. (2012). *Undemocratic and Arbitrary: Control, Regulation and Expropriation of India's Forest and Common Lands*. New Delhi: SPWD; Washington, DC: Rights and Resources Initiative.
7 www.downtoearth.org.in/dte/userfiles/images/2-Forest%20clearance-1.pdf. Accessed 29 January 2014.
8 www.cseindia.org/userfiles/GRP%20factsheet%20Full.pdf. Accessed 29 January 2014.
9 'we are mountain people; if we go somewhere else, we will die', stated by a tribal boy of the Kondh tribe, Rajender Vadaka, who, along with other members, visited JNU to seek solidarity during their protest march to New Delhi against the Vedanta Refinery Plant in Niyamgiri.
10 'Policies for Tribal Development: Analysis and Suggestions' prepared for NAC by Dr N.C. Saxena, http://chittabehera.com/Rehabilitation/Orissa%20Displaced%20Study/Displacement%20Scenario%20Ch-9.pdf. Accessed 16 March.
11 And what exists is C-M-C, where C stands for commodity and M stands for money.
12 Capabilities described by Sen, A. (1996), as alternative combinations of functioning from which a person can choose. (*India, Economic Development and Social Opportunity*. New Delhi: Oxford University Press).
13 'Policies for Tribal Development: Analysis and Suggestions' prepared for NAC by Dr N.C. Saxena. http://chittabehera.com/Rehabilitation/Orissa%20Displaced%20Study/Displacement%20Scenario%20Ch-9.pdf.
14 Ibid.
15 *The Indian Express*, 9 July 2009.
16 Retired professor and environmental scientist of School of Life Sciences, Sambalpur University, Odisha.
17 *The Down to Earth*, 31 July, 2008, Acid Rain in Orissa.
18 This cluster crossed the CPCB-developed Comprehensive Environmental Pollution Index (CEPI) scored greater than 70 on a scale of 0 to 100.
19 *The Times of India*, 21 October 2012.
20 Professor of School of Life Sciences, Sambalpur University, Odisha.
21 *The Down to Earth*, 31 July 2008, Acid Rain in Orissa.
22 M.B. Shah Commission Report (2014): Odisha's Mines of Scams Exposed. *The Down to Earth*, 28 January.
23 *The Economic Times*, 24 April 2014.
See http://pib.nic.in/newsite/erelease.aspx?relid=78503. Accessed 5 August 2015.
24 See http://pib.nic.in/newsite/erelease.aspx?relid=78503. Accessed 5 August 2015.
25 Sharing the Wealth of Minerals, A Report on Profit Sharing with Local Communities, CSE, www.cseindia.org/userfiles/Sharing%20the%20Wealth%20of%20Minerals.pdf. Accessed 5 August 2015.
26 The company paid 85 lakh to the main opposition party, while the ruling Congress got only 30 lakh. Maharashtrawadi Gomantak Party got 2 lakh while Shiv Sena got 1 lakh (*The Times of India*, 15 October 2011).
27 M.B. Shah Commission Report (2014): Odisha's Mines of Scams Exposed. *The Down to Earth*, 28 January.
28 *The Times of India*, 15 October 2011.
29 Though all are guided by self-interest, it is not an issue. What is important is what should or should not be the self-interest.

References

Association for Democratic Reforms. (2014). *Who Funds Political Parties? 90 Percent of Donations in 2013–2014 Came from Corporate*. New Delhi: ADR, 25 December.

Bhaduri, A. (2014). *Development by Dispossession*. Valedictory Lecture, GIDS, IPEA Conference, Lucknow, 16 November.

CSE. (2009). *Rich Lands, Poor People: Is Sustainable Mining Possible*. New Delhi: Centre for Science and Environment.

Desai, S. and V. Kulkarni. (2008). Changing Educational Inequalities in India in the Context of Affirmative Action. *Demography*, vol. 45, pp. 245–270.

Directorate of Economics and Statistics, Government of Odisha. (2005). *Economic Survey 2004–2005*. Bhubaneshwar: Planning & Coordination Department, Government of Odisha.

Directorate of Economics and Statistics, Government of Odisha. (2012). *Statistical Abstract of Odisha 2012*. Bhubaneshwar: Directorate of Economics and Statistics, Government of Odisha.

Dreze, J. and Sen, A. (2011). Putting Growth in Its Place. *Outlook*, 14 November.

Frank, A. G. (1970). The Wealth and Poverty of Nations. *Economic and Political Weekly*, Special Number, pp. 1179–1180, July.

Ganesan, K. (1999). Corruption in the Political Process: A Case for Electoral Reform. In S. Guhan and S. Paul (Eds.), *Corruption in India: Agenda for Action*. New Delhi: Vision Book, p. 7.

Haan, A. D. and A. Dubey. (2005). Poverty, Disparities, or the Development of Underdevelopment in Orissa. *Economic and Political Weekly*, p. 2328, 28 May–4 June.

Heston, A. and V. Kumar. (2008). Institutional Flaws and Corruption Incentives in India. *Journal of Development Studies*, vol. 44, no. 9, p. 1254.

India Labour and Employment Report. (2010). *Pre-Launch Announcement*. New Delhi: Institute of Human Development (IHD), p. 8.

Kumar, A. (2014). Interrogating the Anti-Graft Platform. *The Hindu*, 6 February.

Kurup, A. (2014). *Tribal Law in India*. New Delhi: Critical Quest, p. 10.

Lange, O. (1963). *Political Economy: General Problems*, vol. 1. New York: Pergamon Press Book, The Macmillan Company, p. 12.

Lipton, M. (1990). Urban Bias. In G. M. Meier (Ed.), *Leading Issues in Economic Development*. Oxford: Oxford University Press, pp. 337–338.

Myrdal, G. (1958). *Rich Lands and Poor: The Road to World Prosperity*. New York: Harper.

Nayyar, G. (2009). *The Nature of Employment in India's Services Sector: Exploring the Heterogeneity*. Discussion Paper Series. Oxford: Department of Economics, University of Oxford Press, p. 5, September.

Padel, F., A. Dandekar and J. Unni. (2013). *Ecology and Economy: Quest for Socially Informed Connection*. New Delhi: Orient Blackswan.

Patnaik, P. (2010). *Globalisation and Social Progress*. Annual Convention of NAOP and International Conference on Mind, Culture and Human Activities. Jawaharlal Nehru University, New Delhi.

Pitt, W. (2009). *The Little Book – The Origin of God*. Bloomington, IN: Wesley Lloyd Cann, Author House, p. 223.

Rao, M. G. (2009). Regional Development for Inclusive Growth. *The Business Standard*, 6 October.

Singh, R. (2010). A Note on the Current Political Situation: Some Issues and Conclusion. *Marx Series*, no. 11, p. 5.

Tripathi, P. S. (2011). Sacrificial Lambs. *The Frontline*, vol. 28, no. 12, 17 April.

6 Gender and the mining sector

Mapping the praxis of women workforce in the mining sector

Debabrata Baral

Introduction

Gender inequality and gender discrimination are few of the social evils, which have been hiding behind cultural ethos or legislative frameworks. Empowerment of women has been one of the toughest challenges. At the global level various advocacy group are spreading awareness to end gender discrimination, e.g., the United Nations. It have included 'Gender Equality' as a necessary principle to achieve sustainable development by 2030. While gender discrimination in employment is a sad but an undeniable fact. Although, there are various sectors that have seen feminization of work and gender segregation of workforce in different sectors also do exist. With reference to the mining sector, this chapter will engage and analyse the ways through which gender segregation operates in availing employment opportunities.

Around two decades back, the report of the World Summit on Sustainable Development had outlined the importance of the mining sector and stressed the importance of women participation in the mining sector. Section 46 of the report states, to quote,

> 46 Mining, minerals and metals are important to the economic and social development of many countries. Minerals are essential for modern living. Enhancing the contribution of mining, minerals and metals to sustainable development includes actions at all levels to:
>
> . . . (b) Enhance the participation of stakeholders, including local and indigenous communities and women, to play an active role in minerals, metals and mining development throughout the life cycles of mining operations, including after closure for rehabilitation purposes, in accordance with national regulations and taking into account significant trans boundary impacts.
>
> (United Nations, 2002: 37)

Here, it would be interesting to refer, to a study on a small-scale mining project in Papua New Guinea (Javia and Siop, 2010). This study suggests that, first, women manage the small-scale mining projects better than their male counterparts. Second, the health, safety and environmental concerns associated with the mining projects are more important to the female as compared to their male counterparts. Third, the incomes earned by the female are spent on children and family as compared to the males, who primarily spend on drinking, prostitution, gambling, etc. Apart from this, the contribution of mining sector in terms of revenue and employment generation cannot be ignored. But as of late, mining sector is generally criticized for lacking gender equality. Traditionally, mining operations have been a male-dominated sector. Cultural and biological factors have propagated and facilitated bias against women, which has resulted in the exclusion of the female workforce from the majority of the mining activities. It is in this context that this chapter studies the women working in the mining sector, to highlight and understand the contexts of discriminatory practices that perpetuate gender inequality in the mining sector.

Here, it is relevant to differentiate between large-scale mining projects (hereafter will be referred to as mining sector) from artisan and small-scale mining hereafter will be referred as ASM). ASM projects are quite informal in nature. It is based on traditional practices with skills passed on over generations (Eftimie et al., 2012). Out of the 40 million workers engaged in ASM, around one third or half are women and girls (GIZ, 2019). A report on the global participation of women in mining suggests that less than 10 per cent of women are employed in the large-scale mining projects while around 40 per cent of females are employed in artisanal and small-scale mining projects (Richard et al., 2017). However, the focus of this chapter is to analyse and review practices of large-scale mining projects where the participation of women is less than 10 per cent. Even though women have started making inroads in getting employment in the mining sector, still the mining industry has largely been male dominated. Mining work includes both underground and above-ground activities. Historically, the males carried out underground mining activities while the female were marginally employed in the 'above ground' work activities. They were employed and engaged in activities relating to either human resource, finance, laboratory work or other administrative roles. This preferential selection of employees in the mining sector contributes to gender inequality and impedes women economic empowerment. Although, mining sector is a site where gendered power relations operate, but one cannot ignore the fact that this biasness towards female workforce was slowly addressed at different levels in different locations. But before entering into this discussion, let us first have an overview regarding the status of the women workforce in the mining sector in India and also at the global level.

I

The status of women in the mining sector: in India and at the global level

There has been exclusion of women from the underground mining activities throughout history. Maintaining gender equality in a male-dominated sector is quite a challenge for a large number of countries. Legislative restrictions and working shifts predominantly exclude the participation of women. But still few countries are taking proactive steps in addressing and maintaining gender equality. This section gives a bird's-eye view on the status of women in the abstractive industry in countries such as India, Indonesia, Canada, Australia and South Africa. These countries are chosen due to their size and influence of the extractive industry on their national economies.

Women workforce and the Mines Act, 1952, of India: an outline of the gendered division of labour

A mining law can unlock the potential of women. But there seems to be a gender division of labour in the mining sector. In India, women were alienated from the mining sector by legislations, which were enacted to bar them from certain mining areas. The relationship between the women workforce and the mining industry is extremely interesting. First, it can be stated that there has been a structural bias with respect to the employment of women in the mining sector. The section 46 of the Mines Act, 1952, outlines the conditions and restrictions on the participation of the women workforce in the extractive industry, to quote,

> 46 Employment of women. – (1) No woman shall, notwithstanding anything contained in any other law, be employed –
> (a) in any part of a mine which is below ground;
> (b) in any mine above ground except between the hours of 6 A.M. and 7 P.M.
> (2) Every woman employed in a mine above ground shall be allowed an interval of not less than eleven hours between the termination of employment on any one day and the commencement of the next period of employment.
> (3) Notwithstanding anything contained in sub-section (1), the Central Government may, by notification2 in the Official Gazette, vary the hours of employment above ground of women in respect of any mine or class or description of mine, so however that no employment of any woman between the hours of 10 p.m. and 5 a.m. is permitted thereby.
>
> (Government of India, 1952: 28)

Both state and private players conduct mining operations. This law is equally binding for both the sectors. The above-mentioned clause should be looked at with reference to Article 16 of the Indian constitution. Article 16 guarantees equality of opportunity and forbids discrimination. To quote,

> 16 Equality of opportunity in matters of public employment
> (1) There shall be equality of opportunity for all citizens in matters relating to employment or appointment to any office under the State
> (2) No citizen shall, on grounds only of religion, race, caste, sex, descent, place of birth, residence or any of them, be ineligible for, or discriminated against in respect or, any employment or office under the State
>
> (Government of India, 1950: 7)

Although there has been a structural bias with reference to the women participation as a workforce in the extractive industry. But it should not be generalized. There are few enterprises that have been working towards gender equity. For example, Coal India had started a program to extend the age of retirement from 50 to 55. But due to the restrictions of women employed in mining sector, it has around 26,000 women working in nontechnical position. The nontechnical positions generally include 'peon', 'para medical staff' and 'sweepers'. Although it plans to replace the unskilled women employees who have opted for voluntary retirement with their sons (Sengupta, 2014). The structural bias as outlined in the Section 46 of the Mines Act, 1952, was addressed in February 2019. Through a notification, the Government of India, revised its stand and allowed women to work in underground mining operations and also to undertake night shifts. But the Government of India also attached certain conditions. To Quote

> (b) in the case of women employed in any mine below ground,-
> i the owner of a mine may deploy women between the hours of 6 am and 7 pm in technical, supervisory and managerial work where continuous presence may not be required.
> ii the deployment of women shall be after obtaining the written consent of the concerned woman employee;
> iii the women so deployed shall be provided with adequate facilities and safeguards regarding occupational safety, security and health;
> iv the deployment of women shall be subject to the framing and implementation of Standard Operating Procedures on the basis of the guidelines issued in this regard by the Chief Inspector of Mines from time to time;
> v the deployment of women shall be in a group of not less than three.
>
> (Ministry of Labour and Employment, Government of India, 2019: 1)

Definitely, it took some time, but the legislation is definitely a positive step in addressing gender discrimination.

Women in the extractive industry: mapping the praxis at the global level

A study on the mining sector of Peru, Poland, Tanzania and Papua New Guinea outlines the patterns of distribution of benefits and risk. Whereas man benefits through employment and income while, women bear the harmful 'environmental' and 'social impacts' (Eftimie, Heller, and Strongman, 2009). During the world wars, there was an increase in the employment of women in the mining sector. Women were engaged in heavy-duty activities like 'dragging', 'pushing trucks' or 'covering coal'. But after 1950, it changed, man again started dominating and took over the duties that the women were initially undertaking in the mining sector (Bradley, 1989). Although, international advocacy groups like Oxfam, Action Aid, Rio Tinto group, etc., were trying to build awareness and promoting rights, participation and empowerment of women working in the mining sector. But still at the global level, the status of women in the extractive industry is immersed with biases and restrictions. *First*, there were laws restricting the participation of women the underground activities of the mines, e.g., England and Zambia. Even in Indonesia, in order to work in open-cut mines, women need to take permission and submit letters certified by their father and husband. Second, in Australia, the employment and wage structure is quite gendered. As per WEGA,[1] during 2014–15, only 16 per cent of the workforce consisted of women primarily employed as machinery operators, drivers, technicians, etc., but with reference to clerical or administrative jobs, the women made up for around 77.4 per cent of the entire workforce. To add, there exists a wage gap. A gap of around 23.7 per cent existed between the men and women working in the coal mining sector. This gap reduced to 13.3 per cent with reference to the clerical or administrative work. Third, South Africa is known for its gold, diamond, platinum and, more recently, the coal extractive industry. Until 1994 the mining law in South Africa prevented the employment of women in underground activities. South Africa has been proactive in taking steps to include women in the mining workforce. It has proposed quotas, even acts like 'Mineral and Petroleum Resources Development Act of 2002' and the 'Socio Economic Empowerment Charter' safeguarding the interests of the women in the South African mining industry. The failure to abide by these acts would lead to the nonrenewal of the mining license. Fourth, in Canada, as per WIM,[2] the females constitute 14 per cent, and males constitute 86 per cent workforce of the mining industry. Mark Scott, who was working as human resource superintendent, at Vale Inco, Manitoba Operations at Canada, also highlights the lack of diversity in the mining sectors. To quote,

> We need to do more in the industry as a whole to encourage and support diversity – gender, generational, ethnic – whatever the case maybe. It has long been an industry full of white dudes and we're not going to survive if that's how we continue to think.
>
> (Mining Industry, Human Resource Council, 2011)

There had been a shift in the praxis of women in the mining sector. Legislations and war were few structural factors that governed their participation in the mining sector. Apart from that, there were other socio-cultural factors also that influenced their participation. The following section outlined it.

II

Mapping the socio-economic-cultural contexts for exclusion of women from the mining sector

Apart from the policy perspective, there are other factors responsible for low participation of women in the mining sector. In the early days, due to socio-cultural reasons, women were not encouraged to work in the mines. It can be argued that the social structure of the society (even at global level) has been extremely discriminative to the women and propagated male dominance. This section outlines the various contexts that discouraged the female participation as workforce in the mining sector.

Colonialism, extractive industry and gendered power relations

The expansion of colonial structure into the mining sector has not only impacted the socio-economic status of women, it has also made them relatively powerless as compared to other traditional systems. First, before the advent of the colonial rule, women were involved in their traditional gender roles, e.g., fetching water, preparing food and undertaking small-scale farming activities. Colonialism led to an expansion of an extractive industry. This establishment of colonial rule proved to be quite disadvantageous for the women. As, most land were categorized as private properties, hence it debarred people from using it. Women were excluded from accessing the mineral-rich areas to perform their traditional gendered roles. Moreover with the substitution of the surface mining activities with underground mining activities, it further facilitated exclusion of women from the labour workforce. Second, in South Africa, during the colonial era, spouses were prohibited from staying together. This led to the emergence of the well-known concept of Hostel system. The women stayed back in their home and engaged in unpaid agricultural activities. The expansion of mining sector has deeply impacted the livelihood and economic activities of the women (Moyo, 2010).

Traditional caregiver roles entangle the family work-life balance

Women have been performing the role of caregivers. This traditional-historical role often contradicts with any new role that the women pursue. The traditional division of labour often segregates the role of the man from the woman. A career in the mining sector often contradicts with the primary role of women as a caregiver. It becomes difficult for females to maintain a good work-life and family balance. The mining sector often has its own constraints in terms of flexibility, long working hours, remote sites and the expectations of doing overtime work. These expectations are expected irrespective of the worker's gender. But since a higher percentage of women assume the role of caregiver as primary, hence these issues restricts the women as compared to their male counterparts. Here one needs to think: why do women have to balance the family and work-life? Has the society not evolved enough to talk about equal participation of male and female? For how long should the bias division of labour on the basis of sex be upholded?

Cultural myths

Historically women have been demonized. Apart from the structural restrictions, women have also fought against quite a few cultural biases. For example, it was believed that the precious stones would disappear if the women stepped into the mines (Bradley, 1989). At the same time, there were other beliefs that getting intimate with the women right before going to work would invite accidents is quite a dominant myth in many places globally. Hence the mine owners would generally restrict or exclude women from the mining premises. Definitely these mythical stories perpetuate cultural bias. But, why does these cultural biases get unchallenged in the era of enlightenment is a question to think. What do these cultural biases reflect on the nature of the society and the mind-set of the people propagating these myths? It is unfortunate to hear about the gender-insensitive cultural myths, but it is really more dangerous to see them perpetuating in the modern era.

Infrastructural limitations

Definitely, ergonomics and anthropometrics determine the participation of the social groups or human body participation. Lack of appropriate ergonomics also restrict women from carrying out certain mining operations (Hermanus, 2007). At the same time, infrastructure design can also be discriminative for few social groups. For example, the construction around the mining sector has a male bias. The lack of female toilets, changing rooms and proper lights in the tunnel, demotivated the women workforce from joining the underground mining activities (Kandare, 2017).[3] Here one thing that came to the forefront is that gender equality can be restricted in the absence of proper architectural or infrastructural design. Hence the normalisation of gender-biased infrastructure needs to be revisited at every level not only in the mining sector.

Masculinity

Mining operations are characterised by 'risky working conditions', 'hard work' and 'dangerous environment'. Hence it is associated with masculinity and the profession of man. A reading into the social construction of technology shows how the technology at time behaves and becomes gender-insensitive. With reference to the mining sector, women are generally regarded as unfit to undertake hard labour. Hence mostly the mine owners prefer to engage and employ men in their underground workforce. But unfortunately these assumptions are extremely problematic as it assumes all men are stronger than all women. A reading into gender definitely suggests that physical activity influences the level of testosterone in the body. Hence the masculine nature of work in the mining sector needs to be revisited.

The stigma surrounding working in the mines

Apart from structural restrictions and cultural biases, there are a lot of stigmas surrounding the jobs in the mining sector. In general, it is believed that people who are uneducated, immigrants and rural mass take up jobs in the mining sector. These stigmas further demotivate the educated lower middle class or middle class from thinking about a career in the mining sector seriously. Hence, government and other agencies to overcome these stigmas should convey various programmes and orientations highlighting the importance in pursuing a career in the mining sector. Quite recently, the program titled '100 Global inspirational women in Mining' started by Women in Mining is definitely a step forward to remove stigmas and promote gender diversity. It will also further act to attract and retain women workforce in the mining sector (Women in Mining, n.d.).

Remote locations

Predominantly mines are located either on the outskirts of city or in some remote locations. At the same time, long working shifts also discourage a section of the women workforce who is entangled in the family-work life balance. Hence remote locations mean additions to their transportation and commuting time. Women generally have limited time to discharge duties of a caregiver, if working as a mineworker. Hence squeezing their already tight schedule to take time out for travelling to work is extremely difficult. Hence, the absence of proper transportation network, discourages people, especially women participating in the mining sector.

III

Addressing exclusionary practices and facilitating women participation in the mining sector

Addressing the discriminatory practices in the mining sector is like stepping towards gender equality and women empowerment at some level. Definitely there have been legislations and international organisations are pioneering the cause of women economic empowerment through workforce participation. But it's a long, drawn-out battle in which the society needs to be reminded that the gender disparity needs to be addressed at various time intervals. Banking upon previous literature and own research, a few ways of addressing gender discrimination in the mining sector are suggested.

Corporate governance: inclusion through policies

Progressive mining laws can definitely contribute in empowering and addressing gender bias in the mining sector. For example, South Africa is one of the few countries that leads in terms of employing women in the mining sector. Certain policies of South Africa, e.g., The Mineral and Petroleum Resources Development Act (28 of 2002) (MPRDA) and the accompanied Broad-based Socio-economic Empowerment Charter aimed to rectify previous inequalities and disadvantages in the mining sector and specifically provide for the inclusion of women in core mining activities. According to the act and the charter, the mining industry was supposed to achieve a quota of 10 per cent women in core mining activities by 2009 (Botha, 2013). According to the Chamber of Mines (CoM) 2017 fact sheet, it is estimated that about 57,800 women were employed in the industry from 2015 to 2016, compared with 11,400 in 2002. Women currently represent more than 13 per cent of employees in the local mining industry, thereby exceeding the mining charter's requirements (Breytenbach, 2017).[4]

Vision and initiatives by international organisations

The practice within the mining sector should be reoriented with the United Nations' 'sustainable development goals', which talks about achieving gender equality and addressing discriminatory practices. To quote,[5]

- 5.1 End all forms of discrimination against all women and girls everywhere
- 5.5 Ensure women's full and effective participation and equal opportunities for leadership at all levels of decision making in political, economic and public life
- 5.A Undertake reforms to give women equal rights to economic resources, as well as access to ownership and control over land and other forms of property, financial services, inheritance and natural resources, in accordance with national laws

Apart from the vision documents, UNDP has granted a US$5 million loan facility for women miners in Zimbabwe. These initiatives go a long way in breaking stereotypes and facilitating women empowerment.

The way forward: scheme for redistribution of power

1 There should be a constant monitoring and evaluation framework regarding the participation of women in the mining sector. This will outline trends and challenges faced by the women miners at different time intervals.
2 The male counterparts need to be educated that mining is not a gendered profession and space, communication and sensitiveness to the other gender needs to be a part of orientation programs that need to accompany, every new and old man miner in the sector.
3 Since women miners also perform the traditional caregiver roles, hence steps should be taken in facilitating adequate childcare facilities.
4 Awareness regarding their health and occupational hazards needs to be highlighted.
5 The UN sustainable development goals and national legislations that empower women participation in the economic workforce and mining sector should be effectively implemented. It should not just be a vision document.
6 Organisations or groups similar to the 'Indigenous Women in Mining Australia', 'Pauktuutit-Inuit Women of Canada', and 'Waanaleru-Organization of Indigenous Women from the Amazon', etc., needs to be supported at the national level to promote women professional development and make them aware of their rights in the mining sector.
7 As outlined previously, legislations, socio-cultural factors and ideologies play an important in propagating gender discriminations; hence an approach engaging with state, international organisations and social structures is the need of the hour. An inter-related approach will be more fruitful than treating gender as an independent variable.

Notes

1 WGEA, or Workplace Gender Equality Agency, of Australian government has documented the gender issues in the Australian mining sector. The report was downloaded from www.wgea.gov.au/wgea-newsroom/gender-equality-spotlight-mining. Accessed 18 November 2018.
2 WIM stands for Women in Mining. It's a national nonprofit group founded in 2009 looking after and advancing the interest of women in the mining community across Canada.
3 http://genderlinks.org.za/news/promoting-gender-equality-in-the-mining-industry/.
4 http://m.miningweekly.com/article/s-african-mining-industry-advances-gender-diversity-transformation-targets-still-to-be-improved-2017-08-04.
5 Quoted from the UN Sustainable Development Goals on Gender Equality, available at www.un.org/sustainabledevelopment/gender-equality.

References

Botha, D. (2013). *Women in mining: A conceptual framework for gender issues in the South African mining sector*. Thesis submitted for the degree Doctor Philosophiae in Sociology on the Potchefstroom Campus of the North-West University, Bokone Bophirima, North West University.

Bradley, H. (1989). *Men's Work, Women's Work: A Sociological History of the Sexual Division of Labour in Employment*. Cambridge: Polity.

Breytenback, M. (2017, August 4). *Women representation increases from 'extreme minority' to 13%-plus of SA's mining workforce*. Retrieved from Creamer *Media's Mining Weekly*: https://m.miningweekly.com/article/women-representation-increases-from-extreme-minority-to-13-plus-of-sas-mining-workforce-2017-08-04/rep_id:3861.

Eftimie, A., K. Heller, and John Strongman. (2009). *Mining for Equity: The Gender Dimensions of the Extractive Industries*. Washington, DC: World Bank.

Eftimie, A., K. Heller, J. Strongman, J. Hinton, K. Lahiri-Dutt, and N. Mutemeri. (2012). *Gender Dimensions of Artisanal and Small-Scale Mining A Rapid Assessment Toolkit*. Washington, DC: World Bank.

GIZ. (2019). *Encyclopedia of Gender and Mining*. Bonn: Deutsche Gesellschaft für Internationale Zusammenarbeit (GIZ) GmbH.

Government of India. (1950). *The Constitution of India*. New Delhi: Government of India.

Government of India. (1952). *The Mines Act, 1952*. New Delhi: Central Government.

Hermanus, M. (2007). Occupational Health and Safety in Mining: Status, New Developments and Concerns. *The Journal of the South African Institute of Mining and Metallurgy*, vol. 107, pp. 532–542.

Javia, I. and P. Siop. (2010). *Paper on Challenges and Achievements on Small Scale Mining and Gender: Papua New Guinea*. New York: Wau Small Scale Mining Training Centre.

Kandare, M. (2017, October 4). *Promoting Gender Equality in the Mining Industry*. Retrieved March 24, 2020 from Genderlinks.org: https://genderlinks.org.za/news/promoting-gender-equality-in-the-mining-industry/

Mining Industry, Human Resources Council. (2011). *Women in Mining*. Kanata, ON: Mining Industry, Human Resources Council.

Ministry of Labour & Employment, Government of India. (2019, February 4). *Ministry of Labour Notifies Rules To Allow Employment of Women in Mines. Now Equal Employment Opportunities for Women in Mines*. Retrieved March 24, 2020 from pib.gov.in: https://pib.gov.in/newsite/PrintRelease.aspx?relid=187977

Moyo, T. (2010). Extractive Industries and Women in Southern Africa. *BUWA! – A Journal of African Women's Experiences*. Open Society Initiative for Southern Africa.

Richard, S., W. Treasure, J. McQuilken, A. Mihaylova and J. Baxter. (2017). *Women in Mining, Can a Mining Law Unlock the Potential of Women?* London: Adam Smith International and International Women in Mining.

Sengupta, D. (2014, September 18). *Coal India Relaxes Norms for Voluntary Retirement Scheme for Women*. Retrieved March 24, 2020 from *The Economic Times*: https://economictimes.indiatimes.com/news/company/corporate-trends/coal-india-relaxes-norms-for-voluntary-retirement-scheme-for-women/printarticle/42750102.cms

United Nations. (2002). *Report of the World Summit on Sustainable Development: Johannesburg, South Africa, 26 August–4 September 2002*. New York: United Nations.

Women in Mining. (n.d.). *100 Global Inspirational Women in Mining*. From African Leadership Institute. https://alinstitute.org/images/downloads/WIMTop100.pdf. Accessed 12 May 2019.

7 Land acquisition and development-induced displacement in Odisha

A study on development projects in Western Odisha

Narendra Kumar Behera

Introduction

In the era of planned as well as neoliberal periods, one primary factor of production, i.e., land, has become the centre of discussion among policy-makers, bureaucrats, academics and researchers more than any other factor. Above all the common people have come to focus their attention on it more than ever before. The unlimited desire of the government and capitalist to acquire land by any means has become the centre of controversy at different parts of the country at different time periods. In general, mega projects and large dams are synonymous with the idea of development. The coalition among capitalists, politicians, bureaucrats, contractors and pressure groups from urban consumers used to push for the espousal of these mega projects which require large land areas and causes large-scale population displacement and environmental degradation. The snatching away of land and common property resources (CPR) from the people living in the interior parts of the country severely affects and dismantles the life and livelihood of the people who are adversely affected by these projects. These big projects are embedded with huge social costs which very often get neglected and relegated to the background in the name of development paradigm.

Development projects demand acquisition of land. Land is acquired by the government under the colonial Land Acquisition Act (LAA) 1894 on the grounds of *eminent domain and public purposes*. The British were all set to modernise the then-capital city, Calcutta, but they were ill-equipped with legal provisions of the state rights over individual land and its acquisition for government purposes. The first All India Act VI of 1857 was passed where landowners may be required by the legislature to surrender some of their rights they possess over their land for a purpose of public utility. Subsequently, a well-defined all Comprehensive Land Acquisition Act (LAA) covering the whole of British India came into force on the first day of March 1894 as the Act 1 of 1894. This act empowered the state under the clause of 'Eminent Domain' and 'Public Purpose' to acquire privately owned land. The evolution of 'public purpose' as one of the primary bases for eminent domain emerged only gradually. Moreover, the analysis also reveals that eminent domain principles go back at least 80 years prior to the LAA of 1894, and extensive legal debates about the existence of the provisions for sovereign claims to land were raging around the turn of the nineteenth century (Bhattacharyya, 2015: 47). Even if scholars have turned to the exceptional status of eminent domain laws from the LAA to RTFCTLARRA, perhaps a far grimier proposition can be found in the recent argument 'that under the Indian Constitution eminent domain is not exceptional power given that the right to property is not a fundamental right' (Ibid., p. 53).

Until 2013, this law was being followed by the states in the matter of land acquisition and distribution of compensation to the landowner. The legal holders are only entitled to get the compensation on the basis of a land valuation fixed by the government taking note in the sale deeds of that area. People having no title on land and dependents on CPR are discounted from the purview of the act. 'To determine land valuation, four methods are used across the world to reach at appropriate compensation. These are (a) evaluating the market value of land (b) evaluating the net value of income from the land, (c) determining original land use value as set by state, and (d) arriving at land value through negotiation' (Mahalingam and Vyas, 2011: 96).

All across the world, the state is empowered to acquire land for public purposes in lieu of payment of compensation to the landowners. This power, terms and conditions are exercise as per the directives of the constitution as in case of Australia and China or as specified in enacted laws as in the case of Hong Kong, Malaysia and Singapore. The term 'public purpose' also varies across country. In the case of France, Japan, China, Mexico and India, it is an explicitly enumerated situation and project under which land can be acquired or appropriated by the state for public purposes. In the case of Malaysia, Brazil, US, UK and Singapore, the 'public purpose' is subject to interpretation and potential dispute. 'The principle or philosophies that guide land acquisition in most countries can be classified into three main categories – the "value to the owner principle", the "just compensation principle" and the "reasonable compensation"' (Ibid., p. 95).

Regarding compensation, the parliament redefined compensation as a fixed amount and 'specified that the principles on which, and the manner in which the compensation was to be determined or given could not be called in question in any court on the ground that compensation provided by law was not adequate. The debate about compensation did not end with that and continues to remain relevant, contentious and unsettled even to this day' (Bhattacharyya, 2015: 47).

In addition to the LAA 1894, there are 16 more central acts which causes land acquisition and displacement. These are the Land Acquisition (Mines) Act, 1885; the Indian Tramways Act, 1886; the Works of Defense Act, 1903; the Forest Act, 1927; the Manoeuvres, Field Firing and Artillery Practice Act, 1938; the Resettlement of Displaced Persons (Land Acquisition) Act, 1948; the Damodar Valley Corporation Act, 1948; the

Requisitioning and Acquisition of Immovable Property Act, 1952; National Highway Act, 1956; the Coal Bearing Areas Acquisition and Development Act (CBAADA), 1957; the Ancient Monuments and Archaeological Sites and Remains Act, 1958; the Atomic Energy Act, 1962; the Petroleum and Minerals Pipelines (Acquisition of Right of User in Land) Act, 1962; the Metro Railways (Construction of Works) Act, 1978; the Railway Act, 1989; the Electricity Act, 2003; the Special Economic Zones Act, 2005 and the Cantonments Act, 2006. Among all these acts, the LAA and the CBAADA 1957 have caused much more land acquisition and displacement than any other act. After industrialisation gathered momentum, particularly with the onset of New Economic Policy, 1991, private companies, both domestic and foreign, entered the race for getting hold of land in various parts of the country. They themselves entered the land market and started acquiring land at the prevailing market price. But what became more treacherous, the state became an agent for the private sector in the name of industrialisation and higher gross domestic product (GDP).

The intense controversies over land acquisition and displacement over the last several decades have compelled the government of India to go for a new law. 'The long march in October, 2007 of more than 25000 displaced, landless dalits and tribal from Gwalior to New Delhi to pressurise the central government to form a national lands commission and formulate a national land reforms policy was the culmination of many years of struggle, despaired and hope thousands of land less people' (Pai, 2007: 10). The new Right to Fair Compensation and Transparency in Land Acquisition and Resettlement & Rehabilitation Act 2013 (RTFCTLARRA) was passed by the parliament with substantial changes to the LAA of 1894. It is for the first time that resettlement and rehabilitation of project-displaced people became a right and legal entitlement of the affected population is allowed through a legal status. The new law is likely to address the problem of land acquisition and displacement in a progressive manner than earlier.

Western Odisha

Odisha is a state of two in one. Out of 30 districts, 11 districts come under West Odisha. Geographically the state has been divided into hill districts of Western and Southern Odisha and Coastal plain districts of eastern Odisha. The coastal districts of Odisha compared to the hill or Western districts are in a much more advantageous and privileged position both in political and economic aspects. In view of large mineral deposits and rivers, a number of large-scale industries and dams have been constructed in these districts, such as the aluminium industries at Hirakud, Damanjodi; the Hindustan Aeronautic Ltd. at Sunabeda; the Steel Plants at Rourkela and Sambalpur, Cement plants at Bargarh, Jharsuguda and Rajgangpur; ordinance factory at Saintala; refractory at Belpahar and Rajgangpur and thermal power stations at Banharpali. In the 1950s, one of the world's largest artificial lakes, i.e., Hirakud Dam, Rengali Dam, Indrabati Dam, Kolab Dam, etc. have been built at different time periods. All these projects have acquired huge amounts of cultivable land and forest land and caused large-scale population displacement from West Odisha.

Magnitude of displacement

Land acquisition coexists with the evils of population displacement. Researchers like Professors M. Cernea, Walter Fernandes and others have tried to evolve a database for the displaced people of different projects in India. In India, of the 20 million people displaced since 1947, it is estimated that 75 per cent of them have been impoverished due to development projects (Downing, 2005). During the last two decades of the previous century, the magnitude of force population displacement caused by development programme was of the order of 10 million people each year or some 200 million people globally during that period. [Cernea, 2000: 11]

Sainath says, 'It's happened in India, where in the period 1951–90, over 21.6 million people suffered precisely that fate – displaced by just dams and canals alone. Add mining that has dispossessed 2.1 million people and you have the population of Canada. Further, industries, thermal plants, sanctuaries and defense installations have thrown at least 2.4 million human beings out of their houses. That's around twenty-six million Indians' (Sainath, 1996: 71). This data clearly indicates huge population displacement has taken place due to different development projects in the country. Experiences show that displaced people are destined to go without adequate resettlement and rehabilitation measures. As a result, they become a potential source of migration as a by-product of development projects. They are thrown to the space of landlessness and joblessness which is termed as involuntary or forced migration.

The conservative estimates of displaced people and their rehabilitation in India is presented in table 7.1, which shows 213,00000 number of displaced

Table 7.1 Conservative Estimate of Displaced Persons by Various Categories of Projects India (1951–1990)

Sl. No.	*Type of project*	*Number of displaced*	*Number of rehabilitated*	*Backlog*
1	Dams	1,64,00,000	41,00,000	1,23,00,000
2	Mines	25,50,000	6,30,000	19,20,000
3	Industries	12,50,000	3,75,000	8,75,000
4	Sanctuaries	6,00,000	1,25,500	4,75,000
5	Others	5,00,000	1,50,000	3,50,000
	Total	2,13,00,000	53,80,000	1,59,20,000

Source: Fernandes 1994: 22–32

people, out of which only 53,80,000 (25.25 per cent) have been rehabilitated during 1951–90 in India. Among all the displacing agents, dams top the list.

Table 7.2 shows a few cases of displacement and amount of land acquired for public sector projects and private industries established during the pre- and post-reform periods in Western Odisha. In this context, it may be pointed out that while acquiring land, the quality and the need aspect of land is not taken into consideration. In the case of the Hirakud Dam project, there was the acquisition of 1,83,593 acres, but it lost good-quality agricultural land amounting to 1,15,128 acres in the reservoir forever. There is an excess acquisition of land by a number of projects only in the name of development. This is going to threaten the food security in future. Table 7.2 shows that the maximum amount of land acquisition and displacement has been caused by dams, followed by industries and coal mining. With the adoption of New Economic Policy, 1991, the domestic private sector and multinationals have assumed the role of industrializing the state, mainly through the mineral-based industries rather than through any value-additive industries. Industrial houses, such as Bhusan, Vedanta and Aditya Birla, are going to add more to land acquisition and displacement through their mining and industrial operations in Western Odisha. The controversy over Vedanta's mining in Niyamgiri has shown the aggressive capitalism for the use of natural resources in West Odisha. According to latest information, 10,226.437 hectares of forest land have been diverted for mines, industries and infrastructure projects in the state. Out of which, the share of forest land diverted for such purposes in West Odisha is 3718.281 hectares (Dhritri; 9th Jan., 2012). This shows that land is greatly diverted for non-agricultural purposes.

Table 7.2 Dams and Displacements

Name of project	*Total land acquired acre*	*No. of villages affected*	*No. of families affected*	*No. of people displaced*
Hirakud Dam	1,83,593	291	26,501	1,60,000
Upper Indravati Dam	32,477	105	5,301	18,500
Rengali Dam	1,02,672	263	11,289	46,570
Upper Kolab Dam	28,375	49	3,179	15,890
Rourkela Steel Plant	19,277	30	4,251	23,400
Bhusan Steel	1,315	13	164	854
IB Thermal Power	1,406	04	147	748
Ib Valley Coal Mine	74,740	18	110	8,049
OCL India, Rajgangpur	1,133	03	13	105
VAL, Lanjigarh	2,060	09	125	600
Total	4,47,048	785	51,080	2,74,716

Sources: Reddy, 1992: 76, Pandey, 1998; Sabar, 2010

People's voice

> "Let it not be said of India, that this great Republican a hurry to develop itself, is devastating the green mother earth and uprooting our tribal population"
>
> – From the speech of the president of India, K.R. Narayanan, 25 January 2001.

As long as people keep themselves mum, there is no problem, but as soon as they start affirming their rights, they face state brutality and repression. Land acquisition and displacement induce the affected people to voice against displacement on account of several factors, like disruption of economic and social fabric, inadequate and improper resettlement and rehabilitation measures, denial of project benefit to the displaced people, etc. Sacrifice and pain, the real cost undertaken by the displaced persons, are neither recognized by the society nor even by the beneficiaries of the project concerned. It has been an observed fact that the project authorities and displaced people have no common economic compulsion to 'work together'. In fact, it has become a day-to-day column of most of the state's newspapers to focus the problem of displaced people of different dams, industries and mining projects that are protesting and demanding better resettlement and rehabilitation measures from the authority.

Long back in the 1920s, nonviolence resistance against displacement under the leadership of Senapati Bapat against the construction Mulshi-Peta Dam near Pune is the best-known organized fight against displacement. The struggle was appropriated by the freedom fighter. Although they opposed the British on this ground, the national leaders had themselves internalized the concept of eminent domain and other colonial value systems of divide and rule, rulers and ruled, etc. When they became the decision-makers of independent India, the freedom fighters who had supported the Mulshi-Peta struggle continued to use the same colonial legislation to displaced people in the name of national development (Murickan et al., 2003: 3).

The construction of Hirakud Dam was ultimately recommended as an independent dam by Mr. H.C. Prior, and the foundation stone was laid on 15 March 1946 by Sir Hawthorne Lewis, the then-governor of Orissa. A second foundation stone was laid on 12 April 1948 by the first prime minister of India, Pt. Jawaharlal Nehru, a great protagonist of gigantic model of development. He told the villagers while laying the foundation stone for the project, 'if you are to suffer, you should suffer in the interest of the country'. His words turned into reality, and the people suffered in all respects and were denied the benefit of Hirakud water for which they sacrificed everything in the name of nation-building.

The history of displacement will remain incomplete without covering the Hirakud Dam. The construction of Hirkud Dam in the river Mahanadi saw the first large dam project in Odisha built as an anti-flood measure to save the coastal people. With the announcement of the project in 1945, there were mass protests by the people of Sambalpur district. Bharat Nayak, a retired deputy collector, opposed the project on the grounds of hilly terrain, loss of cultivable fertile land and minerals and huge displacement. As a mark of protest, 30,000 people demonstrated in front of the governor of Orissa at Sambalpur. If necessary, people were prepared to separate Sambalpur out of Orissa. On 10 November 1946, I.P.C. 144 was declared, which remained in force for three months. The withdrawal of local congress leaders, betrayal of leaders like Budhuram Dube and the imposing image of congress party led to the failure of protest movement against Hirakud Dam and ultimately led to the completion of the dam in 1957. There was a proposal to construct the second large dam downstream of the Mahanadi at Tikarpada. The large-scale agitation in the 1960s against the dam at Tikarpara, which would have displaced several thousands of people in the present districts of Sonepur and Boudh, forced them to abandon the Tikarpara Dam.

The causes of displaced people have been brought to the light more successfully by the Narmada Bachao Andolan (NBA) against the construction of Sardar Sarovar Project. The leadership of Medha Patkar is considered as a symbolic voice of displaced people in the country. A few years back, she supported the cause of the affected people due to the construction of South Korean steel project POSCO in the district of Jagatsinghpur of Odisha.

On 21 July 2011, the government of Odisha signed a MOU with National Hydro Power Corporation (NHPC) and Orissa Hydro Power Corporation (OHPC) to set up three hydel projects in the districts of Sambalpur, Sonepur and Boudh downstream of the river Mahanadi in Western Odisha. The government declared that the proposed plants would have an installed capacity of 320 MW and that Odisha would receive 12 per cent of the output free of charge. The government also announced that 1 per cent of the cost of the power generated will be spent on peripheral development activities in the region. It is known as the Sindhol-I (100 MW), Sindhol-II (100 MW) and Sindhol-III (120 MW) hydroelectric projects. The government also announced that the power project would provide ample employment opportunity apart from the economic development in the region. Perhaps the government of Odisha has not learned any lesson from the worst resettlement and rehabilitation of the oustees of Hirakud and Rengali Dams, and it will be a top task to go for the proposed project at this juncture. The euphoria of sacrifice has lost its ground in the age of increasing awareness and strong voice against displacement. The government set a subcommittee to look into the Sindhol project. After the report of the subcommittee in December 2011, the government announced the annulment of Sindhal projects. In the 1980s, there was a massive protest by the local people and environmentalists against then-public sector aluminium company BALCO to carry out mining operations at Gandhamardan Mountain of Bargarh-Balngir districts. In spite of a beginning by the company, it had to shut down its operations before the public agitation. Thus there are a few cases of successful agitation and unsuccessful move against projects in West Odisha.

Violence and brutality are also associated with land acquisition and displacement. The brutal incidences of the past decade relating to Kashipur, Kalinganagar, of Odisha and Singur, and Nandigram, of West Bengal, are worth mentioning. The police firing at Kalinganagar killed 13 tribal people (January 2006) due to construction of Tata Steel, which was likely to displace 443 families. In case of Kashipur, Singur and Nandigram, a number of people died due to police firing. In 2001, 10 tribal people were killed in a police firing in the protest against the KoelKaro Hydro Power Project. Similarly on 6 December 2008, one person was killed, and several were injured in a police firing near Dumka, Jharkhand. Thus history shows a number of cases where bloodshed has taken place for land acquisition and displacement. On 7 May 2011, Bhatta and Pasaul (U.P.) saw violent clashes with the police and government officials on one side and the residents on the other. Eight people, including two policemen, were killed, and around 100 went missing (Mahaprashasta, p. 125). On Tuesday, 9 August 2010, the Pune rural police opened fire on the farmers protesting a water pipeline project from the river Pavana to industrial township of Pimpri-Chinchwad. As a result of the police's violent actions, three protestors died, and scores were injured and hospitalized (Roy, 2011).

The (peoples) movements have brought to light the tremendous loss of resources: forests, cultivable agricultural land, money, etc. due to development projects and policies. It is a highly subsidized development which glosses over the huge cost the nation pays in the form of loss of green forest, pure air and water, fertile land, livelihood and social disruption. If these costs were computed, these projects would reflect their burden and prove counterproductive for the nation (Sangvai, 2007: 114). The voice of the people needs to be considered with a human consideration rather than ignoring them in the name of development alone.

Consequences of Land Acquisition and Displacement

In India, of the 20 million people displaced since 1947, it is estimated that 75 per cent of them have been impoverished due to development projects (Downing, 2005). The Land Acquisition Act has failed to address several economic, social, cultural, psychological and physical aspects of the displaced people. Once displacement takes place successfully, whatever may be the policy of R&R, they become marginalised, their voice remains unheard, and they become rootless and suppressed ruthlessly. The democratic rules of right to equality and right against exploitation fail to operate for the victims of development. Their sacrifice for the cause of development became the forgotten story of the past, and they slip down the economic and social ladder. The widespread impact of displacement upon the displaced people is largely negative in term of economic and social consequences. The environment too goes unheeded. The economic structure of the displaced people collapses. Based on the issues of resettlement, Professor Michel M. Cernea has evolved eight major impoverishment risk factors arising out of displacement. These are (i) landlessness, (ii) joblessness, (iii) homelessness, (iv) marginalisation, (v) food insecurity, (vi) increase in morbidity and mortality, (vii) loss of access to common property and (viii) social disarticulation. Other risks like the risk of education, risk in shift of occupation and risk of loss of livestock are also very much associated with displacement. Again to quote Cernea, 'Expropriation of land removes the main foundation upon which people's productive systems, commercial activities livelihoods are constructed. This is the principal form of decapitalisation and pauperisation for most rural and many urban displaces, who lose this way both natural and manmade capital'. (Cernea, 1999: 17). The draft National Tribal Policy (NTP) 2006 also admits the alienation of tribal land is the single-most-important cause of pauperisation of tribal.

The best examples are the uncared victims of development projects like Hirakud and Bhakra Dams. In case of displaced of Hirakud Dam, only 11 per cent could be resettled without any proper rehabilitation measure. They had to struggle hard in remote areas and barren land. Many of them perished in the process of their struggle. During my field visit, people have narrated their misery during a post-displacement period. Here I wish to present two such experiences of displaced people.

Case 1

Sri Debendra Gupta, aged about 84, a freedom fighter and formerly a resident of Fatapali near Rmpela in the submerged zone of Hirakud Dam, narrated the story about the construction of dam before the research team. He, along with Chitamani Gupta and Arjun Gupta, took part in the Quit India Movement of 1942 and were imprisoned for nine months. Now Sri Debendra Gupta lamented that the promise of sweet and honey to the displaced people by the government has remained a daydream even after 50 years of its existence. Daipayan Gupta supported the project in a meeting held at Bargarh for the greater interest of the state in the form of irrigation, electricity, industry and flood control. But he lamented that no benefit is provided to the people of submerged areas who sacrificed their land and underwent severe hardship. No promise has been fulfilled by the state. His submerged village, Fatapali, was far better than the present site of resettlement at Kalmi-Nua-Mura. In term of land fertility, one acre of land at Fatapali is equivalent to three acres of land in Kalmi. Here, he has no good quality land. He led the villagers to the Kalmi camp. For him, sacrificing for the country as a freedom fighter and land for HDP are in equal footing, and the benefit from the project has never come to them.

Case 2

Sri Mangulu Charn Biswal, a retired high school headmaster and a noted writer of Sambalpuri drama, opted for self-resettlement at Baradunguri. As a resident of Pitapali, a submerged village, he has expressed that displacement has brought tragedy to the DPs. Although the name of his village name was Pita (bitter), in reality it was Mitha (sweet) in all respects. And now they are in an infertile area where agricultural output is far below the submerged village. The social and cultural ties peoples' prosperity without proper compensation; resettlement and rehabilitation are buried forever. The conditions of village deities of submerged villages remain uncared without proper measure for reconstruction of temples. It is seen that there was the presence of number of Lord Jagannath temples, which indicates the spread of Jagannath culture in the submerged area. It is noticed that the village Pitapali was declared as a partially submerged village. But actually it became a fully submerged village, except the village forest, where a few poor DPs have resettled. The village temple of Lord Jagannath is seen during summer, and now it has become a picnic spot. But the deity's temple has not yet been constructed, and the *gountia*, or village lord, in spite of his economic degradation, is taking personal care only. The resettled DPs near the reservoir depend on fishing as their main occupation with no other source of livelihood. The other DPs of the village have undertaken self-resettlement at different existing villages of Sambalpur district. In the post-displacement period without food security, people were forced to consume non-food items for their survival. Bamboo shoot (Kardi) became their principal vegetable. Pitapali, a well-established village, was shattered like a card house, and all displaced families resettled in different villages and towns and became unknown to one another. The social fabric of the village was lost forever.

Whom did the project benefit?

A natural question comes from a sensible citizen. Who has benefited from the project at the cost of the displaced people? The reservoir has turned a fertile area and a civilisation into Salila Samadhi (cremation in deep water). The report on the benefits of the Hirakud Dam has not properly evaluated in terms of the social cost, loss of forest, fertile land, agricultural output, occupation, health and tragedy of the displaced people. They have never been settled in the command area. All resettlement camps were established in forests and inaccessible areas. This shows that the government had never intended to provide irrigation benefit of the project to the DPs. On the contrary, the people in the command area of present Bargarh, Sonepur districts have benefited basically from irrigation. In our country, there is underpricing of water for irrigation, and no measure has ever been taken to recover the project cost and pass a part of such proceeds to the displaced people. It is also a fact that a large number of farmers from Andhra Pradesh and Telengana could purchase large tracts of land in the tahasil of Attabira, Bargarh, Bheden and Dungripali and enjoin the benefits of Hirakud water. The local Odiya farmers were reluctant to go for winter paddy with Hirakud canal water. They were having a misconception that paddy cannot be grown by 'BalalaPani', i.e., flow water and chemical fertilizer. That is why they were throwing bags of chemical fertilizer supplied to them free of cost by the government onto the road. It is the farmers from Andhra Pradesh who taught them the skill of double-cropping through irrigation and chemical fertilizer. In fact, they have dominated the agricultural production, especially paddy, in the command area. The lost forest in the reservoir has never been compensated through aforestation measures. The closure of canals in the tail reach area has reduced the net command area. The project benefit was overestimated; on the contrary, the social and environment cost and perspective yield of the submerged agricultural land were underestimated. These experiences clearly indicate that development projects do create marginalisation, and project benefit is not passed on to the displaced people. This has happened with the Adivasis of Rourkela, who lost their land for the Rourkela Steel Plant but did not get any benefit. The advantages were hijacked by the people of coastal districts and neighbouring states. Experiences show that development projects create a marginalised section of the people who face exclusion rather than inclusion to the process of development. Development-induced displacement endangers human rights. The World Commission on Dams estimated that by 2000, 40–80 million people had already been forcibly displaced as a result of large dam projects alone.

McCulley (1998), in the context of large dams, says the permanent inundation of forest, wetlands and wildlife is perhaps the most obvious ecological effect of a dam. Reservoirs have flooded vast areas; at least 40,000 square kilometers have been lost worldwide. Yet it is not only the amount of land lost which is important, but also its quality. River and flood plain habitats are some of the world's most diverse ecosystems (p. 36).

The social activist and organizer of NBA, Medha Patkar, told *Frontline*, 'It is not land acquisition that is the chief issue. The main issue is of planning and development. Anything and everything are being called a project in the "public interest". What could be worse when even the government statistics, in the Economic Survey of India, estimates that more than 60 lakh hectares has been taken in the last 15 years and hardly any among the poor has been benefited out of this development. It so happens that the rural and urban poor and not the elites of the country have to sacrifice always for such development. And this is leading to a scenario of structural violence of the state against violence of the people' (Mahaprashasta; 2011: 128).

Laws and policy on land acquisition and displacement in Odisha

The government of Odisha did not have any rehabilitation policy for a long time. Due to the lack of a basic framework for rehabilitation, the ousted, especially during the period from 1950 to 1970, have suffered a lot, and a number of them have perished in the changed condition of post-displacement. 'It was found in 1988 that even after 32 years of filling of Hirakud reservoir compensation amounting to Rs.15 crore rupees were to be paid to 9,913 claimants who lost their lands. A number of cases are yet to be disposed even after sixty year of its existence. In the case of Machhakund Hydro-electric project, no rehabilitation provisions were made for 300 displaced scheduled caste families. Only 450 families, which are 30 per cent of the total tribal families displaced belonging to scheduled tribes, were rehabilitated. Similarly, the Rourkela Project (Steel Plant) rehabilitated 53.6 per cent of its total number of displaced families. There was no clear-cut principle under which the land was allotted to each family for the purpose of rehabilitation' (Patnaik, 1996: 125).

It is fact that there was no resettlement and rehabilitation (R&R) policy for the displaced people of Odisha. They were dealt with the limited provision of compensation under LAA 1894, which was quite insufficient, inappropriate and unjust towards the displaces. The dam projects had no R&R policy until 1973. It is only the agitation of Rengalioustees that forced the government for a policy in 1973 and subsequently in 1990 and 1994. In case of industrial and mining units like RSP, HAL, NALCO and Ordinance factory, they have their own policy to deal with the displacement.

On 14 May 2006 (Notification No.18040-R&REH-1/2006), the government of Odisha declared the Orissa Resettlement and Rehabilitation Policy (ORRP) following the Kalinganagar massacre (2 January 2006) in which 14 tribals were shot dead in police firing. The policy is somehow an improved version and shall apply to all projects for which private land has been acquired under LAA 1894, as well as for which land is acquired through negotiation under the policy. The ORRP 2006 has identified five different types of projects where displacement occurs via industrial projects, mining projects, irrigation projects, national parks and sanctuaries, urban projects and linear projects like roads, railways, power lines and other projects.

The project authority will make special efforts to facilitate skill upgradation of the displaced people. The policy has the provision to provide employment to one member of each displaced family in case of industrial and mining projects and one-time cash assistance up to Rs. 5 lakh to those displaced families who have lost all land, including homestead land, in the following categories: (i) displaced families coming under Category (i) 5.00 lakh; (ii) displaced families coming under Category (ii) 3.00 lakh; (iii) displaced families coming under Category (iii) 2.00 lakh; and (iv) displaced families coming under Category (iv) and (v) 1.00 lakh.

However, certain areas of concern still prevail, e.g., the involvement of intermediaries like IDCO and IPCOL has raised various questions. It is said that the tribal were paid Rs. 22,000 to 37,000 per acre by the Industrial Development Corporation of Orissa, which in turn sold the land to TATA at Rs. 3 to 3.5 lakhs per acre. The displaced tribal feel that the said compensation paid to them was below the current market price (Sahoo, 2006: 134). The ORRP 2006 has failed to address the cause of dispossession and deprivation of sustainable livelihood of the displaced people in general and the Adivasis in particular. In exercising the state sovereign power, it has been acting as a broker for the private corporate sector. The burning examples of such cases are Tata Steel at Kalinganagar and POSCO Steel near Paradip Port in Jagatsinghpur district. Let the land of Orissa be not hijacked by the corporate world to serve their vested interests. The policy does not provide any means of free, prior and informed consent of the affected families before the process of land acquisition starts. There is no mandatory provision on the part of the state to provide land to the displaced people. The ORRP 2006 is meant for the likely-to-be displaced families but remain silent about the 1.5 million already displaced during the past few decades. The improper implementation of ORRP 2006 has also come under judicial scanning of the Orissa High Court in the case of Kalinganagar industrial estate (*The Telegraph*, Oct. 25 2011). Even after more than 60 years of the Hirakud Dam project, a number of displaced people are yet to receive their compensation. God knows when their cases will be finalized.

Here a question arises: why are the displaced people dealt with through a policy which is not enforceable? How long will their sacrifice be out of the orbit of law? Let the policy be given a legal status by the government so these provisions will have a legal dress. Their sacrifice will get at least a legal status after six decades of independence. Realizing the absence of national law to provide adequate and just resettlement and rehabilitation and compensation for the loss of livelihood of the displaced people and the high public concern on the problem of land acquisition issue throughout the country, the much-discussed 'The Right to Fair Compensation and Transparency in Land Acquisition, Rehabilitation and Resettlement Act, 2013' (RFCTLA R&R, 2013) was finally passed in the parliament and became an act from 8 September 2013. Ultimately the rights of the displaced people and project-affected people got the status of an act after six decades of independence and causing much more damages to the displaced people of different projects. Among all the displaced people, the displaced people of dams are the worst victims of development projects. In this act, three positive things have come: (i) R&R receive a legal status by substituting policies; (ii) land acquisition can take place, provided 80 per cent of the affected families give their consent for public purpose and 70 per cent for public-private partnership projects; and (iii) the role of gram sabha has been given priority in the acquisition of land in the scheduled areas under the Fifth Scheduled referred in the constitution of India. Besides these, the act has enhanced the rate of compensation, special provision for multiple displacements, return of unutilized acquired land, share in the sale of acquired land, etc. has been added. Special provisions have been made of landless and ST and SC. Infrastructural development for the need of the resettled displaced people has also been emphasized. One significant change is the reduction of the powers that the district collector enjoyed under LLA 1894.

Benefit-sharing mechanism

The financing of post-displacement rehabilitation through a benefit-sharing mechanism is slowly being embraced as legitimate and incremental to individual compensation paid on a family-by-family basis. Countries tend to use this mechanism for investments in welfare of the displaced group as large collectives, through area development programmes around reservoirs. In sum, the advantage of using economic rents and project benefit is that the financing necessary to avoid displacees pauperisation becomes a part of the economics of the displacing project itself (Cerenea, 2007: 1037). The passing of project benefit is being practised in a number of countries. For example, in Colombia since the early 1990s, 1 per cent of benefits from the hydropower plant is directed towards the development of the areas into which the displaced reservoir population were related. In Brazil, royalties are paid throughout the power plant lifetime for the sustainability of the affected population. In 1985, China's State Council decided to create a post-resettlement development fund in which contributions from power companies will be deposited for the benefits of displaced people. The findings of World Bank's studies show that the post-resettlement measures adopted by China have been able to decrease the incidence of impoverishment, despite the increase in the number of displaced people. Japan has adopted land-leasing experiment while renouncing the process of expropriating lands required for reservoirs. Above all, it is a comprehensive policy for land acquisition and R&R of the displaced people. Instead of land acquisition, the land lease policy is far better to provide project benefit to the landowner in a sustainable manner. Nothing has been provisioned for the past victims of the development projects. It should have followed the Chinese policy in this respect to restore and achieve comprehensive development goals for the project-displaced people as a whole. The RFCTLA R&R, 2013, although coming after much water has flown in the river of land acquisition and displacement, is still a welcome step in the history of Indian legislation. Nevertheless the benefit-sharing mechanisms adopted by different countries, if adopted in case of Indian cases of displacement, would have become more comprehensive and people-oriented.

Conclusion

Commenting on the World Bank-assisted Narmada project, S. Parasuraman and colleagues write, 'The progress made by the SSP [Sardar Sarovar Project] does not seem to be very different from India's experience with major irrigation and power projects: while main civil works somehow get completed, creation of the necessary infrastructure to realise benefits of the projects remain uncertain' (Wade, 2011: 62). This statement clearly shows that secondary importance is usually paid to the causes of displacement and their resettlement even in the twenty-first century.

The past record of least satisfactory R&R has developed a sense of betrayal among the displaced people of most of the projects in the country; hence there is growing resistance. The incremental nature of R&R is not the solution to the growing problem of development-induced displacement.

There is the need of human touch. Let us consider them as 'Great Sacrificers' for nation-building and be a part of enjoying the fruit of development. Let the next generation be proud of parents' sacrifices and equally enjoy the fruit of development. The colonial politico-bureaucratic pattern of development should find an alternative mode of development, i.e., to ameliorate the plight of teeming Indians through education and health rather than selling the country to the MNC/TNC and domestic, large industrial houses through the back door.

Displacement should be avoided or to be as minimum as possible. The fertile land and populated areas should be out of the industrial establishment. The displaced people should be provided land-based rehabilitation along with replacement cost of land rather than market-determined price for the acquired land. The resettlement and rehabilitation measures need to precede the construction of projects. Education and training must be imparted to the affected population before the commencement of the projects so as to prevent hijack of jobs and other benefits by the outsiders. The reservation of seats in the important educational institutions of the country for the children of displaced people is the need of the days to avoid risk of education of the children. A time-bound measure is needed to achieve all-round development of the affected area. Above all, a corruption-free administrative mechanism is highly necessary to percolate the desired economic and social benefits to the bottom of the society. Social Security measures like family pension need to be introduced to all categories of displaced people, irrespective of the nature of the projects. Insurance coverage in respect of health, life and property should be provided to the victims of all development projects. Land in the command area of irrigation projects must be acquired to resettle and rehabilitate the displaced people of that project concerned. The corporate house must adhere to their commitment by discharging the corporate social responsibility (CSR) in a vigorous way, particularly towards the displaced people. The displaced people of other projects should also be taken in a normative manner so that their deprivation of economic development is minimized and brought back to the mainstream. To finance displacement, measures like collection of special assessment from the project benefit area, particularly in case of irrigation projects, can also be taken. Last but not least, before chanting the mantra of development, the act for acquisition of land and R&R should content the provision of adequate measure to protect the environment so as to make provision of finite resources for the future generation and to achieve the course of sustainable development.

References

Bhattacharyya, D. (2015). History of Eminent Domain in Colonial Thought and Legal Practices. *Economic and Political Weekly*, vol. L, no. 50, 12 December.

Cernea, M. (Ed.). (1999). *The Economics of Involuntary Resettlement: Questions and Challenges*. Washington, DC: World Bank.

Cernea, M. (2000). Risks Safeguard and Reconstruction: A Model for Population Displacement and Resettlement. *Economic and Political Weekly*, 7 October.

Cernea, M. (2007). Financing for Development, Benefit Sharing Mechanism in Population Resettlement. *Economic and Political Weekly*, vol. XLII, no. 12, 24–30 March.

Dhritri. (2012). Diversion of Forest Land for Mining, Industries etc. *Odiya Daily*, 9 January.

Downing, T. (2005). *Rights for the World's Evicted: Are Development Projects Harming the People They Are Meant to Help?* www.ted-downing.com.

Fernandes, W. (1994). An Activist Process Around the Draft National Rehabilitation Policy. *Social Action*, vol. 45, pp. 277–298.

Mahalingam, A. and A. Vyas. (2011). Comparative Evaluation of Land Acquisition and Compensation Process across the World. *Economic and Political Weekly*, vol. XLVI, no. 32, 6 August.

Mahaprashasta, A. A. (2011). Fight for Land. *Frontline*, 3 June.

McCulley, P. (1998). *Silenced Rivers*. New Delhi: Orient Longman.

Murickan, J. et al. (2003). *Development Induced Displacement*. New Delhi: Rawat Publication.

Orissa Resettlement & Rehabilitation Policy. (2006). Revenue Dept. Govt. of Orissa, Bhubaneswar.

Pai, S. (2007). Janadesh 2007: The Land Question. *Economic and Political Weekly*, vol. XLII, 10–23 November.

Pandey, B. (1998). *Depriving the Underprivileged for Development*. Bhubaneswar: Patnaik, S. M. (1996). *Displacement Rehabilitation and Social Change*. New Delhi: Inter India Publications.

The Right to Fair Compensation and Transparency in Land Acquisition, R&R Act, 2013, Ministry of Rural Development, Government of India, 8 September 2013.

Reddy, I. U. B. (1992). *Displacement and Rehabilitation*. New Delhi: Mittal Publication.

Roy, S. S. (2011). The Maval Land Struggle. *Economic and Political Weekly*, vol. XLVI, no. 35, 27 August.

Sabar, B. (2010). Development induced Displacement and Human Rights Violation in Orissa: An Anthropological Insight. *Social Action*, vol. 60, no. 2, April–June.

Sahoo, T. (2006). Industrialization and Displacement in Orissa, Adivasi, vol. 46, no. 2, pp. 18–24.

Sainath, P. (1996). *Everybody Loves a Good Drought*. India: Penguin.

Sangvai, S. (2007). The New People's Movements in India. *Economic and Political Weekly*, 15–21 December.

Wade, R. H. (2011). Muddy Waters: Inside the World Bank as It Struggled with the Narmada Project. *Economic and Political Weekly*, vol. XLVI, no. 40, October.

Part II

Development, displacement and dispossession

Selected case studies

8 Development, displacement and disposession

A study of POSCO India transit camp

Debabrata Baral

POSCO-India, a polarizing development project?

Since the day POSCO-India signed the Memorandum of Understanding (hereafter will be referred as MoU) with Government of Odisha, there has been controversies and conflicts. Initially, the three main stakeholders involved in these controversies are (i) POSCO, the mining project. (ii) The Ministry of Environmental and Forestry of Government of India. This body is responsible to evaluate the social and environmental impact of the project and grant required licenses accordingly. (iii) The members of the local community. The people delimited in the proposed POSCO-India project site. This section will outline the positions of each of the stakeholders regarding the mining project.

The Project

POSCO, the parent company of POSCO-India, signed a project with the government of Odisha on 22 June 2005. It planned to establish an integrated steel plant worth 51,000 crores. The details of the project as stated in different sections of the MoU is given below. To quote,

1 M/s POSCO having its registered office at 1 Koidong-Dong, Nam-Ku, Pohang-City, Kyungsanbuk Province, Republic of Korea, (hereinafter referred to as POSCO, which expression shall, unless repugnant to the context or meaning thereof, include its successors, executors, administrators, representatives and permitted assigns), is proposing to set up an Integrated Steel Plant of a total capacity of 12 million tonnes per annum in the State of Orissa at Paradeep, in Jagatsinghpur district. . . .

4(1) The Company is desirous of developing and operating the following facilities on the basis described in this MoU in the State of Orissa with proposed investment of around US$ 12 billion or Rs.51, 000 crores. . . .

> (2) The Company is also desirous of developing and operating the following related infrastructure based on the needs of the "Steel Project", on the basis described in this MoU:
>
> i Mining facilities in the areas allocated by the Government of Orissa/ Government of India (the "Mining Project");
>
> ii Road, rail and port infrastructure (the "Transportation Project"), including the dedicated railway line from the mine-belt to Paradeep;
>
> iii Integrated township; and
>
> iv Water supply infrastructure (the "Water Project").
>
> (3) The Steel Project will be located at Paradeep. The Mining Project will be established at the mining site(s) that are identified as the mineral resources for the Company . . .
>
> (Government of Odisha, 2005: 1).

> 5. (ii) The Company will require approximately 4,000 acres of land (hereinafter referred to as the "Land") for the purpose of setting up the Steel Project and associated facilities, including the port facilities and a storage yard for coking coal . . .
>
> (Government of Odisha, 2005: 3).

The above portions of the MoU clearly state that POSCO is going to establish an integrated steel plant of 12 million tonnes per annum capacity. The value of the project is 51,000 crores. The integrated mining project will be located in Jagatsinghpur district of Odisha. This project includes mining activities and building infrastructure for transportation and township. It also requires infrastructures in water or, to be more precise, port facilities. The project requires a 'Minor Port'. The project is planned in two phases. The first phase of making crude and finished steel will begin after the company takes possession of the land and other licenses required for the projects are cleared. The government of Odisha identified a coastal stretch of land in Erasama Block of Jagatsinghpur district in Odisha. It was proposed that the port would be built on the point where Jatadhar River meets the Bay of Bengal Sea. The port is proposed to be located in Dhinkia village. It may be noted that just about 10 kilometers away from the Jagatsinghpur Gram Panchayat, there has been a Port.[1] Irrespective of this fact, the government has in principle, approved the construction of another port in the same district. This project as a development project has got a huge backing from the side of the government.

Resistances against the project and its Fractions

POSCO-India requires 4,004 acres of forest land. From it, around 3,566 acres are officially classified as forest land. Land for the proposed POSCO-India project is located in the Erasama district. The land selected for the project falls in six villages. These villages are located in the coastal part of

Jagatsinghpur district. The impacted village and the Gram Panchayat are; Noliasahi, Bhuyanpal and Polanga village of Gadakujang Gram Panchayat; Dhinkia and Govindpurof village of Dhinkia Gram Panchayat; and Nuagaon of Nuagaon Gram Panchayat. But, at the same time during August–September 2005, the people residing in the proposed site, started to oppose the establishment of POSCO-India. Since then, POSCO-India has been surrounded by a lot of controversies. The establishment of the proposed project seemed to have polarized the people residing in the proposed project site. On one hand, there has been a strong resistance against the establishment of the project. While on the other hand, there were fractions of people who eventually agreed to give their land for the proposed development project. These led to conflicts between these two groups. Hence, eventually the people who agreed to support the integrated steel plant were forced to move out of the villages. They were later relocated in a transit camp.

The Institutional Perspective on the project

From the perspective of the central government (Government of India) and the state government (Government of Odisha), establishing POSCO-India project has always been a priority. As in 2010, the Union of India granted in-principle approval to the POSCO-India project. This in-principle approval was granted despite the fact that the ordinary people residing in the proposed project site were resisting the establishment of the project for the last five years. The Ministry of Environment and Forestry of Government of India states, to quote,

> MOE&F & POSCO project in Orissa – An update
>
> 1 On June 26, 2007, the Orissa Government applied to the Central Government for permission under the Forest Conservation Act, 1980 to divert 1253.225 hectares of forestland for establishment of an integrated steel plant and captive port by POSCO-India (user agency) in Jagatsinghpur district of Orissa.
>
> 2 After careful considerations, the MOE&F gave 'in-principle' approval for the said diversion on September 19th, 2008 subject to fulfillment of certain conditions.
>
> (Ministry of Environment and Forests, Government of India, 2010)

While, on 3rd January 2011, the Ministry of Environmental and Forest gave the final clearance for the Steel-cum-captive Power plant, Captive minor port etc. The Minister of state, independent change and Environment and Forestry granted the final clearances to the project. But he added few safeguards. To quote,

> Undoubtedly, projects such as that of POSCO have considerable economic, technological and strategic significance for the country. At the same time, laws on environment and forests must be implemented

seriously. Every such case presents its own unique set of circumstances and requires a distinctive solution. In this case,

i The 28 additional conditions imposed as part of the environmental clearance for the steel-cum-captive power plant;
ii The 32 additional conditions imposed as a part of the environmental clearance for the captive minor port; and
iii The pointed assurance sought from the state government in keeping with its obligations under the Forest Rights Act, 2006,
– provide comprehensive package of measures to ensure that this project will not be detrimental from an ecological and local livelihood perspective. In any case, the conditions imposed are going to be closely monitored.

(Ministry of Environment and Forests, Government of India, 2011)[2]

The Union of India passes the POSCO-India project with certain safeguards. Definitely giving the inprinciple approval and then the final approval highlights the inclination of the government's towards the project. But at the same time, the prevalence of discontent and conflict in the proposed site cannot be undermined. This conflict had led to the displacement of a section of the community which later agreed to favour the establishment of the project. The next section will elaborate in detail the reason for the establishment of POSCO-India transit camp.

POSCO-India transit camp: a social history

This section maps the changing perception of the people residing in the POSCO-India transit camp, e.g., a shift from initially aggressively resisting the project, to accepting the project, then getting sceptical of the project. The POSCO-India transit camp was established in 2008. It hosted around 52 families, and 217 people are residing in it. POSCO transit camp resembles a small settlement. There were small concrete houses with tin sheets as rooftops. Roughly the houses were 15 feet by 15 feet. One family gets one room in the transit camp. Living conditions in the transit is very tough. There is no adequate supply of drinking water. There is one toilet, which is now broken. During the rainy season, the roof leaks as it is made of tin. While in summer, it becomes intolerable as there are no windows in the room for any sort of ventilation. Even in winter, dewdrops starts getting accumulated in the room. There were some banana trees and a small toilet outside the settlement.

Contending political mobilisation: the context for changing public perception on POSCO: from Anti-POSCO to Pro-POSCO

As per respondents, there have been various groups involved in mobilising and influencing the opinion of the local community. But the state election in

2008 damaged the unity of people. People started questioning the leadership of PPSS. Hence after 2008, there was a change of public opinion regarding POSCO-India. To quote a resident,

> This is a centrist-leftist plot. Few leftist leaders came to Dhinkia village and stayed there. They started mobilizing people against POSCO. Soon after that leader from the centrist party and also from the ring wing political party reached the site with their associates. They asked people not to support POSCO. People got swayed away by the centrist-leftist nexus. Now we are the ultimate victims of their politics. The Orissa government is silent, while the atrocities of the POSCO-Protirodh Sangram Samiti leadership are increasing. They are forcing people to protest. People were protesting for 300 days per year, and those people who were not going to the protest were fined. Now 90 percent of the people want POSCO so that they can be free from the atrocities of the anti-POSCO leadership. The election was the turning point in this movement. The political difference between centrist political party and the leftist parties resulted in violence. This later broke the unity of the people, and made a section of the people pro-POSCO.

The POSCO-India transit camp is located in Badagabapur. This camp was established by POSCO-India as a temporary measure to rehabilitate the people displaced by conflicts in its proposed project site. This transit camp was initially started to house people supporting the establishment of the development project. The people residing in the camp claimed that they were forced into exile. In 2007 the resistance against POSCO-India turned violent hence The villagers took shelter in the camp. A resident of the camp narrated, to quote,

> This transit camp is made for the 52 families that were displaced by the anti-POSCO leadership. On June 26, 2007 the anti POSCO leadership displaced us from our own village. We went to the Kujang police station; we wept before the Superintendent of Police[3] and the collector. We pleaded them to rehabilitate us but they did not resettle us. Then we went and resided in the compound of the nearby Girls College for 8 months. While in 2008, POSCO with the Chief Minister's approval built this transit camp for the 52 displaced families.

Quite surprisingly, as per the narrative mentioned above, it seemed quite a sizeable section of the village was displaced and were grieving. Here one tends to think about the role of the Grievances Redresser mechanisms of the government of Odisha. To quote,

> Public Grievance Cells have been functioning at various levels of Administration, starting from the level of Hon'ble Chief Minister, Departmental Secretaries and Heads of Departments, down to the level of District

> Collectors, Sub-Collectors, Tahasildars, Block Development Officers and other field functionaries of different departments.[4]
>
> (Government of Odisha, 2012: 1)

To quote further,

> Hon'ble Chief Minister has been emphasizing on holding of joint hearing of grievances by the Collector and the Superintendent of Police along with other district level officers. Accordingly joint hearing of grievances is being taken up in each district by the Collector and the Superintendent of Police on every working Saturday. A consolidated report is sent to the office of Hon'ble Chief Minister on the same day after review of the grievance position of all the districts.
>
> (Government of Odisha, 2012: 4)

This section states the context, of the local community members favouring POSCO during 2007–2008. Generally scholars involved in social movements base their analysis from a synchronic perspective. But with reference To the Social Movement against Posco a Diachronic study of culture, i.e., culture within a social movement is highly recommended.

Lived experiences matter: interrogating policies and safeguards on land acquisition

In terms of policy, land acquisition for any development projects in Odisha are undertaken through the Orissa Resettlement and Rehabilitation Policy 2006.[5] The objective of the policy resonates with the objectives of the National Rehabilitation and Resettlement Policy of 2007. This policy safeguards the people and talks about sustainability of the local community and environment. To quote,

1. to avoid displacement wherever possible and minimise it exercising available options otherwise,
2. to recognise voices of displaced communities emphasizing the needs of the indigenous communities and vulnerable sections,
3. to ensure environmental sustainability through participatory and transparent process and
4. to help guiding the process of developing institutional The impacts of development project are generally evaluated in two phases i.e. during the establishment and after the establishment of the project. A review of the rehabilitation and resettlement provisions or through a survey of the socio-economic-ecological conditions of the people gives an impression of the impact of the development project.

(Government of Odisha, 2006: 1)

But at the same time, an interaction with the people in the POSCO-India transit camp suggested that the National Rehabilitation and Resettlement Policy of 2007 was either not properly implemented and was insufficient. Hence this section, states the lived experiences of people to outline the various aspects that land acquisition policy need to address and incorporate.

Unsustainable financial assistances

The National Mineral Policy of India celebrates and refers to the 'Odisha Model' in terms of relief and rehabilitation. To quote,

> the Orissa package offers various types of assistance to families that have been displaced or affected by different types of projects. For those affected by mining, project assistance includes: employment to one family member in the project or cash assistance ranging from Rs 1 lakh to Rs 5 lakh with option for 50 per cent of cash assistance in the form of convertible preference shares; training for self-employment; homestead land subject to availability or Rs 50,000 for relocation elsewhere; a house or housing assistance up to Rs 150,000; and shops or service units to those who opt for self-employment with preference to handicapped persons, ST and Scheduled Castes (SC). In addition to assistance specific to mining projects, certain types of assistance common to Project Affected People (PAPs) of all projects have also been listed. These include: maintenance allowance of Rs 2000 per month per family for one year; assistance of Rs 10,000 for a temporary shed; and transportation allowance of Rs 2000 in lieu of free transport to habitation site. For tribal PAPs this would also include preferential allotment of land and resettlement as far as possible in compact areas.
>
> (Planning Commission, Government of India, 2016: 73)

But, in the transit camp, a sum of rupees 4000 per day is totally paid to the entire 52 families, which comprises of 217 people. Each family was paid only rupees 20 to sustain their needs for a day. This figure again contradicts with the safeguards assured in the Orissa Relief and Rehabilitation Policy of 2006[6] and the National Mineral Policy of 2006.

Dispossessed by the 'temporality' of the rehabilitation and resettlement schemes

According to residents of the transit camp, the temporary measures offered by the government were not going down well by the villagers who had eventually agreed to sell their land to POSCO-India. They are now finding it difficult to sustain their lives, sending children to schools or even finding daily wage work. The people in the camp don't have a job. Their piece of land lies inside the village. But due to conflict they are unable to enter. They are shelter-less.

Moreover, because of their transit camp status, they are socio-culturally discriminated. As no one wants to given their sons or daughter for marriage to the people residing in the transit camp. A resident remarked, to quote,

> We are unemployed. Here people are dying of hunger. Narayan Ojha had died of hunger; even his widow was not given any compensation.

The government administration is silent on the issue of rehabilitation. The narratives of these people are again going against the Orissa Resettlement and Rehabilitation Policy of 2006, which states that if people are displaced or if there is loss of agriculture land due to the establishments of the industrial projects, then a member of the affected families will be eligible for employment in the project. To quote,

> (a) Employment: Families shall be eligible for employment, by the project causing displacement or loss of all agricultural land. For the purpose of employment, each original family will nominate one member of such family. The project proponent will give preference to the nominated members of the displaced/other families in the matter of employment. The order of preference will be as follows:
> (i) Displaced families losing all land including homestead land,
> (ii) Displaced families losing more than 2/3rd of agricultural land and homestead land,
> (iii) Displaced families losing more than 1/3rd of agricultural land and homestead land,
> (iv) Displaced families losing only homestead land but not agricultural land,
> (v) Families losing all agricultural land but not homestead land,
> The Project authority will make special efforts to facilitate skill upgradation of the nominated member of each displaced/other family to make him/her employable in their project.
>
> (Government of Odisha, 2006: 5)

Here it should be added that, the former, the minister of state had said that there is no provision regarding the number of employment in the Memorandum of Understanding (MOU) signed by the government of Orissa with POSCO-India Limited.[7] So, does the Odisha Rehabilitation and Resettlement Policy of 2006 remains just a promise away from its practice?

Non-transparency in compensation disbursal: the seeds for emergence of resistance

The lived experiences of the people residing in the transit camp were further countering the significance of the safeguards that were assured in the Orissa

Resettlement and Rehabilitation Policy of 2006.[8] The resistance against the establishment of the project was initially started in all the seven villages from where land acquisition was planned. According to the spokesperson, the people initially resisted POSCO-India, as they were not eligible for compensation. To quote,

> Nearly 80–90 percent people live on betel cultivation which is on government land. If POSCO comes, then government will take away the government land and people will get no compensation as they were cultivating on the government land. Look at the case of Rourkela, workers the government till now did not resettle them. This is why, we were Anti-POSCO. The proposed POSCO plan will displace 100 houses in Patana village which is in Dhinkia Gram Panchayat. Police cannot enter Dhinkia even though 80 percent villagers are supporters of POSCO. There is a law and order problem in Dhinkia.

Contrary to the dominant literature that suggests, development projects bring growth and welfare. This section concludes that the people who have agreed to give land and cooperate with the development project failed to get adequate support either from the government or the development project. They were gradually sidelined and subjected to a condition of impoverishment. Here a reference to Poulantzas would be very significant. As he argues, there are two perspectives through which one could understand the nature of the state. The first perspective looks at the state as a thing or instrument; therefore the state is seen as a passive tool in the hands of a class or some particular faction. In this perspective, the state has little autonomy. The social class acts to influence the state by forming itself into various pressure groups. The dominant class influences and absorbs the state and its specific powers. The second perspective views the state as a subject, which means the autonomy of the state and its specific powers are considered to be absolute (Poulantzas, 1972). In the context of POSCO-India, it seemed as if the state would largely fit into the first category, as the government of Odisha and the Union of India were more interested in facilitating the establishment of POSCO-India, irrespective of the fact that people are opposing the establishment of POSCO-India for over a decade.

The way forward: few recommendations

From the research and subsequent field visits of the transit camp, this chapter offers three suggestions outlined subsequently.

(Un) Represented: media and the local voices

First, listening and locating the concerns of impacted people are of utmost importance. For example, the people of the transit camp had selected a person to express their views to the outsiders. On getting the assurance that the opinion of the people of the transit camp will not be manipulated and be stated precisely, the spokesperson started his interview. The spokeperson, who very clearly stated, to quote,

> POSCO is in news because of various reasons. So a lot of press reporters, media persons, political groups, academicians come here regularly and enquire about it. As the numbers of visitors to the camp were increasing so the people in the transit camp has appointed me to speak on behalf of the people and present their views. The media and political groups manipulate the original voices of the people. I will share my experience with you only if you commit that you will not manipulate or interpret my statements and be honest in reporting my interview.

The opinions of people at the ground level are of utmost importance. Although, reflecting, analysing and speaking on behalf of these local communities is extremely important. But at the same time, one should also have the patience to listen and understand the issues, concerns and aspirations of the local community members.

Addressing the gaps in implementation

The issues and concerns faced by people in the transit camp has already been addressed in the Orissa Resettlement and Rehabilitation Policy of 2006. But, the non-transparent and improper implementation of the said policy has definitely played a major role in the changing perception of the people over the development projects, and in this case aggressively resisting it.

Functional alternatives

Definitely development projects have a functional value to the larger society; it also has certain dysfunction for certain sections of society. These impacted people bear the rough side of development projects. Hence it is highly recommended that development projects should have a detailed provision of functional alternatives for the local people, in terms of livelihood and employment, especially to the uneducated Project Affected People (PAP). The members of the local community should be trained, financed and made aware of the alternatives they can avail in case their livelihood and socio-economic life structure gets impacted.

Notes

1 POSCO-India plans to build a port as part of its integrated steel plant project. The port is initially planned to be built where the Jatadhar river meets the Bay of Bengal.

2 The abstract is taken from the document titled 'POSCO: Final Order and Other Relevant Documents' dated 31 January 2011. This document was downloaded from the Ministry of Environment and Forest on 23 May 2014 on 3:30 p.m. The web address currently available is: http://www.indiaenvironmentportal.org.in/files/Posco-final-orders-02052011.pdf.
3 Superintendent of police.
4 Quoted from the Annual Report on the Activities of Public Grievances and Pension Administration Department for the year 2011 and 2012, pp. 1–4. www.odisha.gov.in/publicgrievances/PGPA_AnnualReport/Annual_Report-2011-12.pdf. Accessed 24 March 2014 at 2.29 pm.
5 Downloaded from http://orissa.gov.in/e-magazine/orissaannualreference/OR-Annual-2009/pdf/313-322.pdf.
6 Announced vide Government of Orissa, Revenue Department, no. 18040/R, R & REH-1/06, dated 14 May 2006.
7 http://pib.nic.in/newsite/AdvSearch.aspx.
8 Announced vide Government of Orissa, Revenue Department, no. 18040/R, R & REH-1/06, dated 14 May 2006.

References

Government of Odisha. (2005). *Mou Between GoO and M/s POSCO*. New Delhi: Government of Odisha.

Government of Odisha. (2006). *Orissa Resettlement and Rehabilitation Policy 2006*. Revenue Department. Bhubaneshwar: Government of Odisha.

Government of Odisha. (2012). *Annual Report on the Activities of Public Grievances and Pension Admistration for the Year 2011 and 2012*. Public Grievances. New Delhi: Government of Odisha.

Ministry of Environment and Forests, Government of India. (2010). *MoE&F & POSCO Project in Orissa – An Update* (F. C. Division, Ed.). New Delhi: Government of India.

Ministry of Environment and Forests, Government of India. (2011). *POSCO: Final Order and Other Relevant Documents, 31st January 2011*. Jairam Ramesh, Minister of State (Independent Charge) and Environment and Forest, 2011. New Delhi: Government of India.

Planning Commission, Government of India. (2006). *National Mineral Policy. Report of the High Level Committee*. New Delhi: Government of India.

Poulantzas, Nicos. (1972). The Problem of Capitalist State. In Robin Blackburn (Ed.), *Ideology in Social Sciences*. London: Penguin Books.

9 Impact of displacement on social life

A case study from Talcher Coalfield

Suravee Nayak

Introduction

The means to development and the goals of development are observed to be contradictory to each other at times. High economic growth, supposedly to be the panacea for all ailments in an economy, sometimes goes beyond what is expected. Undoubtedly growth is the means to development, with industrialisation and commercialisation as its key tools. However, these weapons of growth have caused unsatisfactory and complex consequences when it comes to development. The important question to be asked here is what we mean by development in true sense. We certainly need a definition of development which goes beyond the realms of few indicators of wealth which does not necessarily tell us the difference between a developed nation and a developing nation; simultaneously it also does not substantiate the ongoing quality of life lived by the people out there.

Nevertheless, developing countries like India have been following the development regime provided by the Western development thinkers who suggested that industrialisation, globalisation and commercialisation have the potential to alleviate problems like poverty, unemployment, poor standard of living, illiteracy and malnutrition. To initiate these path-breaking and welfare-providing terminologies, large tracts of forest land and agricultural land are acquired by the state under the umbrella of 'public purpose', displacing millions of people from their dwellings and sources of livelihood.

This extraction of resources demands acquirement of huge land mass which causes massive involuntary population resettlement.[1] And it has been found that the extraction of resources has negatively affected the livelihood strategy of poor households (Shylendra and Rani, 2005). It has also been established that landless, small and marginal farmers are more affected than that of the landed (MIDS, 1996, as cited in Parasuraman, 1999). Bromley (1985b) argues that the displacement also turns the poor people further poor in resources, apart from increasing the number of poor.

There are three different categories of developmental projects according to the nature and extent of displacement (SC & ST, 1990, as cited in Parasuraman, 1999), which results in displacement of various scales. Those are irrigation and hydro-electric projects, industrial, power, mining and port projects and infrastructural projects. In India, around 50 million people have been displaced due to development projects in over 50 years (Negi and Ganguly, 2011: 6). Around 21.3 million development-induced Internally Displaced Populations (IDPs) include those displaced by dams (16.4 million), mines (2.55 million), industrial development (1.25 million) and wildlife sanctuaries and national parks (0.6 million) (IDMC, 2007, as cited in Negi and Ganguly, 2011: 6). In India, around 113,000 hectares of forest tract have been diverted for mining since 1980 (Kothari and Shrivastava, 2012).

Coal mining-induced displacement

As India is bounded by all other sources of energy, coal is given the status of national importance, and it has become the base of industrial growth among all other mineral resources. 'In particular, Coal formed the basis of accumulation of capital, industries and national wealth, though the contribution of mining to GDP is less than 3 percent' (Lahiri-Dutt, 2014: 15, 21). 'Some 400 million people are still without access to electricity, while countless more have limited access' (Ramesh, 2015: 414), which pressurises the increase in the production level of coal even more than earlier times. Presently, India is the third-largest producer of coal in the world with approximately 267 billion tonnes of coal reserves after China and USA (CIL, 2016).

Government-controlled Coal India Limited (CIL) is the single-largest coal producer in the world and dominates the domestic coal supply market with an 80 per cent market share; though captive coal mining has been allowed for industries. 'CIL's environmental track record was abysmal – mining over and above its permissible limits in some coal blocks was par of course, or its remedial efforts to address the adverse impacts of mining virtually non-existent' (Ramesh, 2015: 378). As 90 per cent of India's coal is produced from open-cast mines, this requires acquisition of large tracts of land, often from agricultural or tribal areas. This leads to a lot of displacement and loss of livelihoods among the people.

Study area

Coal India Limited (CIL) produces coal through seven of its wholly owned subsidiaries in India, and one of its subsidiaries is Mahanadi Coalfields Limited (MCL) which operates in the state of Odisha with two major coal-bearing areas that are IB Valley Coalfields and Talcher Coalfields, being sixth-major coalfields of India with high quarrying potentiality because of high ratio of coal to non-coal strata (MCL, 2007). There are eight open-cast and three underground mines in Talcher Coalfield. Talcher area is one of the fastest-growing industrial centres of India (Garada, 2013a; Mckinsey, 2014). As per 2011 Census, there is a total of 97,968 population, of which 51,567 (53 per cent) are male and 46,401 (47 per cent) are female and of which 18,807 (19 per cent) belong to a scheduled caste and 8,655 (9 per cent) belong to a scheduled tribe in Talcher block.

As mentioned previously, Odisha has the second-highest coal reserves, and Talcher is one of the fastest-growing industrial complexes. It is very much evident that the coal capitalism has been successful in expanding its terrains at Talcher. In this context, it is necessary to analyse the impact of such rapidly growing coal capitalism on the social lives of the displaced people of Talcher. Although it is debated in academics that the impact of displacement is multidimensional, this chapter examines the impact of displacement on the social coordinates of the people, given the fact that displacement leaves a long-standing social cost for everyday survival of the displaced people.

Methodology

An extensive field survey has been carried out from September 2015 to December 2015 in four villages of Talcher, Odisha. There are three categories of villages that have been taken for the study, for which four villages have been surveyed. The first category is the displaced village which is defined as that village where the households have completely lost their homestead land and either partly or completely or did not lose agricultural land. The second category is the affected village which is defined as that village where the households have completely or partly lost their agricultural land only. The final category is the least affected village which is defined as that village where the households have not lost either their homestead or agricultural land partly or completely for coal extraction.

For the first category, two displaced villages, namely Arisa[2] and Poddo, have been chosen for the study. The two displaced villages which have been chosen have different socio-economic characteristics, and hence, the nature of impact of displacement can be analysed by making a comparison between the displaced villages. One affected village named as Manda has been selected, and one least affected village named as Chakuli has been selected for the study. By way of method, a case-control approach is adopted to conduct this study. The Chakuli village is considered as the control village, and the affected and displaced villages are the cases.[3] The sampling method adopted for displaced villages is snowball sampling as the displaced households have moved to different places. The sampling method adopted for the affected and least affected village is representative sampling. The list of households in these two villages was prepared by the recommendations of the village committee comprising of members from different socio-economic groups.

A total of 583 households and 3,216 individual samples have been drawn from the four villages. The samples drawn from the Arisa village is 78 households out of 184 households by visiting 9 sites in Talcher; from the Poddo village is 108 households out of 421 households by visiting 12 sites in Talcher; from the Manda village is 187 households out of 806 households;

from the Chakuli village is 210 households out of 536 households. The data has been collective of both quantitative and qualitative nature. The analysis of the data collected has been done by using simple statistical tools, and narratives have also been illustrated in this chapter.

Impact of displacement on social life

In this chapter, we shall try to understand the impacts of displacement on social life using the framework of social reproduction of labour.[4] Social reproduction refers to those structures and activities that diffuse social inequality from generation to generation (Doob, 2013). A poor labour household continues to reproduce the generation for the labouring class. 'In this respect, the capitalist economy changed the meaning and objectives of the social system: the independent household produced the reproduction of its members, the capitalist economy uses the reproduction of the labouring population for the accumulation of capital' (Picchio, 1992: 9).

This chapter is divided into seven sections. The first section throws light onto the education attainment and the level of education attained in the displaced and affected households. The second section highlights the new forms of food insecurities developed due to capitalist economies in the displaced households. The third section analyses various facets of social disarticulation taking place in the lives of the displaced people. The fourth section elaborates the loss of civil and basic human rights during the process of dispossession. The fifth section is an attempt to go beyond the general notion of marginalisation and throws light on new forms of marginalisation emerged in the displaced and affected households. The sixth section tries to trace the changes in physical dimension of space of the displaced and affected households. The final section is an attempt to put together the findings of the previous sections and place them in the framework of social reproduction of labour.

Education

The displacement gives rise to the risk of disruption in education among the displaced people. Many studies have found that displacement has a negative impact on the education attainment of the displaced people (Mathur & Marsden, 1998). In this section, we shall trace the impact of displacement on the educational attainment and also on the level of education of the displaced people. The following table shows the current status of educational attainment below the 20 years of age group, which is taken as the education-attaining age group of all the surveyed villages.

From table 9.1, there are two critical observations which can be made. The educational attainment of the Manda village and Chakuli village are similar which clearly shows that the absence of displacement in the Manda village has prevented the village from any abnormal change to take place in

Table 9.1 Current Status of Education (for Age Group <=20) in the Surveyed Villages

Status of education (age group <=20)	*AFF*	*DISP 1*	*DISP 2*	*LE AFF*	*Total*
CURRENTLY ATTENDING	74.22	63.55	85.06	75.09	76.9
NEVER ATTENDED	3.11	21.50	0.65	2.26	3.98
EVER ATTENDED BUT CURRENTLY NOT ATTENDING	22.67	14.95	14.29	22.64	19.13
TOTAL	100.00	100.00	100.00	100.00	100.00

Source: Field Survey, 2015 values in percentage

Notes: 1, 2,3-case village; 4-control village
1) AFF-Affected (Manda) village 2) DISP 1-Displaced (Arisa) village
3) DISP 2-Displaced (Poddo) village 4) LE AFF-Least affected (Chakuli) village

the Manda village. Second, the educational attainment in both the displaced villages is different. As we have discussed earlier, the economic characteristics of the village before displacement were quite different. The Poddo village had already moved into transitioning, and hence dependence on agriculture had decreased substantially.[5] Hence, these households had already started to search livelihood options out of traditional shared economies for which the need of education had already emerged among some households.

To illustrate the case, as Ramakanta, 62 years old, from Poddo village says,

> Most of the people of our village were literate, the sole dependence on agriculture was no more viable. We wanted to get some jobs and at the same time hire labourers for doing agriculture. In this way, we could have benefited a lot.

The village was already doing better in terms of education than other nearby villages.[6] Additionally the job compensation which made them the employees in MCL had facilitated them to educate their children in schools sponsored by MCL.[7] Better employment opportunities, especially in MCL, are the motive of educational attainment in this village.

To illustrate the case, Chandan, 20 years old, from Poddo village says,

> I have completed my ITI course in mechanics from PMIT, Talcher. I donot want to study further. My father is doing some back door arrangements for my employment in MCL.

However, a similar pattern is not found in the Arisa village. This is possibly because many households are still ignorant of the value of education. Their intimacy with the traditional economy has still been intact. They were not much literate before the displacement because they never felt the need of education for sustenance in agriculture.[8] Many respondents have agreed to the fact that their purpose of sending their children to school is the disappearance of agriculture.[9] Similarly the children are also hopeful that the way their parents got employment in MCL without any education, they may also get employment in MCL. To illustrate the case, Chintu, 25 years old, says,

> If the land would have been there, then that would have been mine. So, MCL is responsible for my livelihoods. Why should I study when it is my right to get job in MCL?

Another possible reason could be that the many households in Arisa village could not avail the job compensation for which they cannot afford education for their children.[10] Along with the educational attainment, it is necessary to examine the level of education attained by the displaced villages. The following table shows the level of education attended across all age groups in the surveyed village.

From table 9.2, we can observe that as discussed earlier, the percentage of illiterate people are higher in Arisa village than the Poddo village. The maximum level of education attainment for most of the people across the villages is the secondary. (Refer to table 4.2.) It is a general notion found in these villages that secondary education is the minimum education which one should acquire nowadays, especially for a girl child.[11] However, we can see that in the case villages, especially in the Poddo village, people are attaining education more than the level of secondary education when compared to the control village by various measures. (Refer to table 4.2.) The purpose of attaining higher levels of education is the placement in MCL and

Table 9.2 Level of Education Prevailing in the Surveyed Villages

Level of education	*AFF*	*Village No.*			
		DISP 1	*DISP 2*	*LE AFF*	*Total*
ILLITERATE	19.90	28.40	15.02	19.00	18.74
PRIMARY	11.07	8.52	10.42	9.87	10.25
MIDDLE	9.20	8.83	9.72	17.78	11.65
SECONDARY	29.23	23.34	26.68	32.36	28.50
HIGHER SECONDARY	9.58	11.99	11.31	7.31	9.86
DIPLOMA	5.97	6.62	7.07	2.56	5.53
GRADUATION	8.83	5.99	14.31	5.24	9.60
POST-GRADUATE AND ABOVE	1.12	1.26	1.59	0.49	1.14
TOTAL	100.00	100.00	100.00	100.00	100.00

Source: Field Survey, 2015 values in percentage

Notes: 1, 2,3-case village; 4-control village
1) AFF-Affected (Manda) village 2) DISP 1-Displaced (Arisa) village
3) DISP 2-Displaced (Poddo) village 4) LE AFF-Least affected (Chakuli) village

other industries located nearby. Given the demand of technical education, many ITI colleges (public and private) have opened up in Talcher-Angul.[12] It should be noted that the attainment of higher level of education is only possible if they are availing the job compensation.[13] To illustrate the case, Samanta, 60 years old, from Poddo village says,

> Our children have no other option but to qualify and fit themselves in the industries and for that they need education. Those who study well they try for becoming doctor and engineer, but that is very rarely seen; In our village most of the children opt for technical courses. After all they acquired land, brought these many industries to the area, we bear all sorts of environmental and social costs, they have to give us employment.

Food security

Food insecurity is a risk associated with sudden abruption in food supply to the displaced villages. However, here we shall see that not only the reduced quantity but also poor quality of food intake leads to food insecurity. The people in the Arisa and Poddo villages used to naturally grow fresh fruits and vegetables in their own kitchen gardens, like potato, brinjal, snake gourd, lady finger, pumpkin, spinach, carrot, beans cauliflower, cabbage, tomato, onion, garlic, ginger, green chili, papaya, banana, lemon, bitter gourd, sweet potato, guava, etc. Presently, very few people can afford to have a large homestead land area to have a kitchen garden; hence most of the displaced people do not have a kitchen garden anymore.

To illustrate the case, Meena, 57 years old, from Manda village says,

> I use to grow many vegetables in our kitchen garden. My husband used to work in fields. For rice and vegetables, we did not have to depend on others. Now, for everything we have to depend on market. Other people grow and sell and we buy.

Similarly, Pramila, 51 years old, from Arisa village says,

> We have bought 4 cents of land only. We don't have enough space for living. Where will I grow vegetables?

Those who still have a kitchen garden are not able to grow much variety of fruits and vegetables due to small areas and loss in the fertility of soil due to pollution.[14] Earlier the displaced people never used to put any fertilizer for growing vegetables and fruits in their kitchen garden. Along with this, the people have lost access to food items from various common property resources. They have been forced to depend on the market to purchase the various fruits and vegetables which they earlier used to get freely from forest or used to grow naturally in their kitchen gardens. To illustrate the case, Hadibandhu, 47 years old, from Manda village says,

> Where are those fruits, vegetables? We used to collect mushroom and from lake we used to catch fish whenever we wanted. Now, we have only money to buy onion, potato and rice and sometimes we sustain on pakhala (rice water) only.

As the market is run through cash, this mechanism is very exclusionary as the people with inadequate cash are forced to curtail their consumption baskets accordingly, hence resulting in reduction in nutrition levels and affecting health conditions. With the loss of the quantity of food, the quality has been inferior to what they used to consume earlier. The intake of fertilizer and pesticide-based food products have also impacted their health condition which they could have avoided, given they would not have been displaced and continued their traditional food practice.[15]

With reduction in quantity and quality of food, the displaced people who have got the job compensation have somehow adjusted with market mechanisms of food intake; the real troubled are the displaced people with no job compensation. Hence, the food insecurity is a short duration risk which is likely to reverse with the job compensation, but the quality of food can never be restored to the earlier level.

Social disarticulation

The displacement and land acquisition due to coal mines have led to a severe risk of damaging the social relations. There is an immediate risk of social disturbance not only in displaced but in affected villages as well. The following table shows the family disputes among Manda, Arisa and Poddo people due to the faulty compensation packages provided by the coal mines followed by land acquisition and displacement.

Family dispute

Displacement and Dispossession has also created unending family disputes among the people in Talcher which has been empirically explained by the following table 9.3.

Almost 72.27 per cent people in Manda village, 70 per cent people in Arisa village and 51.01 per cent people in Poddo village have family disputes. The agricultural lands were majorly jointly owned, the unequal distribution of job compensation has led to many conflicts within the family. To withdraw the land compensation money, all the owners of the land have to put in a signature for accepting the money together. In many cases, it has been found that those who do not get the job compensation do not accept the cash compensation by not signing on the documents of cash withdrawal.[16] This

Table 9.3 Distribution Pattern of Family Dispute in the Affected and Displaced Villages

Family dispute	*AFF*	*DISP 1*	*DISP 2*	*Total*
YES	72.27	70.00	51.01	60.92
NO	27.73	30.00	48.99	39.08
TOTAL	100.00	100.00	100.00	100.00

Source: Field Survey, 2015 values in percentage

Notes: 1, 2,3-case village; 4-control village
1) AFF-Affected (Manda) village 2) DISP 1-Displaced (Arisa) village
3) DISP 2-Displaced (Poddo) village 4) LE AFF-Least affected (Chakuli) village

prevents the rest of the owners to avail the cash compensation, which triggers an unending dispute in the family. Sometimes the cash compensation gets forwarded to the court as one of the owners does not sign the document even after years as a protest to get the job compensation, and once it goes to court, it is very difficult to avail the compensation as the beneficiaries need money to fight the case in court, and they have to pay the fees to the lawyer.[17] Many times, nobody gets the cash compensation, and even the protester does not get the job compensation. This fragmentation stays, and the dispute does not come to an end.

To illustrate the case, Tikelal, 63, from Manda village says,

> I have two sons. Both were below 18 years as per cut off date taken for employment. I struggled to get one job after holding several protest by blocking the machine operation in the mine. I use to take axe and seat in front of their machines. Still, I am in pain and agony. Both of my sons want to be employed, I cannot choose whom to recommend for the job. Both fought with me to get the job. My elder son even slapped me and I had a heart attack. I decided not to recommend anyone. Both of them are not staying with me anymore.

The kinship relations also change when one brother is employed in the coal mines and the other brother is not employed in the coal mine as a part of compensation. The brother with higher income-earning livelihood option parts away from the unprivileged brother with an increase in income, better standard of living and so on. The family values start changing.[18] Another family dispute arises between married sisters and brother when a married sister desires job compensation for herself; the brother starts opposing. This leads to dispute between the siblings.

To illustrate the case, Dharam, 38 years, from Manda village says,

> We had a 4 acres of ancestral land where my aunty had share. My father, his three brothers and my aunty were the awardees of the monetary

> compensation but my father said my aunty that she cannot claim on job compensation as she is married. My aunty did not agree and hence, did not sign the documents for cash withdrawal. Without her signature, nobody was able to draw any money. That money was transferred from MCL office to High court. From that day, my father does not have any relation with my aunty.

Integration with the New Locations

The other forms of social disarticulation are the loss of social capital and increase in vulnerability due to dismantling of community which is specific to displaced villages. Social capital refers to the social networks established over the years by the earlier generations (Bourdieu, 1986). Earlier the displaced people used to get immediate help during financial needs, poor health condition, funerals and functions from the community established in the village. Even marriages were mostly channelled through the community. Presently, both of the displaced villages are scattered in many places. Some displaced people have moved out of Talcher, and the rest who stay in Talcher locate in various parts of the area. They have lost all the rich social capital in their new locations. It is very difficult for them to adjust to their new place with new people. They have nowhere to go and pass their leisure time. Especially the aged people of the displaced villages are struggling hard. They don't have their friends with them to share their sorrows, worries and happiness. It has been observed that even after years, the people have not been able to entirely get themselves comfortable in the new location, especially the aged ones. When a household is detached from its community and tries to reestablish in some other place, they have to undergo many threats, sometimes physical threats.

To illustrate the case, Jaga, 62 years old, from Arisa village says,

> After displacement, I stayed for almost 1 year in relative's house. From the compensation money, I purchased a plot of land. I started to construct the house. Every night use to go back to my relative's house. Every morning when I use to come back and see all the construction materials would have been either stolen or the construction would have broken. After four to five such incidents, I stayed back one night to catch the culprits. Around 2 am in the night, few men from the village whom I didn't know by name were stealing the cement bags. I went out and shouted. Then suddenly, they started beating me saying that I don't belong to the village so I should not stay here. After thrashing and four-five slaps, they left and I was speechless with the memories of my village and my people.

Formation of New Identities

There has been a formation of a new identity as 'displaced'. This identity gives notion to the other people that the people who are displaced have no support of their community anymore. In this case, they often try to dominate them,[19] and even they charge money from the displaced people for allowing them to integrate into the new village. However, despite all of this, the displaced households in Arisa village have not been forming any associations or unions for supporting each other. In Poddo village also, the households meet regularly once a week, but for demanding compensation to MCL, not for supporting each other and making their identities stronger by forming any sort of associations. The reason behind such indifference has not been captured in this study due to paucity of time; however, this is an interesting fact of inquiry for further research.

Loss of civil and human rights

There are three basic civil and human rights violation caused in the process of dispossession due to coal mines: right to life with dignity,[20] right to healthy environment[21] and right to adequate means of livelihoods.[22]

There are many events suggesting the violation of right to life with dignity in both of the displaced villages. The people from the Arisa village were evacuated using police force. Due to one employment policy per household, the people of this village did not agree to leave their village as a protest until all the employable persons get the job in coal mines. But they were made to leave their village by the management of MCL. The police controlled the people while the hired bulldozers broke the houses.[23] Now the forced evacuation strategy has changed, as in the case of Poddo village. Whosoever is provided with the job compensation can only receive the appointment letter and join in the coal mines, if and only if he breaks his own house and leaves the village. After assuring the breaking of house, the management allows him to join.

To illustrate the case, Kulamani, 42 years old, from Poddo village says,

> I was selected for working in coal mines but I had to sit for 8 months at home without work because I had not left my village. It is not easy to construct a new house, it takes years. I decided to move to a rented house and finally I was allowed to work.

And even the employees are not allowed to say or protest against the MCL. If they do so, then they have to lose their job. There are instances where if the brother of the employee is protesting for employment, then the employee is not allowed to continue his work unless the protest by his brother comes to an end. To illustrate the case, Mantu, 72 years old, from Arisa village says,

> My elder son was not allowed to work as I was fighting for my younger son's job. Being a father, how I can tolerate the injustice done to my other son. But then my elder son also became jobless because of this, we had no other source of survival. I decided to stop. Now, my younger son

> is working as a watchman, he earns 7,000–8,000 per month. My elder son is a mechanic; he earns 35,000–40,000 rupees monthly salary. I am helpless and deeply pained.

With the increasing operation of coal mines, the pollution levels in the area have risen. The right to healthy environment has been violated and is being violated for all the people in the area. With depleting groundwater, polluted surface water, soil and air compel the people to live in such an unlivable environment.

With unequal distribution of job compensation, loss of agricultural land, increase in unfavourable agricultural conditions and loss of common property resources, violation of right to adequate means of livelihood has taken place. Moreover, the right to livelihood has been turned into various schemes and compensation packages by the coal mines' management. The violation of basic human rights is the most likely risk to occur due to coal mining-induced displacement which is hardly restored, and hence it becomes a long-term forced-upon phenomenon for the displaced people.

Marginalisation

Marginalisation is a risk which is a result of accumulation of many other risks, majorly because of the joblessness. The marginalisation found in the affected and displaced village is the economic marginalisation.[24] The land acquisition and displacement due to mines have pushed some group of people to the edge of the marginalisation. The income disparity is found between the villages, between the households and even within the household. Again within the household, there is income disparity within a generation and between two generations. These new forms of marginalisation have been found across the villages surveyed in the area.

The income of Chakuli village is lower than that of the Manda, Arisa and Poddo villages. The Chakuli village is mostly trapped in low monthly salary income group being in the same area. Even between the displaced villages, the difference in income is considerable. The percentage of people in high- and medium-income groups is higher in Poddo village than the Arisa village. Similar is the case with Manda village. The growth of income across the villages which are affected and displaced is not equal which has brought intra-regional disparities.

The income disparity and difference in well-being strongly exist between the households within a village. The unequal distribution of job compensation has made a clear-cut demarcation of income between households within a village. There are some households within a village where all the employable persons of that household have been provided with the job compensation through various means, and at the same time, there are some households in the same village where none of the employable persons is provided with the job compensation.

To illustrate the case, Burgi, 40 years old, from Poddo village says,

> None of us got compensation from my family. There are households with more than two employment given by MCL. When I tried to protest, the management of MCL charged a false case against me. I am displaced and without any compensation how can I survive, money will finish one day then what about employment.

Another form of marginalisation is found within a household, which is again of two types that are marginalisation within a generation and marginalisation between two generations. The marginalisation within a household occurs when one brother fails to get into job compensation and the other brother gets the job compensation. There are many such cases in Manda, Arisa and Poddo villages.[25] One brother getting employed in a regular salaried job in coal mines as part of compensation package earns a higher income than that of a brother who does not get the job compensation, and hence either remains unemployed or has to make a living out of low income-earning jobs like casual wage labour, contractual jobs and so on. The marginalisation between two generations takes place as job compensation is limited to one generation. The employable youth from the next generation cannot get employment as per the one-employment policy of MCL. Hence, it has been found that the children, including the married children, are dependent on their fathers for their living.

To illustrate the case, Sumitra, 55 years old, from Arisa village says,

> My husband is working in MCL, he is going to retire now. My son is unemployed and he is married. We have to feed him, his wife and their daughter. After retirement, I don't know what will be our condition.

Similarly, Mamta, 52 years old, from Manda village says,

> My husband is working in MCL and he is earning lot of money but I have to share this money with my sons for their survival. They work as casual labours in a coal washery company.

Therefore, marginalisation seems to be a risk which cannot be reversed in a short period of time; rather it is a long-term phenomenon which can only be reduced with a proper source of livelihood.

Physical dimension of living space

Homelessness is the immediate risk pertaining to the displaced people which leads to no particular shelter of their own for at least four to five years for them. The sudden evacuation without being able to construct new houses compelled the displaced people to either rent a house or stay in relatives' houses in both Arisa and Poddo villages. Immediately after the displacement, the displaced people were not able to purchase a new homestead land and construct houses at a stretch; rather it was a stage-by-stage process. The major source of house construction includes the compensation money, the salary earned from the coal mining job and even loans from the financial institution in both of the displaced villages. In this context, this section comparatively examines the previous and current housing conditions in all the surveyed villages. The housing conditions include analysis of homestead land area and ownership of house. The following table shows the previous and current areas of homestead land owned by the people in the surveyed villages.

From the table 9.4, we can reflect upon the living space acquired by the displaced households. The homestead land area holding for displaced households has shifted from one acre and above and 50–1 acre to 5–50 cents and 0–5 cents when compared to the control village. The homestead land area has shrunk significantly for the displaced villages. This implies that unlike previously, they are not able to acquire big plots of homestead lands.

Presently the displaced households from both the villages have majorly 5–50 cents of homestead land. There is an increase from 46.37 per cent to 57.49 per cent in Arisa village and from 57.49 per cent to 90.79 per cent in Poddo village of people having 5–10 cents homestead land. The 0–5 cents landholding has also increased from 28.48 per cent to 39.11 per cent in Arisa village and from 3.72 per cent to 4.05 per cent in Poddo village. The previous and current landholding has minimally changed in the Manda village whereas in Chakuli village, no significant change has been observed in homestead landholding over the years.

The possible reason for such patterns in displaced villages is the lack of monetary power to acquire such big plots of land,[26] loss of agricultural land[27] and also family disputes. Previously the displaced households used to stay together as a joint family on their ancestral property, but due to the increase in family disputes as discussed in the previous section, the joint family system has gradually started to disappear in the displaced households. This argument can be further strengthened by analyzing the following, table 9.5.

From the table 9.5, we can see that though the joint ownership of houses has decreased in all the villages, the decrease is drastic in Arisa (1.52 per cent) and Poddo (13.01 per cent) village. In both of the displaced villages, none of the houses is owned by inherited due to displacement. The ownership of houses has majorly taken a shift to ownership by built considerably, i.e., from 15.45 per cent to 51.82 per cent in Arisa village and from 38.34 per cent to 76.86 per cent in Poddo village. The displacement led to a new ownership pattern of rented quarters owned by MCL in Manda, Arisa and Poddo villages and even resulted in increase of encroachment of government land for building houses in both, especially in Arisa village.

Table 9.4 Distribution of Homestead Land Area in the Surveyed Villages Before and After the Land Acquisition

Homestead land area	*Previous*					*Current*				
	AFF	*DISP 1*	*DISP 2*	*LE AFF*	*Total*	*AFF*	*DISP 1*	*DISP 2*	*LE AFF*	*Total*
0–5 CENTS	34.43	28.48	3.72	22.35	19.33	43.1	39.11	4.05	21.53	22.44
5–50 CENTS	58.08	46.37	69.43	72.94	64.98	47.65	57.49	90.79	72.82	71.66
50–1 ACRE	7.49	18.79	20.95	4.00	12.68	8.08	1.02	2.53	4.94	4.53
1 ACRE AND ABOVE	0.00	6.36	5.91	0.71	3.01	1.17	2.38	2.61	0.71	1.7
TOTAL	100.00	100.00	100.00	100.00	100.00	100.00	100.00	100.00	100.00	100.00

Source: Field Survey, 2015 values in percentage

Notes: 1, 2,3-case village; 4-control village
1) AFF-Affected (Manda) village 2) DISP 1-Displaced (Arisa) village
3) DISP 2-Displaced (Poddo) village 4) LE AFF-Least affected (Chakuli) village

Table 9.5 Distribution of Ownership Type of House in the Surveyed Villages Before and After Land Acquisition

Ownership of house	*Previous*					*Current*				
	AFF	*DISP 1*	*DISP 2*	*LE AFF*	*Total*	*AFF*	*DISP 1*	*DISP 2*	*LE AFF*	*Total*
OWNED- BUILT	5.85	15.45	38.34	23.65	23.49	47.66	51.82	76.86	64.74	55.47
OWNED-INHERITED	18.40	21.82	11.49	26.94	18.46	7.49	0.00	0.00	11.18	4.94
JOINT	67.45	60.30	50.17	47.29	55.01	31.50	1.52	13.01	21.88	19.08
RENTED	0.00	0.00	0.00	0.00	0.00	0.82	3.64	0.00	0.00	0.59
MCL	0.00	0.00	0.00	0.00	0.00	3.75	16.97	4.05	0.00	4.23
ENCROACHED LAND	8.25	2.42	0.00	2.12	2.99	8.78	26.06	6.09	2.12	7.80
TOTAL	100.00	100.00	100.00	100.00	100.00	100.00	100.00	100.00	100.00	100.00

Source: Field Survey, 2015 values in percentage

Notes: 1, 2,3-case village; 4-control village
1) AFF-Affected (Manda) village 2) DISP 1-Displaced (Arisa) village
3) DISP 2-Displaced (Poddo) village 4) LE AFF-Least affected (Chakuli) village

Traditional to market: social reproduction of labour

The loss of agricultural land, which was the primary source of livelihood for the case villages, led to vast occupational changes from agriculture to non-agriculture sector. The agrarian-based economy was an economy where the sectors were interlinked to each other. Similarly, everybody in the economy was dependent on each other for their sustenance. But due to land acquisition and displacement induced by coal mines, this economy was suddenly broken and hence gradually disappeared from these villages. Due to unavailability of any livelihood sources, the people became dependent on the capitalist production system for livelihood. Earlier, they were forced to sell their resources, and now they were forced to sell their labour to sustain themselves. Both directly and indirectly, all the households in these villages became dependent on the capitalist system for their survival. The households who were eligible to get compensation directly became part of the coal capitalism. The landless participated indirectly in the coal capitalism by becoming industrial labourers. The women became indirectly part of the system as well by depending on their breadwinning male counterparts.

The important linkage between the capitalist and the labour became the wages which helped these people to sustain in the market-based economy, where for everything market transaction took place. These wages were not only the price paid as a part of cost of production in exchange of labour for the capitalist economy but for also distributing income among the classes (Picchio, 1992). However, this price is only sufficient for the minimum needs and not for improvement of social life. By breaking all other structures and sources of livelihood sustenance, capitalism has succeeded in making the people dependent solely on the capitalist production system which does not take care of the social life. The people were paid for their labour, and at the same time, they were the consumers of market-based products which sustains the capitalist system. As we have observed in the previous sections, education, food insecurity, marginalisation, living space, etc. are shaping in such a way that the future generation is becoming more and more dependent on such systems, and they have easily accepted such capitalistic system too. As they are not able to find any other forms of employment and they are the ones grown up with the culture of market-produced goods, they are bound to remain in the same working class of the capitalist system. Majority of the young generation of these households have the goal of employment in MCL, and they accordingly try to train themselves.

Conclusion

We have observed that there have been severe changes in the meanings of social life. The education attained by the young generation has been backed by the motivation and purpose of getting employed in industrial jobs, especially in MCL. Starting from the food intake to social construction, from physical dimension of living space to loss of basic human rights, everything has been modified in favour of the capitalist system. At the same time, there are emergences of new forms of marginalisation. Given this, the people are bound to work as the working class in coal mines for fulfilling their market-based necessities with disappearances of traditional ways of living. In other words, coal capitalism has created such conditions of market-based economy by which the young generation are socially reproduced to join the labour force of the capitalist system. The social life of the displaced people has been altered in such a way that they have been forced to depend on the capitalist industries for livelihoods by becoming both inputs of production and the consumer.

Acknowledgements

I am thankful to Dr Vinoj Abraham and Dr P.L. Beena for their valuable comments on the chapter. I must express my gratitude to those 583 respondents for being so kind and making me part of their life events.

Notes

1 'Involuntary population resettlement consists in fact of two sets of distinct but related processes, displacement of people and dismantling of their patterns of economic and social organisation, second, resettlement at a different location and reconstruction of their livelihood and social networks' (Cernea, 1999: 2).

2 It is to be noted that given the sensitivity of the study topic, the original names of the villages and the respondents have been replaced by the pseudonyms.

3 The objective of adopting a case-control method is to trace the impact of land acquisition and displacement induced by coal mines on the cases and to make a comparison between the various changes caused due to coal mines on the cases and the changes occurred normally in the control village with least disturbance to its features.

4 The term 'social reproduction' is first coined by Karl Marx in his pioneering book *Das capital.*

5 For more details, refer to Nayak, Suravee. (2016). *Development and Displacement: A Case Study From Talcher Coalfield.* Unpublished M.Phil thesis submitted to Jawaharlal Nehru University, Centre for Development Studies, Trivandrum.

6 While interviewing, one of the officials in charge of the displacement process of Poddo village said that the village before the displacement itself was much developed than others. The people were literate and aware of the various policies. Some of them were already employed in MCL.

7 There are three to four schools funded by MCL where the children of the employees of MCL can study at a subsidised fees.

8 To illustrate the case, Maguni, 67 years old, from Arisa village says, 'I sent my chidren to school because they were creating nuisance at home. I am not literate, my husband had also dropped school after class 3; We survived on agriculture then, so what we would have done by learning math, history in agriculture?'

9 To illustrate the case, Parsu, 45 years old, says, 'We never imagined that school is so important. My children were helping me in agriculture but after displacement, I had to put them in school. After all, what they would have done at home. Instead, they can study so that they can be employed somewhere'.

10 There are 26.97 per cent displaced households presently staying at an abandoned mining site who could not get job compensation, and none of the household's children are attending school.

11 Many of the respondents from all the villages, including Chakuli village, said that they do not send their daughter for higher studies. They think studying up to secondary is more than enough for a girl child. Rather she should be trained in household works and married off soon. On this account, Rupali from Arisa village, who has just completed her post-graduation at Utkal University, says, 'I have struggled a lot to reach this far. Here, girls are not supposed to study more than matriculation. Many my friends dropped out and got married. I am a post graduate. I want to teach, even now I have to struggle'.

12 Presently, there are 24 industrial training institutes (ITI) in Angul. http://itilist.industrialtraininginstitute.net/orissa-odisha/angul. Accessed 25 June 2016.

13 The job compensation provides them the financial resources to enroll in such technical courses. In this case, they are privileged than the ones who could not get the compensation.

14 To illustrate the case, Chanchala, 65 years old, from Arisa village says, 'For example cabbage, I use to grow and sell. But now I have to buy them from market. They don't even taste the same. They smell very bad sometimes because pesticides'.

15 To illustrate the case, Chanchala, 65 years old, from Arisa village says, 'For example cabbage, I use to grow and sell. But now I have to buy them from market. They don't even taste the same. They smell very bad sometimes because pesticides'.

16 To illustrate the case, Maguni, 38 years old, from Manda village says, 'We had a 4 acres of ancestral land where my uncles had share. My father and his three brothers were the awardees of the monetary compensation but one of my uncle said my father that till he gets the job compensation he won't sign. Without his signature, nobody was able to draw any money. That money was transferred from MCL office to High court. My father does not have any relation with my uncle anymore'.

17 To illustrate the case, Hari, 71 years old, from Arisa village says, 'Due to family dispute, our compensation money was forwarded to high court. After 2 years, we compromised with each other and all my brothers and me, filed case to get that money back. We paid fees to lawyer and spent a lot on travel. After one year nobody else turned up. I cannot bear the cost alone. So I just left fighting for money and thought that I have made a donation to MCL and the Government'.

18 To illustrate the case, Purnadhara, 64 years old, from Arisa village says, 'My elder brother and me used to work in the agricultural fields together, we used to stay together, every sorrows and every happiness was shared between his and my family. But now, he is working in MCL, earning over Rs 40000, staying in a marbled house. Look at me! I am a daily wage labour under a contractor, staying in Indira Awas Yojana granted house and struggling for my minimum survival. MCL destroyed our relation'.

19 To illustrate the case, Chandramani, 45 years old, from Poddo village says, 'We bought a plot in this village just after displacement. We had to pay money for allowing us to stay there. Initially, we did not agree but the villagers said otherwise we won't be allowed to use any common spaces including the cremation ground'.

20 In *Maneka Gandhi v. Union of India*, the Supreme Court gave a new dimension to Article 21 and held that the right to live is not merely a physical right but includes within its ambit the right to live with human dignity. http://timesofindia.indiatimes.com/india/SC-gives-new-meaning-to-right-to-life/articleshow/3720847.cms. Accessed 5 June 2016.

21 Article 21 includes the right to healthy environment. *Any disturbance of the basic environmental elements, namely air, water and soil, which are necessary for 'life', would be hazardous to life* (Mohanty et al., 2011).

22 Article 39 (a), Directive Principle (DP): *The state shall direct its policy towards securing that the citizens, men and women equally, have the right to an adequate means of livelihood* (Mohanty et al., 2011).

23 To illustrate the case, Gopala, 64 years old, from displaced one village recalls, 'We were all asked to come out from our homes by the officials. We came out and saw policemen standing right in front of us. They started controlling us and in no time our homes were crushed by the bulldozers'.

24 Economic marginalisation refers to the backwardness of some section of people in terms of income compared to others in a group.

25 To illustrate the case, Manas, 42 years old, from Manda village says, 'My brother got the job in MCL, but I did not. I protested by blocking the functioning of pumps in the respective coal mine. Then I got an order from the magistrate to employ me in MCL. Till now the order has not being implemented. It's been more than 10 years'.

26 As we have already discussed that compensation is restricted to one generation, only and many grown-up sons (even married with their families) are dependent on their parents, the employment in MCL is the only source of survival for many people. Hence, they spend all the money on their expenditures and hardly save much. So though some people have the job compensation, they do not have enough savings to buy big plots of land. Some of the respondents from the displaced villages also said that for house construction, they have taken loans from banks, and each month they are paying the interest. Additionally those who do not have the job compensation are already poor enough to buy a big plot of land. Hence, lack of monetary power sometimes leads to construction of houses on a small plot of land.

27 For more details, refer to Nayak, Suravee. (2016). *Development and Displacement: A Case Study From Talcher Coalfield.* Unpublished M.Phil thesis submitted to Jawaharlal Nehru University, Centre for Development Studies, Trivandrum.

References

Bourdieu, P. (2011). The Forms of Capital (1986). *Cultural Theory: An Anthology*, pp. 81–93.

Bromley, D. W. (1985a). Common Property Issues in International Development. *National Research Council, BOSTID, Developments*, vol. 5, no. 1, pp. 12–15.

Bromley, D. W. (1985b). Resources and Economic Development: An Institutionalist Perspective. *Journal of Economic Issues*, vol. 19, no. 3, pp. 779–796.

Cernea, M. (1999). Development's Painful Social Costs. In S. Parasuraman (Ed.), *The Development Dilemma: Displacement in India*. Introductory Study. The Hague: Palgrave Macmillan.

Coal India Limited Website. www.coalindia.in/en-us/home.aspx. Accessed 29 April 2016.

Doob, C. B. (2013). *Social Inequality and Social Stratification in US Society*. Upper Saddle River, NJ: Pearson.

Garada, R. (2013a). Contextualizing the Emerging Issues and Dilemmas of Displaced Ecosystem Households: A Case of Coal Mining Industry at Talcher, Odisha (India). *IOSR Journal of Humanities and Social Science*, pp. 22–31.

Garada, R. (2013b). Dynamics of Coal Mining Caused Environmental Crisis Versus Displaced Households' Question of Survival: A Case of Talcher Coal Belt Odisha (India). *Global Journal of Human-Social Science Research*, vol. 13, no. 6.

Kothari, A. and A. Shrivastava. (2012). *Churning the Earth: The Making of Global India*. London: Penguin Books.

Lahiri-Dutt, K. (Ed.). (2014). *The Coal Nation: Histories, Ecologies and Politics of Coal in India*. Surrey, Farnham: Ashgate.

Mathur, H. M. and D. Marsden. (1998). *Development Projects and Impoverishment Risks: Resettling Project-Affected People in India*. Oxford: Oxford University Press.

Mckinsey. (2014). *Putting India on the Growth Path: Unlocking the Mining Potential*. Bangalore: McKinsey & Company, Inc.

MCL Archive. (2007). *Jagruti Vihar, Burla, Sambalpur*. www.mcl.gov.in/Others/ecoalfields.php. Accessed 2 March 2016.

Mohanty Manoranjan et al. (2011). *Weapon of the Oppressed*. New Delhi: Danish Books.

Nayak, Suravee. (2016). *Development and Displacement: A Case Study from Talcher Coalfield*. Unpublished M.Phil thesis submitted to Jawaharlal Nehru University, Centre for Development Studies, Trivandrum.

Negi, N. S. and S. Ganguly. (2011). *Development Projects vs. Internally Displaced Populations in India: A Literature Based Appraisal*. COMCAD Working Papers, 103. Bielefeld: Universität Bielefeld, Fak. für Soziologie, Centre on Migration, Citizenship and Development (COMCAD). https://nbn-resolving.org/urn:nbn:de:0168-ssoar-422011

Parasuraman, S. (1999). *The Development Dilemma: Displacement in India*. London: Macmillan Press Ltd.

Picchio, J. A. (1992). *Social Reproduction: The Political Economy of the Labour Market*. Cambridge: Cambridge University Press.

Ramesh, J. (2015). *Ecology, Growth, and Democracy in India*. New Delhi: Oxford University Press.

Registrar General. (2011). Census of India 2011, Office of the Registrar General Census Commissioner, India. Indian Census Bureau.

Shylendra, H. S. and U. Rani. (2005). *Diversification and Sustainable Rural Livelihood: A Study in Semi-Arid Villages of Western India*. New Delhi: Concept Publishing Company.

10 Land acquisition for mining and social inclusion in Talcher Coalfields of Odisha, India

Saswat Kishore Mishra and Pulak Mishra

Introduction

While changes in pattern of land use and its ownership leading to conflicts of interests across various stakeholders are imperative in economic transition, often such changes result in protests against land acquisition and thus impasse of various development initiatives. The consequences of protests against land acquisition are expected to be far dismal in the Indian state of Odisha which has been facing stiff protests against land acquisition for the proposed mining and mining-based industrial projects.[1] It is observed that the total land acquired as a proportion of its requirement so far in the state is only 27.96 per cent in case of the mining projects and 39.28 per cent for other projects.[2] Given the evidence of socio-economic and human development in mineral-rich economies (e.g., Ejdemo and Soderholm, 2011; Hajkowics, 2011; Fisher et al., 2009), such resistance against land acquisition in the state requires serious scrutiny, particularly considering that Odisha has vast potential of mineral extraction.[3]

The issue is also important in the context of limited potential of agriculture in the state. A large part of geographical area of the state is not suitable for farming, while wide variations in agro-climatic conditions are observed across different regions.[4] Flood, drought and cyclone with varying intensity are regular phenomena in the state.[5] According to TERI (2003), the state has modest to highest level of climate change vulnerability in several pockets. A combination of such extreme weather events has resulted in crop loss in the state during 1999 and 2005 (GoO, 2013), limiting agriculture-based livelihood opportunities in the state and thus causing large-scale outward migration of rural workforce.

Besides, irrigation intensity in the state (30.9 per cent) is seen to be far below the national average (44.3 per cent) (GoO, 2013). The state's degradable land mass constitutes 5.18 per cent of the total geographical area of India, which is higher than that of many of the geographically bigger states like Andhra Pradesh, Uttar Pradesh, Madhya Pradesh and Maharashtra (Ibid.). Hence, growth of non-farm sector is imperative to facilitate inclusive development in the state given its natural advantage of having huge stocks of mineral resources that can be used to expand non-farm sectors through various vertical linkages. In addition, the royalty earned from mining can play a crucial role in promoting growth and development of the state economy.

Over the years, studies in general have concentrated on analyzing the dichotomy in terms of the mode of acquisition (e.g., Dutta, 2011; Sarkar, 2007), amount of compensation (e.g., Ghatak and Mookherjee, 2014; Marjit, 2011; Ghatak and Ghosh, 2011; Bardhan, 2011), possible rehabilitation and resettlement of the displaced people (e.g., Cernea, 2007; Fernandez, 2007), employment opportunity (Mishra and Mishra, 2017), etc. at the local level. The entire approach was that of maximizing net benefits.[6] But the question is whether maximisation of net benefits guarantees maximisation of social welfare. In more recent times, studies have argued for devising various mechanisms of benefit sharing (Soderholm and Svahn, 2015; O'Faircheallaigh, 2013; Cernea, 2008), possible allocation of property rights over land and other natural resources (Sarkar, 2007), direct participation of the affected people in decision-making process (Humphreys, 2000) and efficient use of the regional development investment funds to propel more inclusive development. Yet uncertainty about future work and sustenance can instil in the people a feeling of possible exclusion from the development process. The greater this feeling of possible exclusion, the larger will be the extent of uncertainty among people. Possibility of exclusion during the course of development and its implications, particularly for the socially marginalised communities, has remained largely unexplored in the literature. This is very important considering that a large proportion of these people depend on primary sectors, including various natural resources for their livelihood, and lack of necessary capabilities restrict them from reaping alternative opportunities after land acquisition.

In this perspective, the objective of the chapter is to examine the extent of social inclusion in mining-led development initiatives and its implications for land acquisition. The study is based on primary data collected from Talcher Coalfields located in Angul district of Odisha. The chapter is divided into seven sections. Section 3 makes a critical review of the impact of mining on marginalised communities and the role of institutions therein. While the methodologies applied and sources of data used in the chapter are mentioned in section 3, section 4 attempts to examine the extent of social exclusion and its implications for land acquisition at a household level. An econometric investigation of the impact of mining on household income is carried out in section 5. Section 6 summarises the major findings with their implications, whereas section 7 concludes the chapter and puts forth the scope for further research.

Review of literature: mining, social inclusion and role of local institutions

World Bank (2013) defines *social inclusion* as both an outcome and a process of improving the ability, opportunity and dignity of the people who are disadvantaged on the basis of their identity, to take advantage of and participate in society's economic, social and political processes. In the context of mining-based development initiatives, literature is replete with findings that the disadvantaged people are predominantly the indigenous and other backward communities (e.g., Ge and Lei, 2013; Keenan et al., 2002). It is observed that the indigenous communities residing in mining regions are often specifically excluded from the socio-economic benefits of adjacent mining operations (Ibid.). Taylor and Scambary (2005) have observed that indigenous communities in Pilbara mining region of Western Australia have failed to take advantage of the mining boom in the area. Despite significant expansion of economic activities and employment opportunities in the region, participation of indigenous people in the workforce has risen very little over the past four decades. Similarly, Tiplady and Barclay (2008) have found that indigenous people are under-represented in mining workforce. Even when they find employment in the sector, it is largely in semi-skilled and low-paid positions as labourers and transport workers (Tedesco et al., 2002). Perhaps what is more important is that, in many cases, locations of mines either coincide with or are adjacent to habitants of indigenous communities. Such coincidence creates opportunities for generating wealth and promoting sustainable socio-economic development of indigenous communities.

Making mining-based development process socially inclusive may require appropriate institutional structures. Besides, a lack of accountability on the part of public administration may also result in significant leakages of public expenditures, limiting inclusiveness of the development process. It is observed that capturing political, economic and legal institutions by elites ensure that the benefits of public policy, public investment and public services accrue to the most favoured, aggravating the initial inequality in endowments and opportunities (Bourguignon and Spadaro, 2006; Rajan and Zingales, 2007). A number of studies have shown that institutional environments have significant influence on both the rates and patterns of growth and socio-economic development across countries (Acemoglu, Johnson, and Robinson, 2002, Acemoglu and Robinson, 2008, 2012). Conversely, in the absence of appropriate policy and efforts on the part of the local-level institutions, socio-economic-ecological degradation and subsequent exclusion following mining may be higher.

More importantly, mining directly benefits the landowners (mostly belonging to the coterie of higher caste and literates) as they are eligible for various compensatory packages. But the sharecroppers, labourers, etc., who lack ownership rights over land are excluded from the direct benefits of mining. In addition, weak informal sectors limit livelihood opportunities of these affected people. A large number of studies have documented such exclusion of indigenous communities from socio-economic benefits of mining (Taylor and Scambary, 2005; Tiplady and Barclay, 2008; Tedesco et al., 2002). However, it is also possible that within the landowning community, households are differentially affected depending upon their scale of ownership, amount of land given up and compensation received, present landholding, education level, number of entitled jobs, nature of job, bargaining power and social strata they belong to. This aspect is largely ignored in the existing studies. In this perspective, what follows next is an attempt to examine the implication of land acquisition at a household level.

Methodology and study area

Description of study area and project plant

Talcher, one of the four divisions of Angul district of Odisha, is the second-largest coal-producing regions in India. Talcher Coalfield has 11 ongoing projects and 38.65 billion tonnes coal reserves, the highest in India.[7] Being one of the fastest-growing mining complexes in India, there are a number of underground and open-cast mines in Talcher. While it covers an area of 500 square kilometers, the coal is of lower grade, containing only about 35 per cent of fixed carbon, 40 per cent volatile matter and 25 per cent ash content. Although more than 27,000 acres of land (both private and government land including forest land) have already been diverted for mining, affecting more than 15,000 families, efforts are being made towards further acquisition of land to implement proposed mining-related projects.[8] However, attempts towards land acquisition for mining have caused severe protests by various social groups in recent years.

The coalfields in Talcher are operated by Mahanadi Coalfields Limited (MCL) which is one of the eight subsidiaries of Coal India Limited (CIL), a public sector enterprise. MCL was carved out of South Eastern Coalfields Limited in the year 1992. Recently it became the largest coal producer in India while recording a production of 137.9 metric tonnes (mt) coal at 13.6 per cent growth rate during the year 2015–16.[9] As of now, around 65.38 per cent of the total sanctioned projects have been completed by MCL with sanctioned capital investment of INR 2823.78 crores and 98.08 mt/y production capacity. Presently, MCL operates 18 ongoing projects of 151.33 mt/y capacity with a capital investment of INR 8315.11 crores under implementation in Odisha. Some of the basic features of MCL's employment policy are mentioned subsequently.[10]

1. MCL provides employment to one member from each family sustaining loss of dwelling houses, homestead land and agriculture land, not less than one third of the total holding on priority basis.
2. One member from a family having sustained loss of three acres of non-irrigated land shall be provided employment with 'second priority'.
3. One member from a family sustaining loss of homestead land or total agriculture holdings shall be provided employment 'according to availability'.
4. Rehabilitation of other affected households shall be made through self-employment schemes.

Methodology, data collection and sampling strategy

This study is based on a primary survey of 225 households conducted in seven villages (namely Balugaon, Madanmohanpur, Langijoda, Anadipur, Padmabatipur and Rakas) across two grampanchayats (Kandhal and Padmabatipur) of Talcher block. While the primary survey spanned for around one year during 2014–15, coal mining near these villages has been continuing for more than last five decades. All the sample villages lie within five-kilometer radius from the mining regions. Proportionate stratified random sampling procedure was followed to select the sample households with the sample size of each village being proportionate to the population size of the village.

Description of constructs and tools of measurement

While a set of indicators and measures can be constructed to address inclusion, keeping in view context specificity, the present chapter limits its analysis of social inclusion in terms of impact of land acquisition for mining on income level of households across social groups. The chapter computes Chi-Square values (non-parametric or distribution-free tests) to test the statistical dependence of household income on a set of their social, demographic and economic characteristics. The chapter estimates the empirical model (details given in section 4) by applying the ordinary least squares (OLS) method of estimation for a cross-sectional data set collected from 225 households.

While OLS estimators are unbiased and consistent in the presence of heteroskedasticity, they are not efficient, and the estimated standard errors are inconsistent. Consequently the test statistics using the standard error are not valid. Since in the present study cross-sectional data are used to estimate the models, the t-statistics for the individual coefficients are computed by using White's heteroskedasticity-corrected robust standard errors. This strategy, developed by White (1980) is considered as the most common one for dealing with the possibility of heteroskedasticity. The homoskedasticity assumption implies that the variance of the errors is unrelated to any predictor or any linear combination of the predictor variables. However, homoskedasticity could be violated, even if the magnitude of the error variances is not a function of the predictors in the regression model, a situation referred to as heteroskedasticity of *unknown form* (White, 1980).

Further, variance inflation factors (VIFs) are computed for each of the independent variables to examine if the estimated model suffers from severe problems of multicollinearity, i.e., correlation between predictors. VIFs measure how much the variance of the estimated regression coefficients are inflated as compared to when the predictor variables are not linearly related. In addition, Ramsey's regression specification error test is also carried out to check if there is any omitted variable bias in the estimated models. More specifically, it tests whether non-linear combinations of the fitted values help explain the response variable (Ramsey, 1969). The intuition behind the test is that if non-linear combinations of the explanatory variables have any power in explaining the response variable, the model is misspecified.

Socio-economic implication of land acquisition: household-level experience

Household characteristics

The basic characteristics of the sampled households are given in tables 10.1 to 10.3. It is seen that a majority of the sample households belong to other backward castes (50.7 per cent) followed by scheduled castes (21.8 per cent), general category (17.8 per cent) and scheduled tribes (9.8 per cent).

Table 10.1 Distribution of Sample by Caste Category, Gender, Age and Unemployment

Distribution of sample households by caste sategory		
	Number of households	*Percentage share*
ST	22	9.8
SC	49	21.8
OBC	114	50.7
GEN	40	17.8
Total	225	100
Distribution of Sample by Gender, Age and Unemployment Rate		
Gender	*Number of Persons*	*Percentage Share*
Male	581	53.5
Female	505	46.5
Total	1086	100
Age Group (for total persons covered)		
15 years and below	243	22.4
16–35 years	452	41.6
36–60 years	313	28.8
61 years and above	78	7.2
Total	1086	100
*Unemployment Rate**		
Age group 15–59 years	79	16.8
Total persons	471	
Age group 15–29 years	56	28.6
Total persons	196	

** Includes both sexes between the respective age groups who reported as being unemployed

Source: Primary survey

Table 10.2 Distribution of Sample by Education (for Total Persons Covered)

Level of education	*Number of persons*	*Percentage share*
No formal education	260	25.6
Primary (I–IV)	169	16.6
Middle (V–VII)	141	13.9
Secondary (VIII–X)	306	30.1
Higher Secondary (XI–XII)	99	9.7
Graduation and above	42	4.1
Total	1017	100

Source: Primary survey

Table 10.3 Distribution of Sample Households by Major Occupation, Landholding and Income

Distribution of sample households by major occupation			
Major occupation	*Number of persons*		*Percentage share*
Casual labour in mines	04		1.8
Service at MCL company	102		45.3
Wage labour in construction	90		40.0
Farmer/farm labour	04		1.8
Business/Non-farm	16		7.1
Service (govt./pvt.)	09		4.0
Total	225		100
Range of landholding (acres)			
No. land	112		49.8
0–0.48	40		17.8
0.48–1	13		5.8
Above 1 acre	60		26.7
Total	225		100
Distribution of sample households by income			
Up to 1,00,000	Low	104	46.2
1,00,000–2,30,000	Moderate	43	19.1
2,30,000–4,50,000	High	46	20.4
4,50,000 and above	Very High	32	14.2
Total	225		100

Source: Primary survey

Interestingly, a significant proportion of the respondents are in the age group of 16–35 years whereas a large section of them are found to be unemployed. In particular, the youth unemployment rate (in the age group of 15–29) is critically high (28.6 per cent) in the region. This is very important as generating livelihood opportunity is crucial for people in the age group 15–35 years.

While more than a quarter of the population (about 26 per cent) have no formal education, around 60 per cent have education up to secondary level or less (table 2). More importantly, a large chunk of young mass drops out from schools at early stages of their education, being confirmed of jobs in the mining company (i.e., MCL). These youths belong to those households who were landowners having legal titles and from whom land were acquired. This category of the project-affected persons (PAPs) is entitled to get salaried jobs in the MCL over generations. They are inducted as 'Category-1' workers at entry level, irrespective of their level of education. Thus, no educational qualification is essential for securing these jobs. Possibly because of this, incentive for pursuing education generally lacks in the region.

Notably, the major occupational structure of the people in the region has considerably changed following mining. Table 10.3 shows the distribution of sample households by major occupation, landholding and annual income. Only a slender share of the workforce is engaged in cultivation, and people are either absorbed in MCL (45.3 per cent) or engaged as wage labourers in the construction sector (40.0 per cent). Around 2 per cent of the local people are seen to be working as 'daily' or 'casual' wage earners in the mines under contractors in the unorganized sector. These people largely fall under the category of PAPs who were either sharecroppers, landless tribals (includes those who held traditional right but not legal right over land) or day labourers at the time of land acquisition. As a result, they were not eligible for monetary compensation, rehabilitation or regular jobs in the mines.

Since MCL has limited scope for generating direct employment opportunity and proportion of workforce engaged in construction is too not as high, rate of unemployment is found to be more prominent. While about half of the households have no landholding, a quarter of them has land only up to one acre or less. Prior to large-scale land acquisition for mining and subsequent displacement, people of Talcher were engaged in agriculture, allied activities and hereditary works for their livelihood (Garada, 2013). A significant section of the households (46.2 per cent) are seen to be in the lowest income range, i.e., INR 1,00,000 or less. A sizeable proportion of households (34.6 per cent) are also seen to be in the high-income range or above. This income disparity leads to two important but related questions. Firstly, what determines the level of income of the households in the region? Secondly, does land acquisition for mining play a significant role in this regard?

It is observed that land acquired in excess of 0.5 acres in case of SC and ST households is very less (table 10.4), in fact, no ST household-owned land in excess of one acre in order to give up for mining. The landholding size prior to land acquisition was skewed in favour of the higher caste community. Possibly due to low landholding, not a single ST household received compensation in excess of INR 3,65,000 out of 25 such households (table 10.5). SC households fare only marginally better than the ST households in this regards. The households that were given compensation in excess of INR 3,65,000 largely belong to the general and OBC communities.

Table 10.4 Distribution of Sample Households by Land Acquisition and Caste Category

Amount of land acquired (acres)		*Caste category*				
		General	*SC*	*ST*	*OBC*	*Total*
No land given up		08 (10.0)	13 (16.2)	07 (8.8)	52 (65.0)	80 (100)
0–0.48	Low	11 (16.9)	22 (33.8)	14 (21.5)	18 (27.7)	65 (100)
0.48–1	Medium	–	03 (15.8)	01 (5.3)	15 (78.9)	19 (100)
1 and above	High	21 (34.4)	11 (18.0)	–	29 (47.5)	61 (100)
Total		40 (17.8)	49 (21.8)	22 (9.8)	114 (50.7)	225 (100)

Source: Primary survey

Table 10.5 Distribution of Sample Households by Compensation and Caste Category

Amount of compensation (INR)		*Caste category*				
		General	*SC*	*ST*	*OBC*	*Total*
No compensation		08 (7.3)	28 (25.5)	14 (12.7)	60 (54.5)	110 (100)
0–1,50,000	Low	16 (30.8)	10 (19.2)	07 (13.5)	19 (36.5)	52 (100)
1,50,000–3,65,000	Medium	08 (21.1)	05 (13.2)	01 (2.6)	24 (63.2)	38 (100)
3,65,000 and above	High	08 (32.0)	06 (24.0)	–	11 (44.4)	25 (100)
Total		40 (17.8)	49 (21.8)	22 (9.8)	114 (50.7)	225 (100)

Source: Primary survey

Table 10.6 Pearson Chi-Square Test of Independence

Variables	*Value*	*df*	*Result*
Amount of land acquired and caste Category	50.59***	09	Dependent
Compensation and caste category	26.92***	09	Dependent
Number of jobs in MCL and caste category	49.79***	12	Dependent
Income and amount of land acquired	95.36***	09	Dependent
Income and amount of compensation received	1.160E***	09	Dependent
Income and number of jobs received in MCL	2.048E***	12	Dependent
Income and caste category	45.36***	09	Dependent
Income and average level of education	1.100E***	15	Dependent
Income and major occupation	1.471E***	21	Dependent
Income and size of workforce	35.44***	06	Dependent

N.B.: ***Refers to significant at 1 per cent level of significance

Source: Compiled by authors

Since the value of Pearson Chi-Square statistic (50.59) is significant at 1 per cent (tables 10.6 and 10.7), there is a statistically significant relationship between the amount of land acquired and the caste category of sample households. Also there is a relationship between amount of compensation received

Table 10.7 Likelihood Ratio Chi-Square Test of Goodness of Fit

Variables	*Value*	*df*
Land acquisition and caste category	56.27***	09
Compensation and caste category	30.87***	09
Number of jobs in MCL and caste category	52.52***	12
Income and amount of land acquired	99.09***	09
Income and amount of compensation received	123.48***	09
Income and number of jobs received in MCL	208.61***	12
Income and caste category	48.34***	09
Income and average level of education	101.56***	15
Income and major occupation	173.41***	21
Income and size of workforce	37.26***	06

N.B.: ***Refers to significant at 1 per cent level of significance

Source: Compiled by authors

and caste category of sample households, as the value of Pearson Chi-Square statistic (26.92) is seen to be significant at 1 per cent level of significance. Here, a couple of important questions arise, firstly, whether land acquisition per se increases the income level of land-losing households or whether it is the scale of land acquired that possibly determines the household's income level? This question is also compelling because the MCL provides employment to one member from each family sustaining loss of dwelling houses, homestead land and agriculture land of not less than one third of the total holding. Secondly, it is whether compensation, rehabilitation and resettlement measures have any bearing on the income level of these households?

Given that the largest share of workforce in the region is engaged in MCL, it may be interesting to see the caste distribution of the number of jobs. Table 10.8 shows the distribution of sample households by number of jobs in MCL and caste category. It is observed that the number of jobs in MCL availed by the ST and SC households is, in general, very less as compared to the General and OBC households. For example, the combined share of ST and SC households with one MCL job per household is roughly 15 per cent only. MCL defines 'family' as every male member having attained 18 years at the time of acquisition of land. Only in some cases, women are also treated as a separate family. Since the value of Pearson Chi-Square statistic (49.79) is significant at 1 per cent level of significance (tables 10.6 and 10.7), there is a relationship between number of jobs in MCL and caste category of sample households. But the underlying issue is that demography has not suited the ST households in particular, as none received more than one job in MCL while it was favorable in case of GEN and OBC households. Yet the question is whether more number of jobs in MCL per household has an overwhelming effect on the income level of the households in general?

Given that vast disparity is observed across households in terms of income, compensation received and amount of land given up in the region,

Table 10.8 Distribution of Sample Households by Number of Jobs in MCL and Caste Category

No. of jobs in MCL	*Caste category*				
	General	*SC*	*ST*	*OBC*	*Total*
0	08 (6.7)	35 (29.4)	20 (16.8)	56 (47.1)	119 (100)
1	14 (21.2)	08 (12.1)	02 (3.0)	42 (63.6)	66 (100)
2	14 (46.7)	05 (16.7)	–	11 (36.7)	30 (100)
3	02 (40.0)	–	–	03 (60.0)	05 (100)
4	02 (40.0)	01 (20.0)	–	02 (40.0)	05 (100)
Total	40 (17.8)	49 (21.8)	22 (9.8)	114 (50.7)	225 (100)

Source: Primary survey

an important question arises as to what extent acquisition of land for mining impacts household income. Since both the amount of land given up for mining, compensation received and number of jobs availed in MCL widely vary across households and caste category, it necessitates understanding their possible impact on the level of income. In addition, since education enhances human capability and subsequently aids in gaining productive employment, it will be interesting to see its impact on the level of income as well. What follows is an attempt in this direction.

Impact of land acquisition on income

Table 10.9 shows the distribution of households by income and amount of land acquired. Such an impact represents a significant part of the regional benefits of mining. It is seen that the households that gave up a higher amount of land have ended up in higher income strata and vice versa. But a larger share of households are seen to have given up low amount of land. The value of Pearson Chi-Square statistic (95.36) which is significant at 1 per cent level of significance suggests that there is a direct relationship between household income and amount of land acquired. Therefore, the imperative question is whether the amount of land given up for mining has a positive impact on household income.

Not only the size of landholding but also the compensation, rehabilitation and resettlement benefits received in lieu of acquisition of land can have overwhelming impact on providing sustainable livelihood to households. Over the last many years, the policy measures, and debates have emphasized these measures. Table 10.10 depicts the distribution of sample households by income and amount of compensation received. It is observed that about 35 per cent of households who received compensation up to INR 1,50,000 or less are placed in the lowest income strata. At the same time, about 38 per cent of these households are also found in the high-income ranges.

Table 10.9 Distribution of Sample Households by Income and Amount of Land Acquired

Amount of land acquired (acres)	*Income level (range) (INR per annum)*				
	Up to 1,00,000	*1,00,000–2,30,000*	*2,30,000–4,50,000*	*4,50,000 and above*	*Total*
No land given up	53 (66.2)	18 (22.5)	05 (6.2)	04 (5.0)	80 (100)
0–0.48	42 (64.6)	10 (15.4)	09 (13.8)	04 (6.2)	65 (100)
0.48–1	04 (21.1)	08 (42.1)	04 (21.1)	03 (15.8)	19 (100)
1 and above	05 (8.2)	07 (11.5)	28 (45.9)	21 (34.4)	61 (100)
Total	104 (46.2)	43 (19.1)	46 (20.4)	32 (14.2)	225 (100)

Source: Primary survey

Table 10.10 Distribution of Sample Households by Income and Amount of Compensation Received

Amount of compensation (range) INR	*Income level (range) (INR per annum)*				
	Up to 1,00,000	*1,00,000–2,30,000*	*2,30,000–4,50,000*	*4,50,000 and above*	*Total*
No. compensation	82 (74.5)	19 (17.3)	05 (4.5)	04 (3.6)	110 (100)
0–1,50,000	18 (34.6)	14 (26.9)	15 (28.8)	05 (9.6)	52 (100)
1,50,000–3,65,000	04 (10.5)	05 (13.2)	19 (50.0)	10 (26.3)	38 (100)
3,65,000 and above	–	05 (20.0)	07 (28.0)	13 (52.0)	25 (100)
Total	104 (46.2)	43 (19.1)	46 (20.4)	32 (14.2)	225 (100)

Source: Primary survey

As the level of compensation increases, the proportion of households in the low-income group declines while those in very high-income range increases consistently. However, the households placed in the medium- to high-income groups apparently seem to be unaffected by varying levels of compensation. So it can be argued that the relationship between compensation amount received and income level is ambiguous. The value of Pearson Chi-Square statistic (1.160E) is significant. At 1 per cent level of significance suggests that there is a relationship between income and amount of compensation received by sample households. Therefore, it permits us to understand whether mere entitlement of compensation enhances the level of income in this region.

Employment in MCL plays a crucial factor in strengthening the economic well-being of the households in this region. Table 10.11 shows the distribution of households by income and number of jobs received in MCL. It is observed that around 80 per cent of the households who do not have a single member engaged in MCL is seen to be lying in the lowest income strata. As the number of jobs increases, the income level of households

Table 10.11 Distribution of Sample Households by Income and Number of Jobs Received in MCL

No. of MCL jobs	*Income level (INR per annum)*				
	Up to 1,00,000	*1,00,000–2,30,000*	*2,30,000–4,50,000*	*4,50,000 and above*	*Total*
0	96 (80.7)	19 (16.0)	03 (2.5)	01 (0.8)	119 (100)
1	07 (10.6)	22 (33.3)	29 (43.9)	08 (12.1)	66 (100)
2	01 (3.3)	01 (3.3)	14 (46.7)	14 (46.7)	30 (100)
3	–	01 (20.0)	–	04 (80.0)	05 (100)
4	–	–	–	05 (100.0)	05 (100)
Total	104 (46.2)	43 (19.1)	46 (20.4)	32 (14.2)	225 (100)

Source: Primary survey

across various ranges improves. The value of Pearson Chi-Square statistic (2.048E), which is significant at 1 per cent level of significance, suggests that there is a relationship between income and number of jobs received in MCL by sample households.

On the other hand, more than 80 per cent of households who do not have a single member employed in MCL are languishing at the bottom of income strata. This is quite concerning as it indicates that people in this region exceedingly depend on MCL for eking out a livelihood. It also indicates there is a weak forward linkage of mining industry with the immediate economy, improperly explored informal sector and lack of self-employment schemes. Therefore, this descriptive figure shows that there is a positive relationship between employment in MCL and household income, which requires statistical testing for further corroborating the argument.

Table 10.12 shows the caste distribution of the sample households across varying ranges of income. The value of Pearson Chi-Square statistic (45.36), which is significant at 1 per cent level of significance, suggests that there is a relationship between income and caste category of sample households. It is seen that a significant share of ST and SC households have annual income only up to INR 1,00,000 or less. ST households in particular have barely a marginal presence (4.5 per cent) in the high-income group while hardly figuring in the highest income strata. On the contrary, households in case of GEN and OBC are relatively better placed. This raises a fundamental question whether land acquisition for mining is socially inclusive. In other words, does land acquisition affect different social class differently?

Higher level of education seems to have a positive influence on the household income (table 10.13). Conversely, low level of education is seen to be associated with lower level of income. As the average years of schooling increases, proportion of households in the high-income group also increases. Although no educational qualification is necessary for securing MCL jobs in lieu of land given up, it plays a pivotal role insofar as the

Table 10.12 Distribution of Sample Households by Income and Caste Category

Caste category	*Income level (INR per annum)*				
	Up to 1,00,000	*1,00,000–2,30,000*	*2,30,000–4,50,000*	*4,50,000 and above*	*Total*
ST	16 (72.7)	05 (22.7)	01 (4.5)	–	22 (100)
SC	33 (67.3)	05 (10.2)	08 (16.3)	03 (6.1)	49 (100)
OBC	48 (42.1)	28 (24.6)	19 (16.7)	19 (16.7)	114 (100)
GEN	7 (17.5)	05 (12.5)	18 (45.0)	10 (25.0)	40 (100)
Total	104 (46.2)	43 (19.1)	46 (20.4)	32 (14.2)	225 (100)

Source: Primary survey

Table 10.13 Distribution of Sample Households by Income and Average Level of Education

Average years of schooling	*Income level (INR per annum)*				
	Up to 1,00,000	*1,00,000–2,30,000*	*2,30,000–4,50,000*	*4,50,000 and above*	*Total*
No education	10 (90.9)	–	–	01 (9.1)	11 (100)
1–4	52 (67.5)	14 (18.2)	09 (11.7)	02 (2.6)	77 (100)
5–7	39 (43.3)	21 (23.3)	20 (22.2)	10 (11.1)	90 (100)
8–10	03 (9.4)	08 (25.0)	13 (40.6)	08 (25.0)	32 (100)
11–12	–	–	01 (9.1)	10 (90.9)	11 (100)
13 and above	–	–	03 (75.0)	01 (25.0)	04 (100)
Total	104 (46.2)	43 (19.1)	46 (20.4)	32 (14.2)	225 (100)

Source: Primary survey

internal departmental promotion (thereby meaning higher rank and salary/emoluments/perks) of employees is concerned. Therefore, it can be inferred that education has important bearing on income level in the region. The value of Pearson Chi-Square statistic (1.100E), which is significant at 1 per cent level of significance, suggests that there is a relationship between income and average level of education of the sample households.

Table 10.14 shows the distribution of sample households by income and major occupation. While MCL jobs significantly contribute to the households in the higher income ranges, around 85 per cent of households engaged as wage labour in construction are placed in the lowest income range. About 72 per cent of households engaged in MCL are placed in high or very high-income range. Farming does not seem to be a profitable venture as all households engaged in farming are at the bottom of the income hierarchy. The value of Pearson Chi-Square statistic (1.471E), which is significant at 1 per cent level of significance, suggests that there is a relationship between income and major occupation of the sample households.

Table 10.14 Distribution of Sample Households by Income and Major Occupation

Major occupation	*Income level (INR per annum)*				
	Up to 1,00,000	*1,00,000–2,30,000*	*2,30,000–4,50,000*	*4,50,000 and above*	*Total*
Wage labour in mines	02 (50.0)	02 (50.0)	–	–	04 (100)
Wage labour in construction	76 (84.4)	12 (13.3)	01 (1.1)	01 (1.1)	90 (100)
Service at MCL	08 (7.8)	21 (20.6)	43 (42.2)	30 (29.4)	102 (100)
Farmer/farm labour	04 (100.0)	–	–	–	04 (100)
Business/non-farm	08 (50.0)	06 (37.5)	01 (6.2)	01 (6.2)	16 (100)
Govt./pvt. service	06 (66.7)	02 (22.2)	01 (11.1)	–	09 (100)
Total	104 (46.2)	43 (19.1)	46 (20.4)	32 (14.2)	225 (100)

Source: Primary survey

Table 10.15 Distribution of Sample Households by Income and Size of Workforce

Size of workforce	*Income level (INR per annum)*				
	Up to 1,00,000	*1,00,000–2,30,000*	*2,30,000–4,50,000*	*4,50,000 and above*	*Total*
0	–	–	–	–	–
1–2	74 (56.5)	28 (21.4)	24 (18.3)	5 (3.8)	131 (100)
3–5	30 (32.6)	14 (15.2)	22 (23.9)	26 (28.3)	92 (100)
6 and above	–	01 (50.0)	–	01 (50.0)	02 (100)
Total	104 (46.2)	43 (19.1)	46 (20.4)	32 (14.2)	225 (100)

Source: Primary survey

Higher the size of the workforce, higher may be the possibility of household income and vice versa. Table 10.15 shows the distribution of sample households by income and size of workforce. The value of Pearson Chi-Square statistic (35.44), which is significant at 1 per cent level of significance, suggests that there is a relationship between income and workforce size of the sample households. The demographic dividend seems to be favourable in the region as a large section of households has members in the working-age population. Therefore, it is observed that household income increases with the increase in size of the working-age population.

Differentiated amount of land acquisition has ensured differentiated receipt of compensation amount across households belonging to different social groups. While such skewed accruing of compensation amount is obvious, the ST and SC households are seen to be the least beneficiaries. Generally the number of jobs in MCL plant availed by the ST and SC households is very less compared to higher social groups. A larger share of the sampled households has given up low amounts of land, whereas the households that gave up higher amount of land ended up in a higher-income group. On the basis of descriptive analysis, the relationship between compensation amount received and income level of households is seen to be unclear. But what is certain is that as the number of jobs increases, the income level of households across ranges improves. This descriptive figure also shows that there is a positive relationship between employment in MCL and household income. This requires statistical testing for further corroborating the argument. In comparison, the GEN and OBC households are relatively better placed in terms of income group. Higher levels of education possibly have a positive influence on the household income. Further a large share of households engaged in MCL is placed in higher income range. Higher workforce size also seems to propel household income.

In this background, what follows next is an econometric exercise to understand if income varies depending upon social strata. Such an attempt becomes necessary given that economic inclusion facilitates social inclusion and hence an econometric modelling of impact on income may be crucial in this regard.

Impact of land acquisition on income: an econometric investigation

As it is discussed previously, there are considerable differences in socio-economic and demographic conditions of sample households and the benefits of land acquisitions accrued to them. In particular, it is found that both total income and per capita income varies widely across respondent households. It is therefore necessary to understand how such variations have been influenced by land acquisition for mining. The present section of the chapter is an attempt in this direction. In other words, the objective of the present section is to examine impact of land acquisition on household income controlling various social, demographic and economic (other than income) aspects of respondent households.

Model

The empirical (econometric) model of the present chapter is based on the assumption that household income depends on a set of their social, demographic and economic characteristics. Annual total income (TI) and per capita income of respondent households (PCI) are taken as indicators of mining outcome. If size of the household (FSZ) and share of males in total household members of the age group of 15–59 years (MWFSZ) are included to control demographic characteristics of the households, gender of household head (GHH), caste category (CASTE) and number of family members qualifying tenth standard or above (EQL) for their social characteristics, amount of land given (LG), current landholding (CLH), employment in MCL (EMP), receiving of compensation (RCOM) for economic conditions and rehabilitation and resettlement (R&R) for both social and economic aspects, one can write

$$
\begin{aligned}
\ln TI = \alpha + \beta_1 + CASTE + \beta_2 + \ln LG \\
+ \beta_3 RCOM + \beta_4 R\&R \\
+ \beta_5 EMP + \beta_6 \ln CLH \\
+ \beta_7 MWFSZ + \beta_8 \ln EQL \\
+ \beta_9 GHH + \beta_{10} \ln FSZ \\
+ \varepsilon_1
\end{aligned} \tag{1}
$$

$$
\begin{aligned}
\ln PCI = \alpha + \beta_1 + CASTE + \beta_2 + \ln LG \\
+ \beta_3 RCOM + \beta_4 R\&R \\
+ \beta_5 EMP + \beta_6 \ln CLH \\
+ \beta_7 MWFSZ + \beta_8 \ln EQL \\
+ \beta_9 GHH \\
+ \varepsilon_2
\end{aligned} \tag{2}
$$

Variable description, hypotheses and model specification

Annual total income and per capita income of respondent households are taken as indicators of mining outcome. Here, by per capita income we refer to income per member of a household. The detailed definitions, as well as the expected direction of effects on outcome variable, are provided in table 10.16. A number of studies have emphasized on appropriate pricing structure of land and properly designed rehabilitation and resettlement measures to facilitate land acquisition (e.g., Marjit, 2011; Ghatak and Ghosh, 2011; Bardhan, 2011; Dutta, 2011; Sarkar, 2007). Households who give up land for mining and/or get employment in MCL are expected to be positively affected by mining. Family size, share of working-age population in the family and educational qualification are hypnotized to have a positive impact on mining outcome. The impact of caste category on household income is unclear.

Regression results and discussions

Summary statistics of the variables used in regression models are given in table 10.17, whereas table 10.18 shows correlation coefficients for alternative pairs of these variables. It is found that majority of the independent variables are significantly correlated with the dependent variables. Further, in many cases, the value of correlation coefficient is considerably high.

The regression results are presented in table 10.19. It is observed that the F-statistic is statically significant for both the models. This implies that both the estimated models are statistically significant. Further, high value of Adjusted R^2 indicates that the models have high explanatory power. Since the Ramsey's test statistic is not significant, the estimated models do not suffer from the problem of omitted variable bias. It is also observed that the independent variables do not cause any severe multicollinearity problem as the value of the variance inflation factor is low for all the independent variables.

Table 10.16 Variables Included in the Econometric Model and Their Expected Impact

Variable name	*Abbreviation*	*Measurement*	*Expected impact*
Dependent variables			
Household total Income	TI	Natural logarithm of total income of the household	
Household per-capita income	PCI	Natural logarithm of per capita income of the household	
Independent variables			
Family size	FSZ	Natural logarithm of total number of members in a household	Positive
Share of males in total members of household in age group 15–59 years	MWFSZ	Percentage share of males in total members of household in the age group 15–59 years	Positive
Gender of household head	GHH	Gender of the household head is defined as a dummy variable. It takes a value 1 if the household head is male and 0 otherwise.	Positive
Caste category of the household	CASTE	Caste category of the household is also defined as a dummy variable. It takes a value 1 if the household belongs to the SCs or to the STs and 0 otherwise.	Positive
Number of family members qualified tenth standard or above	EQL	Natural logarithm of number of family members qualified tenth standard or above	Positive
Land given up by the household	LG	Natural logarithm of total land given up by the household (in acres)	Positive
Current landholding of the household	CLH	Natural logarithm of land currently possessed by the household	Positive
Whether any member of the household got employment in MCL	EMP	Taken as a dummy 1= Yes, 0 = Otherwise	Positive
Whether the household received compensation	RCOM	Taken as a dummy 1= Yes, 0 = Otherwise	Positive/Negative
Whether rehabilitation and resettlement done	R&R	Taken as a dummy 1= Yes, 0 = Otherwise	Positive

Source: Compiled by authors

Table 10.17 Summary Statistics of Variables Used for Regression Analysis

Variable	*Observation*	*Mean*	*Std. Dev.*	*Min*	*Max*
TI	225	11.83	1.06	8.01	14.03
PCI	225	10.31	0.97	6.91	12.24
ST	225	0.22	0.41	0	1.00
SC	225	0.10	0.30	0	1.00
OBC	225	0.51	0.50	0	1.00
LG	225	0.40	0.55	0	2.48
RC	225	0.51	0.50	0	1.00
RR	225	0.37	0.48	0	1.00
EMP	225	0.41	0.49	0	1.00
LLA	225	0.26	0.36	0	1.91
STMAG	225	52.01	17.59	0	100.00
QL	225	0.67	0.59	0	1.95
MHH	224	0.90	0.30	0	1.00
FS	225	1.52	0.34	0	2.30

Source: Compiled by authors

In regards to the individual variables, it is found that the coefficients of LG, EMP, CLH, MWFSZ and EQL are statistically significant for both the models. Further, the coefficients of all these variables are positive. This means that variations in total income or per capita income across households at Talcher are caused by the amount of land given up, if any member in the family has got employment in MCL, its current landholding, share of males in total members of age group of 15–59 years and educational qualification of the family members. All these factors influence total as well as per capita income of the household positively. This means that households that have given up more land, got employment in MCL or possess more land after acquisition earn more total as well as per capita income. Similarly, income is higher for households with larger share of males in total members of age group of 15–59 years and more number of educated members in the family.

Furthermore, coefficient of FSZ is also statistically significant and positive for the estimated regression model with total household income as the dependent variable. This implies that, in addition to other variables, total income of a household is positively influenced by the size of the family as well. Thus, both total and per capita income is higher for larger households. However, social identity of the households (i.e., their caste category), receiving of compensation against land acquisition and rehabilitation and resettlement-related initiatives do not have any significant influence on variations in income across households.

From the previous discussions, it is clear that giving up land for mining has benefitted households at Talcher Coalfield of Odisha in respect of their income. Both total as well as per capita income is higher for the households that have given up more land for mining. However, income is also higher for the households that possess more land after acquisition. It is possible that households with larger landholding are better off through acquisition of land for mining. This is very important considering that in many cases,

Table 10.18 Pair-wise Correlation Coefficient of the Variables

	TI	*PCI*	*ST*	*SC*	*OBC*	*LG*	*RC*	*RR*	*EMP*	*LLA*	*STMAG*	*QL*	*MHH*	*FS*
TI	1													
PCI	0.95**	1												
ST	–0.19**	–0.19**	1											
SC	–0.18**	–0.2**	–0.17**	1										
OBC	0.03	0.05	–0.53**	–0.33**	1									
LG	0.56**	0.56**	–0.1	–0.17**	–0.02	1								
RC	0.56**	0.54**	–0.09	–0.10	–0.08	0.70**	1							
RR	0.47**	0.45**	–0.05	–0.25**	0.16	0.52**	0.68**	1						
EMP	0.68**	0.68**	–0.11#	–0.27**	0.03	0.68**	0.78**	0.70**	1					
LLA	0.13#	0.14**	–0.12#	–0.19**	0.05	0.04	–0.11#	–0.16**	–0.01	1				
STMAG	0.27**	0.23**	0.04	–0.05	–0.04	0.03	0.01	–0.01	0.03	0.08	1			
QL	0.58**	0.5**	–0.13**	–0.23**	0.01	0.36**	0.4**	0.41**	0.48**	0.12#	0.17**	1		
MHH	0.14**	0.11	–0.01	–0.04	–0.02	–0.02	0.01	0.04	0.01	–0.04	0.29**	0.12#	1	
FS	0.42**	0.11	–0.04	–0.01	–0.08	0.17**	0.21**	0.2**	0.18**	–0.01	0.18**	0.39**	0.14**	1

Note: **Significant at 5 per cent level of significance; #Significant at 11 per cent level of significance

Source: Compiled by authors

Table 10.19 Regression Results

Variable	*Total income as dependent variable*			*Per capita income as dependent variable*		
	Coefficient	*t-Statistic*	*VIF*	*Coefficient*	*t-Statistic*	*VIF*
Intercept	9.44**	27.90		8.97**	35.47	
ST	−0.24	−1.56	2.21	−0.22	−1.41	2.20
SC	0.03	0.18	1.88	0.02	0.13	1.88
OBC	−0.02	−0.11	2.40	0.01	0.10	2.38
LG	0.30**	2.50	2.24	0.28**	2.32	2.23
RC	0.07	0.46	3.64	0.04	0.26	3.62
RR	−0.10	−0.75	2.60	−0.13	−0.97	2.58
EMP	0.96**	5.44	3.83	1.01**	6.07	3.79
LLA	0.26#	1.62	1.20	0.26*	1.77	1.20
STMAG	0.01**	2.62	1.16	0.01**	2.55	1.14
QL	0.32**	3.09	1.65	0.25**	2.39	1.51
MHH	0.19	1.08	1.12	0.16	0.98	1.12
FS	0.62**	4.03	1.24			
Number of obs.	225			225		
$F_{(12, 211)}$	46.94**			38.14**		
R^2	0.66			0.58		
Adjusted R^2	0.64			0.55		
Root MSE	0.64			0.65		
Ramsey Test	1.66 (0.18)			1.76 (0.16)		

Note: **Significant at 5 per cent level of significance; *Significant at 10 per cent level of significance; #Significant at 11 per cent level of significance

Source: Compiled by authors

resistances against land acquisition are caused by households with either small landholding or no ownership over land.

The results of the estimated regression models have the following important implications: First, since the coefficient of EMP is statistically significant and positive, provision of employment seems to be crucial during the course of land acquisition. One may expect that providing employment against acquisition of land will encourage the households to give up their land as it makes their income higher vis-à-vis others. This is very important particularly considering that compensation against acquisition of land or initiatives towards rehabilitation and resettlement do not have any significant influence of income of the households.

Second, educational qualification of the members of a household plays an important role in influencing its income. Higher education enhances capability of the family members and hence their livelihood opportunities. It also provides them better employment with higher salary. All these result in higher income of the household. Hence, in order to have a smooth process of land acquisition, it is necessary to make efforts towards providing higher and quality education to members of prospective land-losing households. This will not only raise the probability of their inclusion in the development process, but also give them alternative livelihood opportunities and hence necessary confidence. Thus, higher education of household members is very important for making post-acquisition development process inclusive, and appropriate initiatives of the government are likely to play a crucial role in this regard.

Third, income does not differ across households depending on their social identity, i.e., their caste category. This is so possibly because of the provision of employment in the MCL irrespective of social identity and educational qualification of land-losing households. Thus, land acquisition for mining-led development process may not necessarily result in exclusion of socially backward households, particularly when there is provision of employment.

Fourth, compensation against land acquisition, rehabilitation and resettlement-related initiatives have no significant impact on household income, whereas provision of employment and education level of household members play a significant role in this regard. However, provision of employment is restricted only to the landowners who mostly belong to the coterie of higher caste and literates. The sharecroppers, labourers, etc. who lack ownership rights over land are excluded from such direct benefits of mining. In addition, weak informal sector limits scope for alternative livelihood opportunities for these affected people. Hence, improvement in human capability is crucial to raise income level for those who lack property rights over land.

Summary and conclusions

Provision of employment seems to be crucial during the course of land acquisition. Providing employment against acquisition of land may possibly encourage the households to give up their land as it makes their income higher vis-à-vis others. This is very important particularly considering that compensation or initiatives towards rehabilitation and resettlement do not have any significant influence of income of the households. Moreover, educational qualification of the members of a household plays an important role in influencing its income. Higher education enhances capability of the family members and hence their livelihood opportunities. It also provides them better employment. Hence, in order to have a smooth process of land acquisition, it is necessary to make efforts towards providing higher and quality education to members of prospective land-losing households. This will not only raise the probability of their inclusion in the development process, but also give them necessary confidence. Appropriate initiatives of the government are likely to play a crucial role in this regard. In addition, land acquisition for mining-led development process may not necessarily result in exclusion of socially backward households, particularly when there is provision of employment since income does not differ across households depending on their social category.

In Talcher, coal mining has disrupted the local peasants' access to agro-economy and their common property resources by causing severe pollution (Garada, 2013). Behera and Mohanty (2009) find that the coals of this region are highly prone to spontaneous combustion. Evidently, the Central Pollution Control Board has declared Talcher as a climate change hotspot as a consequence of rapid growth of mining and mining-based industries. In downstream areas of river Brahmani, the traditional fisherman lost their livelihood as the toxic effluent wastes were released by the mining to the river. While 27.7 per cent of the total forest area in Talcher has been diverted for coal mining, another 38.4 per cent of the area is likely to be lost in the region (Garada, 2013). Therefore, it is necessary to have a deeper understanding of what determines peoples' willingness to give up land for mining in this region and whether a possible adverse impact of mining on natural resources, biodiversity and ecology plays an important role in this regard. Moreover, mining companies in many countries have undertaken initiatives as part of their CSR to either improve the socio-economic-environmental conditions of the local communities or to reduce the adverse effects of mining. The government of India has also passed legislation, i.e., the Companies Act, 2013, which mandates a certain class of profitable companies to spend at least 2 per cent of their average annual profit during last three years for corporate social responsibility (CSR) activities. It is therefore important to understand the extent of adverse ecological consequences of mining in Talcher and the role of CSR both in their internalisation and possible minimisation of social exclusion. In addition, understanding the role of social/community level organisations in furthering social inclusiveness is also crucial. It is possible that jobs are given across castes due to pressure from such organisations. It is also possible that scope for social inclusion is higher, as MCL is a public sector subsidiary (PSU). If so, issues are likely to be critical for private enterprises which paves a way for future research.

Acknowledgements

This paper is based on insights from the first author's PhD thesis and findings of the authors' recently published works.

Notes

1 For the details on incidences of protests against land acquisition, see Mishra (2016).
2 For details in this regards, see the official web portal of the Industrial Infrastructure Development Corporation (IDCO), Government of Odisha, Bhubaneswar. Information from www.idco.in/2009/orgsubsection.aspx?content=Land. Accessed 27 October 2015.
3 Odisha is one of the largest mineral abundant states in India. It contains nearly 17 per cent of the total mineral deposits in the country (Government of Odisha, 2012–13). The state alone constitutes around 25.82 per cent, 32.53 per cent and 56.36 per cent of the country's total reserve of coal, iron-ore and bauxite, respectively (Ibid.). In addition, there is heavy concentration of chromites, manganese and graphite in the state. The state is the country's largest mineral producer in terms of value of mineral production (IBEF, 2012)
4 For example, while the South Eastern Ghat records an average annual rainfall of 1710 mm per year, it is 1352 mm in the Western Undulating Zone. Similarly, maximum temperature in the Western Central Table Land is 40 degrees Celsius as compared to 34 degrees Celsius in the Eastern Ghat High Land. Likewise, there are considerable variations in minimum temperature and soil conditions across different agro-climatic zones of the state.

5 See the report on Status of Agriculture in Odisha (2008) for the details in this regard.
6 Net benefits = Total benefits of the project - (Losses - Compensation).
7 For details in this regard, see the official website of Directorate of Mines, Government of Odisha. www.orissaminerals.gov.in/Mines/default.aspx?GL=Ghome.
8 Office of the Block Development Officer (BDO), Talcher (as on 29 April 2012).
9 For details in this regard, see *Business Standard*, 4 April 2016.
10 For details in this regard, see the official website of MCL. www.mcl.gov.in/Welcome.php.

References

Acemoglu, D. and J. Robinson. (2008). *The Role of Institutions in Growth and Development*. Commission on Growth and Development. Washington, DC: The World Bank.

Acemoglu, D. and J. A. Robinson. (2012). *Why Nations Fail*. New York: Crown.

Acemoglu, D., S. Johnson, and J. A. Robinson. (2002). Reversal of Fortune: Geography and Institutions in the Making of the Modern World Income Distribution. *Quarterly Journal of Economics*, vol. 117, no. 4, pp. 1231–1294.

Bardhan, P. (2011, April). Land Acquisition: Currently a Major Stumbling Block for Development Policy. *Development Outreach*.

Behera, P. and G. Mohanty. (2009). Peroxy Complex and Crossing Point Temperature of Talcher Coals: An Adducer to Assess the Spontaneous Combustibility Character. *Journal of Scientific Research*, vol. 1, no. 1, pp. 55–60.

Bourguignon, F. and A. Spadaro. (2006). Microsimulation as a Tool for Evaluating Redistributive Policies. *Journal of Economic Inequality*, vol. 4, no. 1, pp. 77–106.

Cernea, M. (2007). Financing for Development: Benefit-Sharing Mechanisms in Population Resettlement. *Economic and Political Weekly*, vol. 42, pp. 1033–1046.

Cernea, M. (2008). Compensation and Benefit Sharing: Why Resettlement Policies and Practices Must Be Reformed. *Water Science and Engineering*, vol. 1, no. 1, pp. 89–120.

Dutta, B. (2011). Balancing the Scales: The Government Has a Crucial Role to Play in a Fair Land Acquisition Policy. *Times of India*, 20 July.

Ejdemo, T. and P. Soderholm. (2011). Mining Investment and Regional Development: A Scenario-Based Assessment for Northern Sweden. *Resources Policy*, vol. 36, pp. 14–21.

Fernandez, W. (2007). *Mines, Mining and Displacement in India*. First International Conference Organized by Australian National University, New Delhi, 19–21 November.

Fisher, E., R. Mwaipopo, W. Mutagwaba, D. Nyange and G. Yaron. (2009). The Ladder That Sends Us to Wealth: Artisanal Mining and Poverty Reduction in Tanzania. *Resources Policy*, vol. 34, pp. 32–38.

Garada, R. (2013). Dynamics of Coal Mining Caused Environmental Crisis Versus Displaced People's Question of Survival: A Case of Talcher Coal Belt, Odisha (India). *Global Journal of Human Social Science*, vol. 13, no. 6.

Ge, J. and Y. Lei. (2013). Mining Development, Income Growth and Poverty Alleviation: A Multiplier Decomposition Technique Applied to China. *Resources Policy*, vol. 38, pp. 278–287.

Ghatak, M. and D. Mookherjee. (2014). Land Acquisition for Industrialization and Compensation of Displaced Farmers. *Journal of Development Economics*, vol. 110, pp. 303–312.

Ghatak, M. and P. Ghosh. (2011). The Land Acquisition Bill: A Critique and a Proposal. *Economic and Political Weekly*, vol. XLVI, no. 41, pp. 65–72.

GoO. (2013). *Economic Survey 2012–13, Odisha*. Government of Odisha. Bhubaneswar: Planning and Coordination Department.

Hajkowics, S. A. (2011). The Relation Between Mining and Socio-Economic Well Being in Australia's Regions. *Resources Policy*, vol. 36, pp. 30–38.

Humphreys, D. (2000). A Business Perspective on Community Relations in Mining. *Resources Policy*, vol. 26, no. 3, pp. 127–131.

IBEF. (2012). *Metals and Mining*. Bangalore: IBEF and ARANCA.

Keenan, K., J. de Echave and K. Traynor. (2002). *Mining and Communities: Poverty Amidst Wealth*. Paper presented at the International Conference on Natural Assets, Political Economy Research Institute and Centre for Science and the Environment, The Philippines, 8–11 January.

Marjit, S. (2011). Guaranteeing Future Claims of Farmers in Land Acquisition: An Option-Pricing Approach. *Economic and Political Weekly*, vol. 45, pp. 80–82.

Mishra, S. K. (2016). *Mining, Social Welfare and Implications for Land Acquisition: Case of Talcher Coalfields in Odisha, India*. Unpublished PhD Dissertation, Indian Institute of Technology, Kharagpur.

Mishra, S. K. and Mishra, P. (2017). Determinants of Households' Resistance against Land Acquisition for Mining: Experiences at Talcher Coalfields in India. *Land Use Policy*, vol. 66, no. 2, pp. 10–17.

O'Faircheallaigh, C. (2013). Community Development Agreements in the Mining Industry: An Emerging Global Phenomenon. *Community Development*, vol. 44, no. 2, pp. 222–238.

Rajan, R. and L. Zingales. (2007). *The Persistence of Underdevelopment: Constituencies and Competitive Rent Preservation*. NBER Working Paper 12093. Cambridge: National Bureau of Economic Research. http://eml.berkeley.edu/~webfac/dromer/e237_f07/Rajan.pdf. Accessed 20 December 2015.

Ramsey, J. B. (1969). Tests for Specification Errors in Classical Linear Least Squares Regression Analysis. *Journal of the Royal Statistical Society Series B*, vol. 31, no. 2, pp. 350–371.

Sarkar, A. (2007). Development and Displacement: Land Acquisition in West Bengal. *Economic and Political Weekly*, vol. 42, pp. 1431–1442.

Soderholm, P. and N. Svahn. (2015). Mining, Regional Development and Benefit Sharing in Developed Countries. *Resources Policy*, vol. 26, pp. 78–91.

Status of Agriculture in Odisha. (2008). *Agricultural Census: 1981, 1985 & 1990/2000/2008*. Orissa, Cuttack: Agricultural Census Commissioner, Board of Revenue.

Taylor, J. and B. Scambary. (2005). *Indigenous People and the Pilbara Mining Boom: A Baseline for Regional Participation*. Centre for Aboriginal Economic Policy Research Research Monograph No. 25. Canberra: The Australian National University Press.

Tedesco, L., M. Fainstein and L. Hogan. (2002). *Indigenous People in Mining*. ABARE eReport 03. Prepared for the Australian Government Department of Industry, Tourism and Resources Canberra.

TERI. (2003). *Coping with Global Change Vulnerability and Adaptation in Indian Agriculture*. New Delhi: The Energy Research Institute.

Tiplady, T. and M. Barclay. (2008). *Indigenous Employment in the Australian Minerals Industry*. Centre for Social Responsibility in Mining. Brisbane, Australia: The University of Queensland.

White, H. (1980). A Heteroskedasticity-Consistent Covariance Matrixestimator and a Direct Test for Heteroskedasticity. *Econometrica*, vol. 48, pp. 817–838.

World Bank. (2013). *Inclusion Matters. The Foundation for Shared Prosperity*. Washington, DC: The World Bank.

11 Development, displacement and resistance movement

A reflection on Kalinga Nagar industrial complex

Dinabandhu Sahoo

Introduction

In fact, it is necessary to paraphrase Marx and Engels' classic opening statement of the 'Communist Manifesto': 'A spectre is haunting the indigenous resource rich world- the spectre of displacement. All the powers of the New World Order: Neoliberal State and Neoliberal Capital are joining forces to exorcise it.' And I can still add another statement from the same 'Communist Manifesto': 'it is high time that those displaced should openly, in the face of the whole world, make their experiences and aims known, and meet the self-serving and technocratic tale of the spectre of Displacement by those in power with a manifesto of their own'. This means that the resource-rich territories mainly inhabited by indigenous or Adivasis communities are more prone to confront displacement in contemporary times. The dislocated need to understand the politics of displacement, experience the plight of those already displaced. They also need to understand the politics of civil society, state and corporation. Then they only can make a manifesto of their own. Displacement is not a new phenomenon; rather it is very common in the history of the growth of civilisation. It is an integral part of Eurocentric modernity and its post-World War II manifestation in Asia, Africa and Latin America. People in the Global South are now compelled to subjugate the continuous conquest of their place and space: economic, ecological and cultural. In the contemporary neoliberal phase of capitalist development, the displacement of commons and indigenous communities living in the resource-rich territories have been multiplied. If such is the result of neoliberal development in Global South, what are its consequences for the uprooted communities? The consequences, as some studies mention, induce a process where the vast majority of dislocated either have been pushed into joining the increasing 'Planet of Slums' (Davis, 2006) where they further experience 'Gentrification' (Smith, 1996) and they are compelled to contest in the urban struggle for space in the city or face a 'double absence' (Sayad, 2004) in their re-territorialisation or they assimilate in a structure of society where they subject heightened inequality, deprivation, marginalisation and cultural genocide (Padel and Das, 2008), de-tribalisation or re/de-peasantisation (Baviskar, 2005; Prasad, 2004).

The process manufactures dissent and discontent that development dislocates contest for not to be exploited, not to be de-territorialized/ re-territorialized, not their livelihood and subsistence base structure makes into capital by the neoliberal agency. When the displaced communities resist the neoliberal development, how does it affect the trajectories of development? Does it bring policy formulation or effective implementation of policy? The last section of the chapter is devoted to answering this question.

I have used the conventional Marxian notion of class and its class and indigeneity (Adivasis) intersection to understand these processes that are emerging in Kalinga Nagar in particular and in the Adivasis resource-rich regions in general. Class represents here as a relation among social groups with unequal power; classes are set in oppositional relationships such that one group's privileges is dependent on another group's disadvantage, one class or group exploits the other or benefits from the other's disadvantage or excludes the other from equitable social and economic rewards (Collins, 1998). In Kalinga Nagar, the dialectic of developmental intervention showed that one class interest is contradictory to other interests. The state has its own intentions, and the ideological apparatus favours a particular class which have a belief that neoliberal development is needed to tackle the region backwardness. The region, on the one hand, is backward, whereas on the other hand it has high potentialities (resource-richness) that favour developmentalism. This dialectic produces a class base movement which can be termed as the conflict between the representative of state developmentalism and the defender of cultural economy (here, Adivasis). The defender of cultural economy has a belief that development should be of their choice but not through imposition as state and other developmentalist wants.

It was 3 January 2006, and I was an undergraduate student in Bhadrak Autonomous College when I read the news of police firing of Kalinga Nagar that occurred in the previous day from an Odiya daily, *The Samaj*. I was then astonished why 12 Adivasis sacrificed their life at the altar of neoliberal development that swept through Odisha. Then an interest formed in my mind: why have the tribals been killed and not the other caste people? My interest gradually took shape when I pursued my PhD in sociology. Interest led me to think of why a development project is always planned in tribal areas. Why do tribals resist development? How do they benefit from such projects? The interest influenced me to study the issues of development, displacement and Adivasis resistance in a neoliberal state.

The data for this chapter was collected primarily as a part of my PhD research using ethnographic fieldwork and case study. The fieldwork was carried out in a whole year from August 2014 to August 2015 in two phases. Interviews and group discussions were conducted during the fieldwork with the leaders, activists, and other members involved in the movement. Case studies were conducted simultaneously during the fieldwork.

The chapter is divided into five sections. The second section of the chapter historically looks at the development intervention and displacement in Kalinga Nagar. The third section elucidates the causes of resistance, collective mobilisation, demands and strategies behind and beyond the resistance movement. The fourth section explains how resistance movement has affected the trajectories of development in Kalinga Nagar Industrial Complex. The fifth section concludes the following discussion.

Historical account of developmental intervention and displacement in Kalinga Nagar

The idea of Kalinga Nagar industrial complex was conceived in the early 1990s on the onset of neoliberal globalisation. Kalinga Nagar is situated in the confluence of resource-rich territories of Sukinda and Danagadi blocks of Jajpur district in Odisha. The Sukinda Valley is popular for its best-quality chrome reserves throughout the world. The mineral resources reserve in Sukinda and its nearby mines like Tamka, Joda, Barbil and Daitari is estimated to be 90 per cent (chrome), 92 per cent (nickel), 3,120 MTs (hematite) and large manganese reserves. All other infrastructural facilities are readily available in and near Kalinga Nagar Industrial Complex (hereafter KNIC) (Sinha, 2008). The state through its neoliberal policies makes easy access to these investment incentives to favour large corporations and industrial houses to facilitate investment-induced growth.

In addition to resource richness and investment incentives, the area was also historically significant for industrialisation. Realizing the resource-rich potentials, in 1964 the government of Odisha had written a memorandum to the central government to establish the second steel plant in the state. (The first was established at Rourkela) (see Meher, 2009). The memorandum identified three places in Odisha emphasising the details of the raw material availability, transport facilities and access to important inputs like water, power, site land and even land for resettlement and rehabilitation of the displaced people. It also invited a team of geological experts to make detailed surveys and feasibility studies before taking any financial decision vis-à-vis other locations in the country (Das, 1992). In the following year in 1965, M N Dastur and Company (hereafter Dastur Committee) conducting detailed study throughout 28 major locations in the country suggested Bonai in Sundargarh district and Nayagarh in Keonjhar district in Odisha to be the best locations in the country for the setting up of steel complexes. Dastur Committee's 1965 report was well examined by the British American Steelworks for India Consortium (BASIC) (Das, 1997). In 1970 the people's representatives from Odisha also demanded in the parliament to set up the second steel plant in Odisha supporting the techno-economic feasibility study favouring the state and backwardness of the state (Lok Sabha Deb. (1970) col. 242 and (Das 1992)). The people's representatives not only demanded further industrialisation of the state, the people's movement organisation, i.e., Ispat Karakhana Sangram Samiti (IKSM, an organisation protesting for the establishment of steel plant) in the same time called a statewide *bandh*[1] for the establishment of a second steel plant in the state. However, the establishment of the second steel plant could not be realised in the state because of 'regional pulls' ground of the federal government and political ad hocism (Balasundaram, 1973). The steel plants later established in South India with lower capacity instead of Odisha.

Apart from these, the significant sections of the population around Kalinga Nagar area are comprised up poor tribals and Dalits who are backward in many aspects. According to Census, 2011, the two blocks, i.e., Sukinda and Danagadi, under which Kalinga Nagar falls, have 37.25 per cent and 30.73 per cent tribes and 11.17 per cent and 21.85 per cent Dalits (scheduled castes) population, respectively. The literacy rate of these two blocks represents 66.74 per cent and 69.35 per cent, respectively, while the district literacy is 86.84 per cent (Census, 2011). The Adivasis population of the acquired area is more than 90 per cent. The Adivasis of the area are mainly of Ho and Santal communities (Dash and Samal, 2008). This phenomenon explains the *resource curse thesis* introduced by Richard Auty. Auty (1993) writes 'new evidence that not only may resource-rich countries fail to benefit from the favourable endowment, they may actually perform worse than less well-endowed countries'. Jeffrey Sachs, who popularizes the thesis, believes that the natural resource curse has resonated through history (Jones et al., 2014).

The tribals of Kalinga Nagar have been migrated from different districts of Chotanagpur in the last part of the nineteenth century and early twentieth century. Lack of irrigation facilities and frequent drought in tribal areas of Chotanagpur region left no option for the tribals but to migrate to other places like tea gardens of Assam and coal fields in the nearby area (Miri, 1993). Land alienation due to state developmental intervention in Chotanagpur in colonial and post-colonial period pushed the Adivasis of the region to migrate to other areas (Prasad, 1988: 77–99). These developmental activities forced the Hos as well as other Adivasis of Chotanagpur as a commodified labour force. Sahu (2007) documented the other story of Adivasi immigration due to drought in Saraikala to Kalinga Nagar. Thereafter some Adivasis also migrated to Kalinga Nagar area, searching for economic opportunities.

Mansingh Purty, an Adivasis of a resettlement colony in Kalinga Nagar locality (age about 74), vehemently stated,

> We are strong and laborious people. Our forefathers came here as contractual labour by the colonial British ruler to construct the Rail road in Eastern Odisha in the last half of 19th century. Since then we are living in this region. The then Sukinda king (Zamindar) permitted us to live here and we make land by cutting forests and are cultivating it. He gave some people patta (Land title) and we were giving Khajana (Tax) in the form of Gotti (bonded labour) to the king.
>
> (Interview 15.12.2014)

In fact, it can be concluded that environmental factors and developmental intervention not only forced the Adivasis to migrate to Kalinga Nagar/Sukinda, but also economic opportunities pushed them to migrate to the area.

The topography of the area was also suitable for Adivasi settlement. The topography of the area consists of undulating land mass with small hills and forests. Small streams, low wastelands and *Patas* (wetland) were the main source of water supply to the area. The main livelihood of the local Adivasis consists of agriculture, especially rain-fed agriculture, i.e., paddy cultivation. After harvesting rice, Adivasis grow pulses like black and green gram, Khesari, maize, kulthi and vegetables. The nearby forests and hills play an important role of supplying firewood and minor forest products like ground nuts, kendu fruits, mango, tamarind, jack fruits, various kinds of leafy vegetables and besides meats of various wild animals and birds. These provided subsistence apart from health and well-being of Adivasis in the area.

Resistance movement in Kalinga Nagar industrial complex

In this section, I'll briefly look into the causes of Adivasis resistance, collective mobilisation, movement demands and strategies and decline of the resistance movement in Kalinga Nagar. I'll focus only on one movement organisation, i.e., Bisthapan Birodhi Jan Manch (BBJM) in KNIC. While examining the causes of resistance, I'll use the conventional Marxian notion of class and its class and indigeneity (Adivasis) intersection. Class represents here as a relation among social groups with unequal power; classes are set in oppositional relationships such that one group's privileges are dependent on another group's disadvantage, one class or group exploits the other or benefits from the other's disadvantage or excludes the other from equitable social and economic rewards (Collins, 1998). In Kalinga Nagar, the dialectic of developmental intervention showed that one class interest is contradictory to other interests. The state has its own intentions, and the ideological apparatus favours a particular class which has a belief that neoliberal development is needed to tackle the region backwardness. It is argued that region has high potentialities, as I discussed earlier, whereas the other who opposed their views and practices of developmentalism. This dialectic produces a class base movement which can be termed as the conflict between the representative of state developmentalism and the defender of cultural economy (here Adivasis). The defender of cultural economy has a belief that development should be of their choice but not through imposition as state and other developmentalist wants. Before explaining how neoliberal development caused resistance in Kalinga Nagar, I attempt to locate historically how colonial and post-colonial exploitation in Kalinga Nagar was the root cause of resistance.

Historical roots of resistance

From the interview with Mansingh Purty, it is evident that the colonial rulers of Sukinda settled the Adivasis in and around the present-day KNIC for making agricultural lands by cutting forests. The rulers also used Adivasis as bonded labour for their profit. Odisha District Gazetter Jajpur writes,

> The system of Bethi, Bagari (Unpaid labour) for the rulers, headmen and officials prevailed to a great extent in all the states (including Sukinda feudatory state). Supply of Rasad i.e free food to officials on tour, also prevailed although later this responsibility was shifted to the Gauntia or headman. Salamis (tax) were levied in various forms. The peasants had no full land rights as in all other states and they were liable to eviction in spite of long possession and enjoyment.
>
> (p. 250)

This was a form of colonial exploitation where one class (the rulers of Sukinda) got advantages from the exploitation of the other class (the Adivasis). Sharma (2006) confirms that in late 1860s in colonial times, Kritibas Bhupati, the ruler of Sukinda, brought Adivasis mainly of Hos from Saraikala-Karsuan region of Chhotanagpur to clean the forests and make the land cultivable. Mahapatra's (1987) study documents a similar story about the immigrant Hos/Mundas. Similarly Das Gupta observes,

> In fact, the rulers of Mayurbhanj, along with those of the other feudatory states of northern Orissa (Sukinda, emphasis own), had invited the immigration of tribal groups along with Brahmins and service castes for both political and economic reasons as these were expected to promote agricultural, industrial and commercial development in the state. The migrant Hos were considered to be better as settled cultivators in contrast to the Bhuiyas who chiefly practised shifting cultivation. . . . Moreover, in contrast to the older settlers who paid a fixed sum as tribute, the immigrant groups had to pay higher tributes and also render compulsory labour service or beth begari.
>
> *(Bonded or indentured labour) (2011: 75)*

The Adivasis of Kalinga Nagar area were subjected to this form of colonial exploitation since colonial times. The Adivasis also worked as bonded labourers for the colonial rulers to pursue agricultural work, forest clearance and other domestic chores of the rulers as well as contractual labour for road and railway construction. This form of exploitation was continued in the whole Sukinda area in the colonial periods. Dalziel settlement report confirms that in Sukinda

> there is an organised system of unpaid labour. Each raiyat has to give his services for one day for ploughing the landlord's nijchas (Zamindar's own land) and for one day for weeding. Services have also to be given for the car festival; the catching of elephants and shooting expeditions.

> In return for these services the raiyats are allowed to take wood from the jungle for fuel and for agricultural purposes.
>
> (p 130)

Apart from colonial exploitation in the form of *bethi begari,* the Adivasis of Sukinda alienated most of their fertile lands that were reclaimed by them from wasteland during the colonial times. Dalziel settlement report writes that there were only 39,011 acres of cultivable land out of the total 2,14,790 acres in Sukinda estate. The king identified 1,06,389 acres of cultivable wasteland for reclamation, and this reclamation of wasteland into cultivable land was only undertaken by the Hos/Munda who migrated from Singhbhum and Mayurbhanj. The rulers granted *patta* for the purpose of reclamation on payment of *salami* allowing a rent-free land for a few years after which the land was assessed to rent (p. 128). Out of these reclamation lands, a few lands were given to the Adivasis, alienating most of the lands. Not only in the colonial period had the Adivasis been alienated from land and exploited by the colonial state, in post-colonial times they have also been exploited, and their land has been alienated by the state apparatus. Jajpur District Gazetteer mentions,

> At present Danagadi Tahasil consist of 126 Revenue Villages. . . . Out of 126 nos of villages RoR (Records of Right) of 104 villages have been published by settlement authority leaving a balance of 22 villages (of 1927–28 settlement) for current settlement.
>
> (P 248)

The Danagadi Tahasil excluded 22 villages for government land settlement that shows that the state used its state bureaucratic apparatus to alienate the people of their land. These 22 villages are mostly Adivasis-dominated villages that are coming under KNIC. Adivasis were alienated of their land rights that they were enjoying since colonial times generation by generation, and they were not provided with *Patta* in the last land settlement of Odisha that conducted in 1980s. This was the deliberate motive of the state to do this for future industrialisation and generate profit out of the alienated lands. The last land settlement in the area was conducted in 1927–28 in colonial times. Most of the Adivasis, except some influential ones, were deprived of land settlement (Sahu, 2007). Not only from colonial and post-colonial state land settlement policies, the people of Danagadi and Sukinda also alienated of *Bhoodan* land distribution scheme from 1993 until now. Not a single land was distributed in the two Tahasils from the Odisha *Bhoodan* Yagna Act since the last two decades. This act was introduced in Odisha in 1953 to distribute *Bhoodan* land to landless families collected through *Bhoodan* movement initiated by Acharya Vinoba Bhave (see Jajpur District Gazetteer). Like land reform programmes, *Bhoodan* movement failed to bring about required changes in the agrarian structure in India. A large number of studies, including official reports, have documented the failure of land reform measures as well as the causes of their failure (Ghosh and Nagaraj, 1978; Bandyopadhyay, 1986). The report of the Task Force on Agrarian Relations of the Planning Commission of India in 1973 acknowledges the failure of land reform programmes in India adopted since independence. The report directly blames the political will of the state governments for its failure. Similarly the exclusion of 22 villages in KNIC for land settlement and the *Bhoodan* land distribution was a deliberate action, and there was lack of political will of the state apparatus for future capitalist development of the territory and super-imposition of capitalist exploitation.

Neoliberal industrialisation and causes of resistance

Biren Jamuda, a local Adivasi activist of the area, asserts,

> Since most of the adivasis in Kalinga Nagar area had no patta of the lands they were cultivating since generations, we had organised two public meetings in the 'Chandia' playground and called Kalinga Nagar ADM (Additional District Magistrate) to be present in the meetings and look into this problem. In both the meetings most of the local adivasis were present, but ADM could not come although he gave consent to come. In the last gathering people vowed not to vacate their land till this problem could not solved. This was happened before Tata Steel coming to Kalinga Nagar.
>
> (Interview 01.02.2015)

The states have used their apparatus in various forms to expropriate the Adivasis of their main source of subsistence and livelihood, i.e., land, water, forests, hills and streams. Harvey (2003) has broadened the Marxian notion of exploitation using the concept 'accumulation by dispossession' to describe appropriation of key livelihood resources, such as land, water, forest and minerals by neoliberal state. In neoliberalism, states are using such types of tactics to expropriate land from the Adivasis. State apparatus provides expropriated lands to the industries that have negative consequences for the traditional employment and livelihoods of the dislocated people because the project destroys more livelihoods than it creates employment. Bhaduri (2016: 65) claims that 'the use of land as a composite proxy for all natural resources implies that a variety of livelihoods are destroyed in the natural sector when land is acquired for industry'. Schumpeter (2012) calls this process as 'creative destruction'. Creative destruction is a continuous process in capitalist development where the dispossession of livelihoods of displaced people continuously outpaces the creation of new jobs through corporate-led industrial development. The process operates like a trap in which an increasing number of displaced people are grasped (Bhaduri, 2016: 67). In Kalinga Nagar, not only the key livelihoods resources of the Adivasis like land, both private and common, several water bodies, forests and hills were appropriated, the industries that came in various phases also could not provide alternative livelihoods to the people. Alternative livelihoods mostly were absent in the mechanised industries, and there was much delay in the commissioning of most of the projects in the area. Nayak and Kujur (2007) confirm that unsure of alternative livelihoods, the people of Kalinga Nagar protested whenever new projects were started. The industries who established their plants first, such as NINL, MESCO, Jindal Steel and Visa Steel, provided few or no employments to the dislocated people (see table no. 2). The resettlement and rehabilitation of the displaced people were forceful and provoking, involving violence. The dissent and discontent of the dislocated people of these plants were suppressed, as there were no strong voices. As a result, some dislocated people have migrated to different areas such as rural, urban and forest areas in search of livelihoods. Some displaced families have also been perished about which the state has no record. An interview with a village community leader reveals that out of 639 displaced families of NINL, 115 families migrated to different districts of Odisha. 30, 20 and 15 families each migrated to Dhenkanal (urban area), Keonjhar (Baranga reserved forest) and Balasore (rural area) districts of Odisha respectively. Fifty families migrated and settled in the same district in the nearby city Jajpur Road. Mishra (2006) well documented these cases and claims that hundreds of families in Kalinga Nagar have been displaced, and many more are expected to be dislocated in the near future. There were 700 families, out of which 250 are living there. There is no news of the rest, the 450 families. So what has happened to those 450 families? Studies conducted by Walter Fernandes (2008) reveals a similar fate of displaced people in India. He writes that only 17.94 per cent of the displaced persons have been resettled in India (see table no. 7). Odisha and Goa have resettled only one third of the displaced people while Gujarat and West Bengal resettled only 23.82 per cent and 11.18 per cent, respectively. Others have either impoverished or perished.

The status of women in Adivasis society is relatively high as compared to women in caste society. It is because women in tribal society participate in productive activities outside the home. Their high status is linked to the land, forest and other common property resources where they derive the livelihoods (Fernandes, 2013: 96; Mathur, 2013: 177; Mohanty, 1998: 82). Due to dislocation and capital accumulation the livelihood resources, tribal women get reduced, and the women without getting any employment or very little employment become housewives. This is a process where Adivasi women become dependent housewives or housewifisation (Mies, 1998, 2014). Housewifisation is a form of exploitation, and it is necessary for capital accumulation to proceed further. The process accelerates due to displacement. Adivasi women depend more on their husband or other male members of their family for their sustenance. The process of housewifisation is also accomplished if industry provides employment or self-help group employment to some women in the resettlement process. Since the new employment is oftentimes low-paid, the women have to depend on their husbands. In Kalinga Nagar, Tata Steel has opened self-help group (SHG) training for self-employment of displaced women. The reality is that few women are attracted for this SHG training since the training is not favourable for tribal women and it provides low profitable employment. In KNIC, employment of displaced women is very negligible, and those who have provided employment in the industries are of low-grade employment. For instance in Tata Steel, out of 306 employments to displaced family, only 19 (6.20 per cent) employment goes to displaced women. Similarly other industries like NINL, Visa Steel and MESCO have provided 6.81 per cent, 6.89 per cent and 4.67 per cent of employment out of the total employment given to displaced family respectively (see table no. 6). Apart from the dislocation situation, the resettlement and rehabilitation policy is designed in such a way that it always favours only a particular class of urban-educated women depriving the illiterate tribal displaced women. The policy also reinforces the process of housewifisation.

Development and industrialisation have also severe repercussions on the environment. In this context, Giddens (1991: 110) states that the ecological threats are the results of socially organised knowledge, mediated by the impact of industrial capitalism upon the material environment. It is the new risk profile that affects modern social life. Beck (1992: 13) argues that 'at the centre lie the risks and consequences of modernisation, which are revealed as irreversible threats to the life of plants, animals, and human beings. Unlike the factory-related or occupational hazards of the nineteenth and the first half of the twentieth centuries, these can no longer be limited to certain localities or groups, but rather exhibit a tendency to globalisation'. Habermas contends that capitalism is the chief culprit of environmental degradation. He states that environmental movements crop up as a consequence of life-world colonisation (Ibid.). In India, the cost of environmental degradation and environmental crisis are disproportionately borne by the poor, tribals, peasants, women and other marginal communities (Rao, 1995). In Kalinga Nagar, most of the perennial streams, rivulets and the low wastelands, common grazing lands, some small hills and village forests that were the livelihood base of Adivasis, farmers have been accumulated and degraded for industrialisation. This has affected the livelihood of Adivasis and biodiversity in the area. The pollutants from the industries in the area are polluting the local water bodies (ponds, rivulets and river *Brahmani*). *Brahmani* is already polluted by Rourkela Steel Plant and other development projects of Odisha and does not contain any fish and prawn (Meher, 2003). In future, similar may be the fate of other rivers in Odisha and the local streams and water bodies in Kalinga Nagar. In KNIC, the affected and displaced Adivasis resettled in the colony. I found kidney disease a common illness. Air pollution is also severe in the area, causing problems like asthma, lung problems and heart disease. Air pollution has also affected the livelihood of the local Adivasis. Shankarsan Behera (a local Adivasi) says about the ecological impact of industrialisation in KNIC,

> We (adivasis) depended upon *Badasuli* hill and forest for collection of wood, sal leaf and firewood. Cows, bullocks, goats and sheep graze in the jungle. Poor adivasis fetch a livelihood by selling those in the local Duburi market. Due to pollution, dusts are covered on the tree leaves of the jungle. Our livestocks are affected by various diseases eating the dust covered fodder. We are no more collecting polluted sal leaves. Dusts are also covered on the surface of our ponds. Bathing on these ponds people are affected by skin disease. Animals are also suffering drinking polluted water.
>
> (Interview 31.10.2014)

Development and industrialisation have also political consequences. For capitalist development state, making nexus with corporations has unleashed a lot of repressive measures like police brutality and police firing. On 16 December 2000 at Maikanch in Kashipur, police killed three Adivasis and wounded many more resisting Utkal Alumina (UAI) bauxite and mining projects. The state government established an inquiry commission under Justice P.K. Mishra. In January 2004, the commission submitted its report that criticised the role of police and district administration. But the state government did not take any action; rather the chief minister threatened that 'forces opposed to the industry will be firmly dealt with' (Sarangi et al., 2005). Similar fate was also in KNIC on 2 January 2006 where police killed 12 Adivasis, wounding 41. After that, there was a lot of police brutality and repression. State government has already set up three commissions subsequently headed by Justice A.S. Naidu, Justice P.K. Patra and Justice P.K. Mohanty, but the report is yet to be publicised. After so many hues and cries, the political power structure of the state government has not changed; rather BJD (Biju Janata Dal) has been voted to power in three consecutive terms after 2006 incident. The political power structure of the BJD is further consolidated. Even the constituency under which KNIC falls was voted for the same political party in all the state assembly elections.

In addition to this, the monetary compensation paid for land acquisition was inadequate. The compensation for land was paid at the rate of Rs. 35,000/37,000 per acre of the land in 1993–94. The state apparatus ignored people representatives' demand of Rs. 1.5 lakhs compensation per acre of land. But the Odisha government, acting like a client, sold these lands to the industries at the rate of Rs. 3.5 lakhs per acre. In compensation principle of development, there is a difference between acquisition economy and livelihood economy. In the development logic, the latter often ignores or undermines the former (Escobar, 1995a). These factors also gave an impetus for resistance movement in KNIC and led to the formation of Bisthapan Birodhi Jan Manch (BBJM) Sukinda.

Demands, strategies and collective mobilisation

BBJM, Sukinda was formed in April 2005 in a gathering called by local tribals in Kalinga Nagar. One elder Adivasis from the local Gobarghati GP (Gram Panchayat) named Chakradhar Haibru was elected as its president. Rabindra Jarika, a post-graduate from Utkal University in Odisha, was a local Adivasi youth of *Chandia* village (one of the affected villages) and elected as its secretary. People of more than 50 affected villages and two Gram Panchayats (GP), namely *Gobarghati* and *Chandia*, which was listed for acquisition by Tata Steel, were its activists. Two GPs were the centre of resistance. Tribals of the Sukinda regions provided sympathy and solidarity to the movement. The organisation formed various hamlet and village committees with a village youth in each village/hamlet as its head. All the people of the hamlet or village remained its members. BBJM had its organisational core committee consisting of eight members. It made ad-hoc alliance and solidarity with various movement organisations and political societies who supported their cause like Lok Shakti Abhijan, a people's organisation fighting against globalisation and for the right to livelihood, Odisha unit, Kashipur Andolankari, Lower Suktel Ekta Manch, Sambalpur Chashi Sanghthan, Posco Pratirodh Sangram Samiti (PPSS), CPI (ML) New Democracy, CPI (ML) Liberation, CPI (M) and CPI (Maoist) and CPI (Janshakti). They performed villages and core committee meetings and discussed the developmental cost on local peoples. They made aware to the local people about the developmental cost burn out of displacement by NINL, MESCO, Jindal and Visa Steel in the area and, to a larger extent, of Hirakud, Rengali Dam and Rourkela Steel Plant. With this discussions and debates, BBJM came to the conclusion that in the contemporary political structure and development model practised by the state, it is impossible by the state to provide a just resettlement and rehabilitation to the dislocated people. The state structure is repressive and exploitative. Development and its consequence displacement are exploitative. Development comes with the costs and sacrifices of a particular class, and often they are Adivasis. While development creates some jobs for a growing middle class, in turn it destroys a lot of livelihoods of the uprooted class. The contemporary development followed by the state is nothing but 'creative destruction' (Schumpeter, 2012). Development projects appropriate the traditional sustainable livelihood resources such as land, water, forests and hills and in turn provide an unsustainable livelihood to a particular class those have formal capability or qualification up to one generation, excluding majority of the dislocates. Like agriculture, it never guarantees livelihood sustainability to the next generation. BBJM and its solidarity organisations made aware of these issues to the activists and common people. Realising displacement and its costs, BBJM demanded the state government to give a 'White paper of all development projects undertaken after 1996 till 2004 in Odisha and particularly in Kalinga Nagar Industrial Complex'. BBJM questioned the Odisha government of 'How many people have the state displaced in the name of development and how many of them have been properly resettled and rehabilitated? What is the condition of those who are not resettled?' BBJM demanded no further displacement in the area and resisted the acquisition of land by Tata Steel. The main motto of BBJM was '*Ame Jamin Chadibu Nahin*' (We won't let our land for acquisition). Adivasis had cognized a sense of place. They declared that the life-world of Adivasis is revolved through *Vitamati* (Habitat), Jal (water), Jamin (land) and Jangal (forest); hence they will not let them for appropriation. During 2005, the BBJM resisted all kinds of activities like land survey, *bhumipuja*, levelling, boundary wall construction, etc., relating to setting up of industries in the Kalinga Nagar. It is necessary to highlight some events that intensified conflict.

On 9 May 2005, Maharashtra Seamless Steel Limited was performing its *Bhoomi Pooja* (Worship of Land) near Gadpur and Bandargadia Village to establish its steel plant. The local tribals violently resisted the event, declaring to stop the project. The police resorted to *lathi-charge* (caning), and women were obstructed on the ground. People broke the police van. The *bhoomi pooja* was abandoned. On 23 July 2005, Tata Steel performed *Bhoomi Pooja* with the presence of then-district collector and superintendent of police (SP). Around 3,000 Adivasis and Dalits protested, and police lodged cases against the leaders of BBJM. The *Bhoomi Pooja* was postponed. But Tata Steel went ahead with the project with assurance from authorities in spite of the violent protests. On 27 July, a notice was served to the people of the area by the state administration to attend a public hearing in Jajpur Road.

On 7 October 2005, Adivasis resisted against the performance of *Bhoomi Pooja* again on the same land by the Tata officials even if accompanied by police force and district administration officials. A constable was reportedly beaten up by the protestors, and according to police, protesters snatched away his gun. On 25 October 2005, Rabindra Jarika, the secretary, was arrested by the Jajpur police while he was returning from attending a tribal conference in Bhubaneswar, the state capital. On his arrest, various organisations, including People's Union for Civil Liberty (PUCL), protested against the government on its attempt to suppress the movement of the people. On 27 October 2005, BBJM and its alliances gheraoed Kalinga Nagar police station, protesting against the arrest. The police reported by trying to arrest the other local leaders of that organisation. On 17 November 2005, in the face of strong resistance by BBJM, the Maharashtra Seamless Steel Limited had suspended its construction work, and later its project was abandoned from Kalinga Nagar.

On 2 January 2006, Tata Steel started the levelling of land early in the morning in the area with the help of state administrative officials like district collector, superintendent of police (SP), and 12 platoons of police force. About 300–400 tribals with traditional weapons like bows and arrows and axes gathered in the area and sent a delegate of four members for a dialogue with the officials. When the delegates were marching ahead, police resorted to tear gas cells. The tribals retaliated by throwing back these tear gas cells. Tear gas cells followed by indiscriminate firing, killing 12 tribals (see table no. 4) and wounding 41 tribals (see table no. 5). This incident intensified conflict in the area. Soon after this, the Adivasis blocked the Express Highway that runs through the area by sitting on a *dharna*at Madhuban Chhaka.

On 4 January, district administration returned the dead bodies to the tribals. They found that the wrists, breasts and genitals of some of the dead bodies had been mutilated. The event further accelerated the discontent among the tribals. On that day, the tribals collectively cremated the dead bodies and vowed in the funeral pyres of the *sahids* (martyrs) not to vacate the lands. In a public meeting near Duburi, BBJM, and attended by its alliance organisations, they articulated a seven-point demand to the government:

1 Put an end to displacement. Five acres of land be given to families who have already been displaced.
2 The chief minister, the finance minister, minister of mines, industry, scheduled caste and scheduled tribe welfare minister be removed from ministry and the minister of finance and chief minister be booked for murder charges.
3 The home secretary and DGP be suspended and SP and collector of Jajpur District and ADM, Kalinga Nagar, be suspended and booked under IPC 302.
4 Declare Rs. 2 million compensation for the family of each dead and Rs. 1 million to the family of each injured.
5 MNCs and monopoly companies be driven out from the soil of Odisha.
6 Adivasis be given the rights over mineral resources, land, water, forests and industry in tribal areas.
7 Unconditional release of leaders and activists of the movement and withdrawal of all cases pending against them.

BBJM Sukinda articulating these demands organised various rallies, campaigns and public meetings in each village of Sukinda and Danagadi blocks for public sympathy and support.

The Adivasis and Dalits from both the blocks, particularly Sukinda, supported the demands of Kalinga Nagar movement. From March 2 to 9, 2006, BBJM convened a cycle rally which is called as *Sukinda Sangram Yatra* (Movement Rally in Sukinda). Organising various public meetings, cycle rally in various villages of Sukinda BBJM successfully organised a big movement conference on 11 March 2006 near Ambagadia hamlet. Many political parties and grassroots movement organisations fighting for displacement and injustice attended the conference. Similar conferences, rallies and demonstrations were organised in Kalinga Nagar industrial complex and in the state capital to justify the demands of the movements. The movement was able to sustain about six years, i.e., from 2005 to 2011. Gradually the movement declined due to the dynamics of state violence and repression, movement fragmentation, consciousness of opportunity of the leaders and internal differentiation both among the Adivasis and non-Adivasis.

Resistance and the trajectory of development

Social resistance has an effect on the development process. Sustained and effective collective action always has an impact on the trajectories of development. However, we rarely find any studies except some scholars like Bebbington (2000), Escobar (1995b) and Oommen (2004). Bebbington (2000: 513) argues that 'People encounter development from their mundane, daily concerns to build and improve their livelihoods, to build places they enjoy being in, to give meaning to their lives through these livelihoods and places, and to maintain and, as far as possible, to extend the degree to which they can exercise control over their conditions of existence. This encounter can sometimes seem like resistance, sometimes like accommodation, and sometimes like self-interest'. Bebbington (Ibid.) criticised both post-structural and neoliberal interpretations for their inadequacy in explaining the full content of development. For him, while post-structural theorists tend to explain development as a process of cultural destruction and homogenisation, neoliberal perspective argues development process as a failure due to insufficient resource use. He contends rather development as a coproduction of resistance. Oommen (2004: 216) argues that 'my notion of social development implies conscious volition and active involvement of the system participants in the developmental process. That is to say, social mobilisation of collectivities is a pre-requisite for their social development'. Further he contends that 'The understanding of this dialectical intertwining between the attributes of a collectivity, the prospects of their mobilisation and the shaping of their consciousness is of utmost importance in analysing the ongoing process of social development' (Ibid.). In Kalinga Nagar, we have a similar story of how development is co-produced due to collective mobilisation. In Kalinga Nagar and in the larger context of development in Odisha, the strong resistance movement supported by civil society influenced the state to formulate the policy and made people participate in the development process. Rabindra Jarika speaks about Kalinga Nagar resistance movement,

> Our movement was able to formulate Odisha Resettlement and Rehabilitation policy 2006. The movement also forced the government for proper implementation of the policy. We, the adivasis got a voice to say about displacement to Tata Steel.
>
> (Interview 08.06.2015)

Jarika claimed that due to police firing, subsequent violent protests and 14 month-road blockade by Adivasis supported by civil society, we were able to force the government to call the BBJM leaders to negotiate the issues with the government. The organised resistance forced Odisha government to bring the Resettlement and Rehabilitation Policy 2006 (hereafter R&R policy) one year before the central government to formulate the policy. Nayak and Kujur (2007) argue that the widespread condemnation of the police firing in Kalinga Nagar compelled Odisha government to formulate the resettlement and rehabilitation policy. The killings of the Adivasis in Kalinga Nagar industrial complex had brought into focus the larger issue of resettlement and rehabilitation of the displaced people displaced by industrial projects. Although in 2005, the state government in consultation with UNDP prepared a draft R&R policy. It was put unused. This draft policy formulation was begun in 2001 due to strong resistance of Adivasis, Dalits and marginal communities resisting mining and industrialisation in different parts of Odisha. In May 2006, the state government finally proclaimed the R&R policy for resettlement and rehabilitation of dislocated people displaced/ to be displaced by industries and other development projects (Government of Odisha, 2006). Mathur (2006) claims that the process of finalising the Odisha R&R policy came in a 'kneejerk reactions' to the Kalinga Nagar police firing. Not only this, the policy was a consequence to counteract the gathering strength of several high-profile movements that stroke the industrialisation process in Odisha. Similarly, in the Sardar Sarovar Project (SSP) conflict, a collective action made a 'chilling effect on the World Bank' which led not only to the Bank to be more circumspect with the funding of the SSP but also has resulted in substantial refinement of its lending codes and policies governing resettlement (Dwivedi, 2006). Resistance movement not only forces the government to formulate policy, but it also compels the government to improve the policies. The anti-Sardar Sarovar Project (SSP) movements in Gujarat pressurized Gujarat government to improve its previous R&R policy (Parasuraman, 1997: 54). Mathur (2008) asserts that the Odisha R&R policy 2006 that came as a consequence of various resistance movements emerging in Odisha is considered to be an improvement of the National R&R policy 2004, and it has also been regarded as the best policy in India (Mehra, 2007).

Resistance movements also provide an opportunity for the government to implement the R&R policy in a better way. The SSP movement in Gujarat influenced the state to improve the R&R implementation process significantly (Parasuraman, 1997: 54). In KNIC in 2006 during the initial phase of protest, only 229 families, or one third of displaced families, got employment in Kalinga Nagar industrial complex out of 815 dislocated families (table no. 2). NINL, a public sector undertaking displaced 639 families, provided only 182 (mere one-third) families with employment. NINL also didn't provide most of the displaced families (79 per cent) homestead land. Three industries such as Jindal, Visa and Rohit even could not provide single employment to the dislocated people. Only 238 (29 per cent) family got homestead land in the R&R colony without basic amenities. Although there were 2005 Kalinga Nagar R&R policy guidelines, the implementation was so hazy. However the R&R policy implementation gradually changed due to the force of strong protest movements, police firing and people's negotiation.

Table no. 3 shows a comparative glossy picture of R&R policy implementation in Kalinga Nagar industrial complex that was the result of resistance movement. In the post-movement period, 1,091 (one-half) displaced families have been provided with employment. Most of the dislocated families have been resettled in R&R colonies (69 per cent) and self-resettlement colonies (28 per cent) with improved infrastructure. NINL that provided only 182 (one-third) employment to the displaced families in the initial phase of protest movement have provided 452 (68 per cent) employment after resistance by BBJM. Jindal, Visa and Rohit Steel industries, who have not provided a single employment, have provided 154 (66 per cent), 29 (74 per cent) and 11 (91 per cent) numbers of employment after resistance. Hence, we can make a conclusion that resistance has gradually improved R&R policy implementation in Kalinga Nagar Industrial Complex. Oommen (2004) argues that the impact of resistance movement on development has also several defects. He comments that social movement operates in the extra-parliamentary space, demanding effective implementation of the existing laws or formulation of new legislation in response to the changing situation. When social movement constitutes a threat to the state or its apparatus, state attempts to use co-option or coercion. While co-option leads to ideological erosion, coercion may produce physical annihilation. The development projects in Odisha in general and Kalinga Nagar in particular have many such instances. One of the instances in KNIC is 2 January 2006 police firing.

Conclusion

Development in the form of industrialisation in Kalinga Nagar is a consequence of neoliberal globalisation. The resource richness of the territory has attracted different metal industrialists to extract the raw materials to generate huge surpluses for state and corporate that is ideologically fuelled and backed by the crony capitalism. Keeping in mind of this political process and ideological position of capitalism, I describe development (investment)-induced displacement in Kalinga Nagar Industrial Complex with reference to political economy of the region. The political economy of the developmentalism is being re/shaped by resource richness, politics of top-down development favouring a particular class, place or space, exploitation or alienation of the Adivasis by colonial or post-colonial state. The political economy of the state generates dissent and discontent, and the dislocated communities resist state politics. The top-down development is executed by the state that often acts for the capitalists or corporate class that can be in the form of transnational or local corporations.

The state developmentalism favouring a particular alien class while transferring its costs and residues to the pre-existing non-capitalist class induces value conflict and resistance. The resistance movement in Kalinga Nagar also emerged as a consequence of exploitation in place or territory. Apart from exploitation in place, other elements that caused resistance in Kalinga Nagar include expropriation of key livelihood resources. The expropriation most of the times has come in the form of creative destruction which has often severe unequal consequences (benefitting few and pauperising many). Besides this, the development logic of the state which itself causes resistance as a development manifestation also transforms the local populace to a peripheral populace within the centre that is going to be developed by the state. The resistance movement has its own course of development, dynamics and politics. The ploys and tactics it applies, the collective mobilisation it manufactures, depends largely on the actors involved in the movement and the structure of the opposite actor/s. Social resistance movement never goes in vain; rather it provides an opportunity to the state and its actors to produce a second thought about the dislocates. The state either formulates or improves its policies to lessen the movement spirit that becomes an obstacle for capitalist accumulation and neoliberal development. Therefore it remains as an essential normative requirement for the social scientist to engage them to understand the politics and dynamics behind and beyond the political economy of developmentalism.

Note

1 Bandh is a formal strike. It is a form of protest that comes under the ambit of social movement strategy.

References

Auty, R. M. (1993). *Sustaining Development in Mineral Economies: The Resource Curse Thesis*. London: Routledge.

Balasundaram, S. N. (1973). Centre-State Relations. In Jag Mohan (Ed.), *Twenty-Five Years of Indian Independence*. New Delhi: Vikas Publishing House.

Bandyopadhyay, D. (1986). Land Reforms in India: An Analysis. *Economic and Political Weekly*, pp. A50–A56.

Baviskar, A. (2005). Red in Tooth and Claw? Looking for Class in Struggles Over Nature. *Social Movements in India: Poverty, Power and Politics*, pp. 161–178.

Bebbington, A. (2000). Reencountering Development: Livelihood Transitions and Place Transformations in the Andes. *Annals of the Association of American Geographers*, vol. 90, no. 3, pp. 495–520.

Beck, U. (1992). *Risk Society: Towards a New Modernity*. London: Sage Publications.

Bhaduri, Amit. (2016). *Malignant Growth*. New Delhi: Aakar Books.

Census. (2011). *District Census Handbook: Jajapur*. Odisha: Directorate of Census Operation.

Collins, P. H. (1998). *Fighting Words: Black Women and the Search for Justice*. London: University of Minnesota Press.

Das, K. (1992). *Uneven Development, Indian Planning and the Strategy of Industrialisation: Case of Odisha*. Unpublished PhD thesis, Jawaharlal Nehru University, New Delhi.

Das, K. (1997). Politics of Industrial Location: Indian Federalism and Development Decisions. *Economic and Political Weekly*, vol. 32, no. 51, pp. 3268–3274.

Dash, K. C. and K. C. Samal. (2008). New Mega Projects in Orissa: Protests by Potential Displaced Persons. *Social Change*, vol. 38, no. 4, pp. 627–644.

Davis, M. (2006). *Planet of Slums*. London and New York: Verso Google Scholar.

Dwivedi, R. (2006). *Conflict and Collective Action: The Sardar Sarovar Project in India*. New Delhi: Routledge.

Escobar, A. (1995a). *Encountering Development: The Making and Unmaking of the Third World*. Princeton: Princeton University Press.

Escobar, A. (1995b). Imagining a Post-Development Era. *Power of Development*, pp. 211–227.

Fernandes, W. (2008). Sixty Years of Development-Induced Displacement in India. *India Social Development Report*, pp. 89–102.

Fernandes, W. (2013). Impact of Displacement on the Tribes. In Sakarama Somajaji and Susmita Dasgupta (Eds.), *Sociology of Displacement: Policies and Practice*. New Delhi: Rawat Publications.

Ghosh, R. and K. Nagaraj. (1978). Land Reforms in West Bengal. *Social Scientist*, pp. 50–67.

Giddens, A. (1991). *The Consequences of Modernity*. Stanford: Polity Press.

Government of Odisha. (2006). http://odisha.gov.in/govtpress/pdf/2006/651.pdf. Accessed 6 January 2015.

Harvey, D. (2003). *The New Imperialism*. Oxford: Oxford University Press.

Jones, Bruce., Emily O'Brien and David Steven. (2014). *The Risk Pivot: Great Powers, International Security, and the Energy Revolution*. Washington, DC: The Brookings Institutions. From Google Books Database. Accessed 22 January 2016.

Lok Sabha Debate in Indian Parliament. (1970). Steel Plant Location in the Country: LS Deb.Col.242.

Mahapatra, L. K. (1987). Ex-Princely States of Orissa: Mayurbhanj, Keonjhar and Bonai. In Surajit Sinha (Ed.), *Tribal Polities and State Systems in Pre-Colonial Eastern and North Eastern India*. Calcutta: Centre for Studies in Social Sciences.

Mathur, H. M. (2006). *Globalization, Displacement, and Impoverishment Risks: Large Corporations and Tribal Peoples in Orissa, India*. Paper presented at the Working Group on Involuntary Resettlement, Environmental Risks and Sustainable Development at IAPS/Bibalex Conference on Environment, Health and Sustainable Development, Alexandria, Egypt.

Mathur, H. M. (2008). Involving Resettlement of Orissa, India: A New Deal for the Displaced in a Globalizing World. *Social Change*, vol. 38, no. 40.

Mathur, H. M. (2013). *Displacement and Resettlement in India: The Human Cost of Development*. London and New York: Routledge.

Meher, R. (2003). The Social and Ecological Effects of Industrialisation in a Tribal Region: The Case of the Rourkela Steel Plant. *Contributions to Indian Sociology*, vol. 37, no. 3, pp. 429–457.

Meher, R. (2009). *How Mineral-Based Industrial Development Marginalizes and Displaces People in India: Three Case Studies*. New York: Edwin Mellen Press.

Mehra, P. (2007). SEZ Controversy: Course Correction. *India Today*, vol. 32, no. 5, pp. 54–55.

Mies, M. (1998). *Patriarchy and Accumulation on a World Scale: Women in the International Division of Labour*. New York: Palgrave Macmillan.

Mies, M. (2014). *Patriarchy and Accumulation on a World Scale: Women in the International Division of Labour*. London: Zed Books.
Miri, M. (1993). *Continuity and Change in Tribal Society*, vol. 43. Shimla: Indian Institute of Advanced Study.
Mishra, B. (2006). People's Movement at Kalinga Nagar: An Epitaph or an Epitome? *Economic and Political Weekly*, pp. 551–554.
Mohanty, M. (1998). Orissa's Tribal People: Politics of Disentitlement. In Sebasti L. Raj and Arundhuti Roy Choudhury (Eds.), *Contemporary Social Movements in India: Achievements and Hurdles*. New Delhi: Indian Social Institute.
Nayak, R. C. and J. M. Kujur. (2007). *State Aggression and Tribal Resistance: A Case of the Police Firing at Kalinga Nagar*. New Delhi: Indian Social Institute.
Oommen, T. K. (2004). *Nation, Civil Society and Social Movements: Essays in Political Sociology*. New Delhi: Sage Publications.
Padel, F. and S. Das. (2008). Cultural Genocide: The Real Impact of Development-Induced Displacement. In H. M. Mathur (Ed.), *India Social Development Report*. New Delhi: Oxford University Press, pp. 103–115.
Parasuraman, S. (1997). The Anti-Dam Movement and Rehabilitation Policy. In J. Dreze, M. Samson and S. Singh (Eds.), *The Dam and the Nation: Displacement and Resettlement in the Narmada Valley*. New Delhi: Oxford University Press.
Prasad, A. (2004). *Environmentalism and the Left: Contemporary Debates and Future Agendas in Tribal Areas*. New Delhi: Left Word Press.
Prasad, R. (1988). *Tribes, a Study in Cultural Ecology and Tribal Dynamics*. New Delhi: Amar Prakashan.
Rao, J. M. (1995). Whither India's Environment? *Economic and Political Weekly*, vol. 30, no. 13, pp. 677–686.
Sahu, B. (2007). Defying the Juggernaut. In R. Kalshian (Ed.), *Caterpillar and the Mahua Flower: Tremors in India's Mining Fields*. New Delhi: Panos South Asia.
Sarangi, D., R. Pradhan and S. Mohanty. (2005). State Repression in Kashipur. *Economic and Political Weekly*, pp. 1312–1314.
Sayad, A. (2004). *The Suffering of the Immigrants*. Cambridge: Polity.
Schumpeter, Joseph A. (2012). *Capitalism, Socialism and Democracy*. London: Routledge.
Sharma, B. D. (2006). *People's Revolt in Kalinga Nagar: A Preliminary Discussion Draft*. New Delhi: Sahyog Pustak Kuteer Trust.
Sinha, B. N. (2008). *Geography of Orissa*. New Delhi: National Book Trust.
Smith, N. (1996). *The New Urban Frontier: Gentrification and the Revanchist City*. London: Routledge.

Part III

Emerging policy gaps

12 Land rights

The penumbral region in Indian constitutional space

Garima Kirti

Introduction

Development-induced displacement poses a conflict between the rights of an individual and the right to development of a community. But this conundrum is just the tip of the iceberg. The crux of the issue is whether the idea of development-induced displacement offends moral and legal principles. The answer to this is buried in a deep-lying structure which can be unfolded only through a specific line of inquiry. At the outset, the understanding of the interconnection between right to land as an intrinsic part of right to life is indispensable. Therefore, the chapter in its beginning seeks to bring out this relationship on the basis of natural rights and fundamental rights. However, while arguing fundamental rights status for land rights under the Indian constitution, the chapter is not sceptic to the fears regarding concentration of wealth and exploitation of poor as a result of such status being accorded to land rights. The next stage of exploration is whether encroachment on land rights allowed within the constitutional framework. If it is, does constitutional correctness necessarily imply moral correctness? Even if the state is successful in justifying displacement of masses for the greater good, is individual consent necessary? If no, then the whole process of displacement amounts to state coercion, and individual dignity and freedom of choice is compromised. An equally relevant query is if the individual does give his/her consent, does it amount to free consent, or it is vitiated by unequal bargaining positions of the individual with respect to the state as well as misrepresentations made by the state in the form of 'rehabilitation and better future' promises. Nonetheless the previous questions, for several past decades, the state has and to this day continues to exercise its power of eminent domain for national and community development, promising individuals that they would be the ultimate beneficiaries in the long run. Hence, the chapter seeks to locate the position of the individual and the faction of displaced masses vis-à-vis the rest of the community. On an optimistic note, if the state has exercised and continues to exercise its power only after applying mindful into the several issues incidental and consequential to displacement, still the ratio of those displaced to those rehabilitated is far from lending consolation to the practice of development-induced displacement. This is where the shoe pinches. In light of this, the chapter attempts to identify past failures and current loopholes in the functioning of the state that has led to a deplorable state of land rights in India. Finally, the several bits garnered out of previous inquiries are joined to pull out the issue of development-induced displacement from the penumbral region of constitutional correctness or incorrectness in Indian legal space and to propose a solution to it.

Research methodology

The chapter is explanatory in nature. The research design employs logical constructs to investigate the problem and arrive at a solution. The right to property is discussed from the perspective of right in incorporeal property, particularly land. It follows analytical approach while referring and quoting material (books and journal) concerning the subject and uses secondary data to prove analysis. Secondary data regarding the displaced and rehabilitated has also been used to demonstrate the gravity and complexity of the problem The author is neutral and unprejudiced in considering political factors concerning the problem of land acquisition.

Right to land vis-à-vis right to life

Right to life is inherent in every human being; it is fundamental and natural to his/her existence. It is a right to which a person enjoys inalienable ownership. Needless to remind, right to life has no meaning in abstraction, a person must have entitlements to adequate means to live it. Right to liberty, livelihood, property, shelter, food, health, education and scores of other rights are the critically essential threads that design into the fabric of human right to life. In the context of the importance of property to life, multiple questions are raised about the nature of right to property and why land as a special resource demands redefining the concept of property in general as well as in the legal sense.

Right to property: a natural right, fundamental right or mere legal right

Natural rights are so constitutive of human existence that any reservation to these would demean human life. According to natural law, scholars' original right to property is vested in the first occupant on the basis of principles of universal law (Blackstone, 1753), on fact and implied assent of all mankind (1753) or on the fact of combinations of one's labour with the land as a common resource, a segment of which is appropriated to the person who mixes his/her labour with it (Locke, 1690: 27–29) or for encouraging productivity and therefore basing the claim over property on individual labour

(Paton, 2004: 539), whereas others like Ahrens Heirich deduce the right to property from the individual's right to act as a free personality (Cohen, 1927). Additionally, natural rights flow from natural state of things, and all people have a 'proper act and end' (Aquinas, 2006). In this light, the right of humans to acquire and hold property as a means to attain dignified and meaningful life as an end holds water to the argument that property rights are natural rights. Practical observations also place right to property within the ambit of right to life. This requires looking into the function of property.

Function of property

The role played by property in a society is multifarious. It may be a source of survival or cause of exploitation. The right to livelihood survives in the womb of the right to property as the latter offers access to and use of resources for securing one's survival. It is therefore the social function of property to contribute to a decent standard of living and a life with dignity, given the existence of just distribution of property in society (Punj, 2014).

Land as a commodity is not just a source of multiple civil rights but around land is built the owner's economic, social and cultural relations and, in the case of the tribal communities, their very identity. Thus, alienation from it is an attack on this totality and affects the whole family and even the community (Fernandes, 2008). In Jharkhand, land has shown itself to be means of livelihood, expression of identity and a symbol for what shape *Adivasi* identity should take in an increasingly commodified world (Sundar, 2009). For tribal peoples who gain food, shelter and livelihoods from communal forests, the relationship with their communal land has been described as 'symbiotic' by the Ministry of Environment and Forests (Prabhu, 2005). Thus, land manifests civil rights as well as social, economic and cultural rights.

Institutionalisation of property rights within the international legal framework and Indian legal system

Right to property as a natural right has been enshrined in various human rights instruments like Article 17 of Universal Declaration of Human Rights, Article I of Protocol I to European Convention of Human Rights, Article 23 of the American Declaration of the Rights and Duties of Man, Article 21 of American Convention of Human Rights and Article 14 of African Charter of Human and People's Rights. However, it means little unless right to property is recognized and protected under domestic legal system. Positioning of property rights under the chapter of fundamental rights is a highly complex and controversial and hence necessitates going down the lane of constitutional history in India.

It is worthy to look at the constitution as it stood before any amendments were made to it. Article 19(1) (f) conferred citizens the right to acquire and hold and dispose of property and formed part of a group of articles under the heading 'Right to Freedom'. Article 31 appeared under the heading 'Right to Property' for the 'Freedom to acquire property' conferred by Article 19(1) (f) would be worthless if a person does not have the right to hold his or her property. Article 31 provides that private property could be acquired by the state only for public purpose and on payment of compensation. Right to free movement under Article 19(1) (d) and right to reside and settle in any part of India under Article 19(1) (e) and Article 19(1) (f) were interlinked is clear from the sequential arrangement of clauses as well as from Article 19(5) which imposes reasonable restriction on all the sub-clauses equally. The right conferred by Article 19(1) (d) not a right implicit or but a special right to move freely throughout the territory of India. This right of free movement is not limited to travelling throughout India because it is accompanied by the further right to reside and settle in any part of India, as also the right conferred by Article 19(1) (f) to acquire, hold and dispose of property in any part of India (Salian, 2002). The aforesaid scheme shows that property rights are intended to be a part of fundamental rights.

Erosion of fundamental right to property

The purpose of constitution (First Amendment) act, 1951, was to rectify the evils of zamindari system, but the purpose got lost in the prolonged tussle between parliament and the judiciary. The fundamental rights case held that though parliament has the power to amend fundamental rights, it cannot destroy the basic features of the constitution (*Keshavanand Bharti v. State of Kerala AIR* [1973] SC 1461). Right to property was not considered to be the basic feature of the constitution. As a result, the Forty-fourth Amendment in 1978 reduced the status of fundamental right to property to a mere constitutional right under Article 300-A. In *Jilubhai Nanbhai Kanchar v. State of Gujarat*, the court reiterated that right to property is not a basic feature of the constitution (AIR [1995] SC 142). Mr H. M. Seervai, an eminent constitutional jurist, is of the opinion that the abolition of the right to property as a fundamental right would destroy other fundamental rights which are embodied in the constitution (Pandey, 2014: 720).

Though there is credibility in Mr Seervai's concerns, such concerns can be conveniently dispelled if land rights are considered alive under Article 21. The court in *M/S Delhi Airtech Services Pvt. Ltd. v. State of UP* held that Article 300-A has been given the status of basic human rights (AIR [2012] SC 573). Article 21 is home to all human rights. It confers on every person the fundamental right to life. The jurisprudence of this article has been vastly expanded by the judiciary. In *Maneka Gandhi v. Union of India*, the court held right to life is not merely confined to physical existence but includes within its ambit the right to life with human dignity (*AIR [1981] SC 746*). Elaborating the view in *Francis Coralie v. Union Territory of Delhi*, the court said that right to life includes right to life with human dignity and all that goes along with it, namely the bare necessities of life such as adequate nutrition, clothing and shelter, freely moving about and mixing with fellow human beings (*AIR [1978] SC 597*). Another landmark decision is *Olga Tellis v. Bombay Municipal Corporation*, which ruled the word 'life' in Article 21 includes 'right to livelihood' also (*AIR [1986] SC 180*). In *Chameli Singh v. State of UP*, it has been held that right to shelter is a fundamental right under Article 21 *(1996) 2 SCC 549*). The connection between right to land and right to life has already been established in earlier sections, both theoretically and practically. Therefore, it is inherently contradictory to view right to food, clothing and shelter as fundamental rights but right to land as mere legal right. Unfortunately in India the courts have refused to include property rights under the chapter of fundamental rights which creates space for easy abrogation of land rights and other fundamental rights incidental to property rights.

Whether state can justify encroachment on the right to land and consequent displacement

No right is absolute, be it fundamental or legal. The state is vested with the power to acquire property under the doctrine of eminent domain, but at what cost? Doctrine of 'eminent domain' is based on two maxims, namely *salus populi supreme lex esto*, which means that the welfare of the people is the paramount law, and *necessita public major est quan*, which means that public necessity is greater than private necessity (*Chiranjit Lal Choudhary v Union of India, AIR* 1951 SC 4, 41 and 54). Further the concept of distributive justice under Articles 38 and 39 and duty of the state to improve living standards of people under Article 47 make out a case for legality of land acquisition (Pandey, 2014: 436–441). Yet another question is: does constitutionality imply morality, and is morality important?

Though morality does not drive modern legal realism, it sets the stage for right and wrong according to space and time. It sanctifies legal principles in a way that infuses legal precepts with justice, reasonability and fairness. Therefore, be it a capitalist state, a socialist state or a mixed state, does it have the sanction to alienate from an individual his natural right and subject it to the ideology pursued by it? According to Immanuel Kant, 'whenever we are confronted with a moral dilemma, we need to consider whether the action would respect the basic rights of each of the individuals involved. How would the action affect the basic well-being and freedom of those individuals? Actions are wrong to the extent that they violate the rights of individuals'. But in certain instances, social costs or the injustice that would result from respecting a right are too great, and accordingly that right may need to be limited (Andre and Velasquez, 1990). This limitation affects a person's life, dignity and livelihood and therefore must provide for fair compensation, resettlement and rehabilitation; their realisation is another grave issue.

However, while circumscribing natural or fundamental rights, does consent of individual assume importance? Under the constitution, waiver of fundamental rights is impermissible, let alone consented deprivation (Jain, 2014: 874–875).

Question of consent

Choice of a person is quintessential to dignity, personality and individuality, and consent is significant to choice. The right to property secures for one a sphere of sovereignty. If we are individuals, required morally, to lead our lives by our judgements, it is crucial that we control the elements with which our lives are lived (Machan, 2005). It is proposed that no system of property rights can survive unless property is infused with moral significance (Merill and Smith, 2007: 1850). This means unconsented taking of property as a moral right is immoral. But consent as a requisite gives rise to holdout problem. The economics of the holdout or assembly problem can be best explained using a model derived by Thomas J. Miceli in his book, *The Economic Approach to Law*. The holdout problem is a term used to describe a property owner who refuses to sell his property and advantages out of it (2004). If it is conceded that consent of a person may be dispensed with, the problem does not end with denying the demanded opportunity of saying yes or no by property owners to the taking of their property; rather it is a wholesome mess-like situation created on account of the displacement that follows which places in jeopardy a number of rights necessary for survival. Therefore, economists must develop a model remedying holdout problems without paralysing individual rights.

Incidence of coercion

Land Acquisition Act (LAA), 1894, had no consent clause. Right to Fair Compensation and Transparency in Land Acquisition, Resettlement and Rehabilitation (RFCTLARR) Act, 2013, provides for 70 per cent consent of affected families for public-private partnership projects and 80 per cent for private company projects, this provision follows majoritarian rule, and consent is subjected to the nature of project, ultimately leading to coercion of the innocent individual who wishes to say no. Also an individual or a small community is too fragile to take up against big public and private corporations, eventually submitting to the resettlement, rehabilitation and developmental promises which remain unrealized. In the case of land acquisition, the basic moral intuition is the same as that which says intentional trespass or theft is wrong. Forcing innocent people to give up their property, even in return for just compensation, may be regarded as morally acceptable only if the benefits of the transaction will redound to all members of the community. But eminent domain is being used to confer disproportionate benefits on few individuals at the cost of many (Merrill and Smith, 2007: 1882–1883). Statistical information would provide better insights into social realities and how individual rights are violated not only at the stage of acquisition but post-acquisition due to non-resettlement and non-rehabilitation.

Social reality: violation of right to life and right to property

Individual rights are compromised to provide for investments in infrastructure (FAO, 2008). Every case of development-induced displacement is unique and needs separate strategies for the rehabilitation and resettlement of the displaced people. Thus, the annals of each development-induced displacement must be studied to rectify the problems related to resettlement and rehabilitation (Garada, 2015: 90). One such principle is that the livelihood of the displaced person or project-affected person should be better after the project than before it because they pay the price of development (Fernandes, 2008).

Cernia points out that displacement from one's land and habitat carries with it the risk of becoming poorer than before. It leads to landlessness, joblessness, homelessness, marginalisation, food insecurity, increased morbidity and mortality, loss of access to common property, social disintegration and violation of human rights (Cernea, 1997). These rights are supposed to be guarded by state. This is paradoxical as they are the ones who violate it.

India has one of the highest development-induced displacements in the world. According to an official figure in 1994, about 15.5 million internally displaced people were in India, and the government acknowledged that some 11.5 million were awaiting rehabilitation. But calculations, on the basis of the number of dams constructed in India and its associated displacement, show that the number of development-related displacement in India may be as high as 21 to 33 million people (Fernandes, 2000). The tribals represented 8.08 per cent of India's total population in 1991, but are estimated to represent 40 per cent of the displaced persons or project-affected persons (Fernandes, 2007: 204). Most pre-1980 projects did not have resettlement plans (Asif, 2000). A study for 1951–1995 completed in six states and other research show that the real number of displaced between 1947–2000 was probably around 60 million (Fernandes, 2004). Hemadri Mander and V. Nagraj in the working paper of the World Commission on Dams in 1999 have stated that it was clear from the start that mega-projects would require the displacement or forced uprooting of substantial populations, policymakers typically viewed these as legitimate and inevitable costs of development, acceptable in the larger national interest (Negi and Ganguly, 2011).

The power of eminent domain has been backed by Bentham's theory of Utilitarianism, 'Greatest happiness of the greatest number'. Utilitarianism is, of course, a moral theory (Merrill and Smith, 2007: 1849). But the idea of development-induced displacement does not conform to it; rather it seems to be a façade where neither the means nor the end is justified.

Failure of the constitutional machinery and constitutional safeguards

In light of previous data, it becomes inevitable to find out the defects in the current system. The Constituent Assembly debates about right to property and eminent domain involved ample discussion on land reforms, but there was no deliberation from the perspective of abuse of power of eminent domain, development-induced displacement or compensation or resettlement and rehabilitation of displaced. A prescient delegate, Shri S. Nagappa, tried to make a distinction between expropriation of a zamindar's land and that of a poor tiller's land and also argued that keeping property rights out of the constitution may help dismantle the zamindars' hold on land in the short term but would harm the 'poor tiller' in the longer term[1] (Gupta, 2012: 464).

When a law is debated, its implications have to be the subject of multidimensional analysis from short-term as well as long-term perspectives. This lapse on the part of Constituent Assembly enabled future parliamentarians to shape up the face of property rights on the constitution as per their whims and fancies.

Parliamentary failure to enact progressive legislation

LAA, 1894, the anarchic legislation, survived for 63 years post-independence. It was amended 17 times by various elected governments to permit acquisition by a company engaged in any industry for public purpose, but no provisions were made for resettlement and rehabilitation, social impact assessment or consent requirement. The Right to Fair Compensation and Transparency in Land Acquisition, Resettlement and Rehabilitation Act, 2013, which provides for fair compensation, resettlement and rehabilitation, social impact assessment and consent clause was passed in much haste by the UPA and has its own demerits (Raghuram and Sunny, 2015: 3–8).

Executive failure: bridge between policy and implementation

In the absence of any provision for resettlement and rehabilitation under the old act, the government formulated the National Policy on Resettlement and Rehabilitation for Project Affected Families, 2003. This policy was later replaced by the National Policy on Rehabilitation and Resettlement, 2007. But neither was effectively implemented.

Studies point to a gap between project planning and implementation. A study by the Parliament Public Accounts Committee in the 1980s showed that no major dam had been built in India at less than 500 per cent cost overrun in a five-year time overrun, and capacity utilisation of most dams was below 50 per cent of what was planned (Singh et al., 1992: 1734). In Andhra Pradesh, the cost overrun was 1,562.04 per cent and 1,217 per cent, respectively, in the Vattivagu and Santhala Dams in Adilabad district

(Fernandes et al., 2001: 179). Poor implementation of projects all the more jeopardized the life and livelihood of the displaced.

Judicial failure: no proactive role

The judiciary is the gatekeeper of fundamental rights. It has the power to declare any legislation whether pre-constitutional or post-constitutional as void if they are in violation of fundamental rights.

Constitutional interpretations and misinterpretations

Land Acquisition Act, 1894, was devoid of constitutional morality. It lacked the basic right to fair compensation, resettlement and rehabilitation, yet it continued to be an instrument of land acquisition.

In *Maneka Gandhi v. Union of India*, Articles 14, 19 and 21, were held to be interlinked. The court failed to discover this in *Keshavanand Bharti v. State of Kerala* while holding right to property out of the purview of basic features of the constitution. As a result, property rights were never analysed in the light of right to life and doctrine of equality. An expanded view of property rights is not without potholes, but constitutional flexibility is a feature of Indian democracy, and it is upon the courts to utilise this flexibility in filtering the benefits out of the provision by putting it to the best possible advantage. Article 14 does not forbid reasonable classification; therefore right to property could be linked to Article 21 to accord protection to the category of people whose livelihood depends on land without committing constitutional transgression. The absence of fundamental right to property disables the displaced from approaching the Supreme Court under Article 32 of the constitution.

The court did attempt to mitigate the evil effects of displacement to some extent but not effectively. In *B D Sharma v. Union of India*, it was ruled that benefits from the dam should not be counted as an alibi to deprive the fundamental rights of the displaced. They should be rehabilitated as soon as they are uprooted. Further, the court provided a time frame by which the rehabilitation must be complete: before six months of submergence (1992 Supp (3) SCC 93).

In *Narmada Bachao Andolan v. Union of India*, it was observed that rehabilitation is not only about providing food, clothes or shelter. It is also about extending support to rebuild livelihood by ensuring necessary amenities of life. Rehabilitation of the displaced is hence a logical corollary of Article 21. On the other hand, the court allowed construction of the dam despite materials presented before the court clearly suggesting the failure on the part of the government to carry out rehabilitation work in *pari passu*, the implementation of the project (AIR 2000 SC 3751, ¶¶158 & 181). The court refused to intervene in policy matters. The petitioners herein had not asked the court to intervene in policy decisions of the government, but to restrain the construction on the ground that the project was not being implemented as it was envisaged, without any rehabilitation. The distinction made by the court between policy decisions and the permissible area of judicial intervention was unnecessary in this context. More importantly, contrary to its own finding, the court itself indulged in commenting on the policy decisions of the government when it presented an unqualified eulogy on the virtues of a dam in Tehri's case (Khaitan, 2009: 116–119).

In *N.D. Jayal and Another v. Union of India*, a petition under Article 32 of the constitution, was filed in connection with safety, environmental and rehabilitation aspects of Tehri Dam. The court rejected the objections, eulogized the benefits of dam and observed that rehabilitation was taking place *pari passu*, the implementation of the project ((2004) 9 SCC 362).

Conclusion

The jurisprudence of property or land rights is constructed on the stones of social, economic and political factors. The analysis of property rights has shown the political elements to have been the most dominant factor in shaping and reshaping their framework. The series of property-centric constitutional amendments followed by scrapping off right to property from the chapter on fundamental rights, the operation of Land Acquisition Act, 1894, for an unreasonably long period of time bypassing precepts of constitutional morality. Absence of consent clause and no provision for resettlement and rehabilitation is proof to this. Although it is argued that the shifting of property rights does not make much difference, as even now the law of acquisition has to be fair and reasonable according to Article 14. On the face of it, this may appear to be a correct proposition, but if this is taken as a rule, it will blur the distinction and higher status accorded to fundamental rights. The placement of the bundle of fundamental rights in a separate chapter of the constitution as a protected set of rights is conclusive of the special approach taken towards these rights; therefore the expansion or constriction of this set by addition or subtraction of rights has profound impact on the set as a whole.

In the law of nature, land is connected to life. But absent legal acknowledgment has given rise to a deceptive truism in the concept of development-induced displacement as a necessary evil. The constitution framers did acknowledge property rights as fundamental but stopped short of considering it as an extended branch of right to life, which made its exploitation easy.

Development-induced displacement is a problem, the solution to which rests on several factors. The reason being it is tied to the concept of property (especially land) rights attached to the land and the role of constitutional bodies in the whole scheme. Resettlement and rehabilitation of people along with fair compensation may at least counterbalance the evil effects of displacement. The adequacy of the proposition is seen as morally and legally questionable given the circumstances where neither is done.

To remedy the situation requires opening a debate on restructuring of the property rights in the light of right to life and other fundamental rights, disturbance to property rights being made subject to minimal disturbance to the human life and dignity which encompasses a gamut of basic rights of livelihood. It is not enough to pronounce resettlement and rehabilitation as a part of Article 21 without broadening the definition of right to land in the context of both owner and dependants. Secondly, right without protection has no meaning. Resettlement and rehabilitation as a solution to development-induced displacement has been futile without any sanction against non-implementation; therefore the provision of resettlement and rehabilitation must be made mandatory under the RFCTLARR Act, 2013. Also a time frame within which resettlement and rehabilitation is to be carried out must be set to avoid loopholes. Thirdly, the burden of interpretation and execution of the constitutional safeguards rests on the three wings of state: the legislature, the executive and the judiciary. Therefore, the ultimate flaw is the missing element of willingness to attach indispensable sanctity to constitutional principles. Social order requires governance by law. A law devoid of moral bits is anarchic and tyrannical. After six decades of foul legislation, the government came up with the RFCTLARR Act, 2013, which was again attempted to be taken closer to the earlier legislation. Though it was withdrawn on account of public uproar, the politics centred around land acquisition sufficiently proves that the people, instead of being ruled by constitutional ideology, are governed by the personal ideology of the power-bearers. Therefore, a necessary transition from personal to constitutional ideology along with integrated and coordinated exercise of legislative, executive and judicial power is required.

The functioning of a healthy democracy is contingent upon honest commitment and willingness to adapt the constitution to changing socio-economic scenario without destroying its fabric. It is development which is inevitable and not displacement. Creativity and balance in law made by the legislature, sound developmental policies and, most importantly, intention to implement such laws and policies is the key to dismantling the concept of development-induced displacement and constructing a new social order wherein development is seen by everyone who loses land, that is, owner and dependants, as an opportunity for a better and improved life. This perception in persons losing land will require creation of faith in the entire system. It would require undoing of injustice already done to millions of displaced by giving them speedy resettlement and rehabilitation and further willingness and readiness to live in the constitutional space where life and livelihood of every person is of supreme importance.

Note

1 Shri Nagappa's comments during the Constituent Assembly Debates. Debates of the Constituent Assembly of India, vol. III (2 May 1947) at 515 [Constituent Assembly Debates].

References

Andre, Claire and Manuel Velasquez. (1990). Rights Stuff. *Santa Clare University*. www.scu.edu/ethics/publications/iie/v3n1/. Accessed 31 December 2015.

Aquinas, Thomas. (2006). *Summa Theologica Part I–II*. The Project Gutenberg ebook, Question 91, Second article. www.gutenberg.org/cache/epub/17897/pg17897.html. Accessed 31 December 2015.

Asif, Md. (2000). Why Displaced Persons Reject Project Resettlement Colonies. *Economic and Political Weekly*, vol. 35, no. 4.

Blackstone, William. (1753). *Commentaries on the Laws of England, Book II 8*. http://files.libertyfund.org/files/2140/Blackstone_1387-01_EBk_v6.0.pdf.

Cernea, Michael M. (1997). *African Involuntary Population Resettlement in a Global Context*. Washington, DC: World Bank, Social Policy and Resettlement Division.

Cohen, R. (1927). Property and Sovereignty. *Cornell Law Review*, vol. 13, no. 8, p. 18. http://scholarship.law.cornell.edu/clr/vol13/iss1/3. Accessed 30 December 2015.

FAO Land Tenure Studies. (2008). *Compulsory Acquisition of Land and Compensation*. Rome: Food and Agricultural Organisation of the United Nations.

Fernandes, Walter. (2000). Pawns in the Development. In S. Parasuraman and P. V. Unnikrishnan (Eds.), *India Disasters Report, Towards a Policy Initiative, Human-Instigated Disasters*. New York: Oxford University Press, pp. 276–279.

Fernandes, Walter. (2004). Rehabilitation Policy for the Displaced. *Economic and Political Weekly*, vol. XXXVIV, no. XII, pp. 1191–1193.

Fernandes, Walter. (2007). Singur and the Displacement Scenario. *Economic and Political Weekly*, vol. 42, no. 3, pp. 203–206.

Fernandes, Walter. (2008). India's Forced Displacement Policy and Practice: Is Compensation Up to Its Functions. In Michael Cernia and Hari Mohan Mathus (Eds.), *Can Compensation Prevent Impoverishment? Reforming Resettlement Through Investments and Benefit-Sharing*. New Delhi: Oxford University Press, pp. 5, 10, 15–16, 20–21.

Fernandes, Walter, Nafisa Goga D'Souza, Arundhuti Roy Choudhury and Mohammed Asif. (2001). *Development-Induced Displacement, Deprivation and Rehabilitation in Andhra Pradesh 1951–1995: A Quantitative and Quantitative Study of Its Extent and Nature*. New Delhi: Indian Social Institute and Guwahati, North Eastern Social Research Centre, p. 179.

Garada, Rabindra. (2015). Development Project Caused Resettlement and Rehabilitation Policy: Overviews on Dam Projects In Odisha (India). *IOSR Journal of Humanities and Social Science (IOSR-JHSS)*, vol. 20, no. 3, p. 90, March. DOI:10.9790/0837-20378997. www.iosrjournals.org/. Accessed 31 December 2015.

Gupta, Priya. (2012). The Peculiar Circumstances of Eminent Domain in India. *Osgoode Hall Law Journal*, vol. 49, no. 3, p. 464. http://digitalcommons.osgoode.yorku.ca/? Accessed 31 December 2015.

Jain, M. P. (2014). *Indian Constitutional Law*, 7th ed. New Delhi: Lexis Nexis, pp. 874–875.

Khaitan, Bulbul and Nitya Priya. (2009). Rehabilitation of Displaced Persons in India. *NUJS Law Review*, vol. 2, pp. 116–119.

Locke, John. (1690). *The Second Treatise of Civil Government*, pp. 27–29. www.constitution.org/jl/2ndtr05.htm.

Machan, T. (2005). Right to Private Property. *Internet Encyclopaedia of Philosophy*. www.iep.utm.edu/property/ Accessed 31 December 2015.

Merrill, Thomas and Henry E. Smith. (2007). The Morality of Property. *William and Mary Law Review*, vol. 48, no. 5, pp. 1849, 1850, 1882–1883. Scholarship.law.em.edu. Accessed 31 December 2015.

Miceli, Thomas J. (2004). *The Economic Approach to Law*. Stanford: Stanford University Press.

Negi, Singh Nalin and Sujata Ganguly. (2011). *Development Projects vs. Internally Displaced Populations in India: A Literature Based Appraisal*. Presented at the ESF-UniBi-ZiF Research Conference on Environmental Change and Migration: From Vulnerabilities to Capabilities, Bad Salzuflen, Germany, 5–9 December 2010.

Pandey, J. N. (2014). *Constitutional Law of India*. Allahabad: Central Law Agency, pp. 436–441, 720.

Paton, G. W. B. (2004). *A Textbook of Jurisprudence*. Oxford: Oxford University Press, p. 539.

Prabhu, Pradeep. (2005). The Right to Live with Dignity. *Seminar*, p. 552.

Punj, Amita. (2014). Development of Special Economic Zones and Its Impact on Labour Rights and Livelihood in National Capital Region. *Shodha Ganga a Reservoir of Indian Theses*, chapter 3, pp. 136–137. http://shodhganga.inflibnet.ac.in/handle/10603/26845. Accessed 16 December 2015.

Raghuram, G. and Simi Sunny. (2015). *Right to Fair Compensation and Transparency in Land Acquisition, Rehabilitation and Resettlement Ordinance 2014: A Process Perspective*. Working paper series of the Indian Institute of Management, Ahmedabad, 3 July 2015.

Salian, Sushantha. (2002). *History of the Removal of the Fundamental Right to Property*, pp. 249, 252. ccs.in/internshippapers/2002/25.pdf. Accessed 2 January 2016.

Singh, Shekar, Ashish Kothari and Kulan Amin. (1992). Evaluating Major Irrigation Projects in India. In Enakshi Ganguly Thukral (Ed.), *Big Dams, Displaced People: Rivers of Sorrow Rivers of Change*. New Delhi: Sage Publications, p. 16986.

Sundar, Nandini. (2009). *Legal Grounds: Natural Resources, Identity and the Law in Jharkhand*. New Delhi: Oxford University Press, p. 7.

13 A review of the audit reports on land acquisition and rehabilitation

Himanshu Upadhyaya

Introduction: auditing land acquisition and resettlement

By reviewing audit findings, this chapter tries to engage with the gap that exists between the policy and performance. This chapter analyses a few audit reports from India's constitutional audit institution dealing with the land acquisition and resettlement processes. Our focus would be on cases of land acquired for industrial development and subsequently allotted by State-level Industrial Development Corporations (SIDCs). While India's supreme audit institute has made detailed comments on the bureaucratic deviations that constrain the safeguards available to landowners and undue favours that are granted by industrial development corporations to corporate entities, there is very little analysis of these audit findings by social scientists and public policy researchers. This chapter presents a few of these audit findings pertaining to West Bengal, Goa and Kerala. It also discusses in some details the performance audits on land acquisition and rehabilitation in case of Odisha.

Performance audit of land acquisition by HIDCO, West Bengal (2008)

In its report for the year ending 31 March 2007, CAG of India had looked at the Rajarhat New Town Project of West Bengal Housing Infrastructure Development Corporation (HIDCO).[1]

The land acquisition process for this project had started in 1999, but as on the date of audit, only 52 per cent of the projected land was acquired. The report notes that, 'even after eight years of existence, the company had yet to acquire and develop 3075 hectares of land in three phases, due to non-preparation of detailed project reports, annual work plans and absence of coordination between land acquisition and development'. CAG auditors also indicted HIDCO for having failed to fix fair and reasonable market prices for land to be acquired under the Land Acquisition Act of 1894. CAG auditors pointed out that due to such wrong calculations, there were cases of short payment of Rs 50.34 crores as compensation to certain landowners. On the contrary, CAG auditors also came across certain cases where HIDCO made excess payment of Rs 67.58 crore to landowners under three mouzas.

CAG auditors also indicted HIDCO for incurring a loss of Rs 78.98 crores because of delays in awarding contracts for land development, unrealistic estimates, selection of non-qualified contractors and failure to arrange the earth required for landfilling. CAG auditors also looked at the resettlement and rehabilitation of ousted families and found out that while HIDCO had started to acquire land in 1999 until 31 March 2007, only 17 per cent families were rehabilitated.

Another CAG audit report on the same project pointed out that HIDCO had incurred an extra financial burden of Rs 42.64 crores in construction of roads due to deviations from norms under IRC guidelines.[2]

Performance audit of land allotments by GIDC, Goa (2009)

In the last week of March 2009, another CAG audit report entered public domain that had put under scanner the land acquisition and allotment by Goa Industrial Development Corporation (GIDC).[3] Audit scrutiny revealed that during the five-year period (2003–2008), GIDC had acquired 43.47 lakh square meters of land and allotted 50.63 lakh square meters of land. CAG audit had examined all allotments to SEZs and all allotments or area measuring more than 10,000 square meters. The audit scrutiny revealed irregularities in 86 cases of allotments measuring 46.27 lakh square meters and estimated the loss of revenue at Rs 102.64 crore. The audit also found that area aggregating 3.13 lakh square meters in respect of 117 allottees had remained unutilised for more than two years. The audit had pointed out that the corporation should have initiated the process to resume the area from the allottees.

In the five-year period (2003–2008), GIDC had initiated land acquisition proceedings for 164 lakh square meters, which was almost equivalent to what it had acquired during a 37-year period (i.e., from 1966 until 31 March 2003). In a previous performance audit of GIDC for the period 1998–2003, CAG of India had observed, 'Saleable land admeasuring 29.57 lakh square metres remained unutilized for period ranging up to 21 years since the said land was acquired'. On 31 March 1998, GIDC was in possession of 36.57 lakh square meters saleable land which had remained unutilised. Despite sitting on such a huge stretch of 'acquired and still un-allotted and unutilized land', GIDC went on to acquire a further 13.71 lakh square meters of land during 1998–2003 period. CAG auditors observed that out of this, as high as 96 per cent (i.e., 8.53 lakh square meters) of land remained unallotted, as on 31 March 2003!

This report that entered public domain in the year 2004 was still not taken up by Goa Assembly's Public Accounts Committee until the year 2009, when another performance audit report of GIDC was tabled in assembly!

Performance audit of land acquisition in Odisha (2011 and 2012)

On 28 March 2011, a CAG audit report was tabled in Odisha state assembly. This CAG audit report on Odisha government (civil) for the year ending 31 March 2010 had presented a performance audit of land acquisition and management. The audit revealed that in 34 cases of land acquisition, 3120.577 acres of private land were acquired for 11 industries, there was underassessment of compensation by Rs 63.98 crores due to erroneous calculation of market rates. The audit explained in detail how land acquisition officers failed to properly assess the compensation payable by ignoring highest sales statistics as well as suppressing highest sales statistics and misreporting of highest sales statistics in many cases (CAG of India, 2011).

The very next year, performance audit of land acquisition and management in Odisha came under the scanner of CAG auditors once again. In an audit carried out during March to September 2011, auditors checked 208 land acquisition cases pertaining to 14 promoters and Odisha Industrial Infrastructure Development Corporation (IDCO) in six selected districts, namely Bhadrak, Ganjam, Jagatsinghpur, Kalahandi, Puri and Sambalpur and 38 files in Resettlement and Disaster Management (RDM) department. This performance audit (CAG of India, 2012: 20) once again pointed out that 'land policy and land use plan had not been formulated by the state government despite commitment expressed in para 18.1 and 18.2 of IPR 2001 and no actions were found on record to create a land bank'. Despite the recommendation during the previous audit, it was again reported by audit (CAG of India, 2012: 21) that 'comprehensive and centralized data on acquisition and allotment of land was not maintained by the department at State level'. This observation comes from a constitutional institution after an entire decade when many of us believed that Orissa state government had started to feel concerned about 'land acquisition with a human face' and 'drafting an R&R policy that meets international standards'! On both these observations, RDM department stated in a reply filed to audit (CAG of India, 2012: 20) in November 2011 that 'the land use plan was not prepared as no guidelines on the same had been prescribed by the state government' and 'such a database was not maintained due to shortage of staff'

Audit (CAG of India, 2012: 21–22) took the notice of 'scale of land required for different categories, and sizes of industries' not being formalized by the government and highlighted cases of 'inconsistent application of the existing non-formalised scales/norms'. Following a rigorous scrutiny of records in industries as well as steel and mines departments, the audit (CAG of India, 2012: 22) observed that 'for the period 1995–2011, 208 promoters had applied for 130677.886 acres of land and Industrial Promotion and Investment Corporation of Odisha Limited (IPICOL) recommended allotment of 120148.092 acres of land in favour of 199 promoters'. The audit (CAG of India, 2012: 22) also observed that 'in case of remaining nine promoters, 9356.144 acres of land were allotted by Collectors/ IDCO even though the actual requirements of these promoters were not assessed by IPICOL'. When several instances of deviations were pointed out by audit, IPICOL stated in a reply filed to audit (CAG of India, 2012: 23) in January 2012 that 'land requirement was assessed by it considering largely the recommendations of the consultant MND as the benchmark and other infrastructural facilities envisaged in the report submitted by the applicant'. Having taken this reply on the record, the audit (CAG of India, 2012: 23) pronounced that 'the reply is only a vague rationalisation of irrational recommendations made by IPICOL for allotment of land to various promoters of industry'.

The audit scrutiny of 184 land acquisition cases (CAG of India, 2012: 25), to ascertain whether the acquisition of land for promoters of industries had met the test of 'public purpose', revealed that 'in 176 cases, 8484.788 acres of private land was acquired at Rs 511.29 crore by the LAOs on the requisitions filed by IDCO on behalf of 12 promoters of industries and one PPP project, wherein notifications issued under Section 4(1) as well as declarations published under Section 6(1) of LA Act had indicated that the acquisitions were being made for "public purpose" by Government at Government cost'. On further examination of records, such declaration was found to be incorrect. It was observed (CAG of India, 2012: 25) that 'since the entire cost of acquisition was paid by promoters/companies, the acquisition had to be made under chapter VII of LA Act, which prescribed the procedure for acquisition of land for companies for restricted purpose'. Replying to this audit finding, RDM department stated in its reply to audit (CAG of India, 2012: 26) dated November 2011 that 'IDCO was acquiring land for industrial purposes for companies and promoters as per the provisions of the IDCO Act'. Having taken this reply on record, CAG of India (CAG of India, 2012: 26) notes without mincing words that 'such reply was not tenable as in all such cases entire cost of compensation were paid by private promoters and no part of the same was met out of public revenue as required under Section 6(1)'.

This audit finding brings forth the modus operandi of land acquisition bureaucracy which exhibited undue haste and indulged in acts of omissions in order to overcome a legal hurdle. This second performance audit also weaves in the amount of research undertaken by auditors as every audit observation is supported with several judicial pronouncements being cited in footnotes. For example, while discussing audit findings in those cases where they brought out misuse of urgency clause under section 17(4) of LA Act, the report (CAG of India, 2012: 26) notes,

> in various judicial pronouncements, the Apex Court have held that as Section 5-A of the Act conferred a valuable right to the land-losers to file objections, they cannot be deprived of their land without their consent and so the State is required to apply its mind while deciding to invoke

> the emergency provisions under Section 17(4) of the LA Act. It has further been held that there can never be denial of the citizens' rights under the specious garb of urgency or necessity. Such pronouncements also required that the procedure laid down in the statute for acquisition of land must be followed to generate the feeling that rule of law prevailed.

Audit scrutiny (CAG of India, 2012: 26) of 85 cases, where land acquisition process was carried out by applying urgency clause (i.e., under provision of Section 17(4)), revealed that 4967.08 acres of private land were acquired between July 2002 to March 2011 for six promoters. By reading provisions of Section 17 (4) of LA Act along with executive instruction issued in September 1985, it was pointed out that several conditions required to be fulfilled were not met. Scrutiny of records (CAG of India, 2012: 27) revealed that 'instead of giving detailed justification for applying such provision, only general remarks like 'the project is being executed on priority basis', 'requirement of land was of emergent in nature', etc. were indicated in the applications by the requisitioning officers'. It was also found (CAG of India, 2012: 27) that 'in all these cases, the land was not put to use even after delays ranging from one year three months to six year three months from the date of publication of notification under section 4(1) against the stipulated time period of six months'. Having taken this reply on record, CAG audit (CAG of India, 2012: 28) pronounced its view that this reply was unacceptable and elaborated why it considered so in following words:

> we were unable to accept this reply, as staff shortages were a preexisting condition and should have been addressed by the RDM Department before going in for acquisitions on emergency basis. The ultimate sufferer was the land-owner who most often was a farmer. We also observed that there was nothing on record to indicate if RDM Department had carried out any due diligence to seriously address this issue. During the period 2006–11, the RDM Department had not even moved Finance Department to address shortage of staff.

The audit (CAG of India, 2012: 42) noticed that 'in four cases, 5293.22 acres of government allotted and acquired private land handed over to IDCO, was lying unutilized for three to 15 years', resulting in what CAG auditors termed as 'hoarding of land'. What is even more shocking is the revelation that out of these four cases, in the case of 'Aditya Aluminium Limited the land was acquired under section 17(4), i.e. urgency clause'!

The performance review (CAG of India, 2012: 46) ends with a last line showing that the commissioner-cum-secretary, RDM department had not bothered to even file a reply to final audit observation. 'The matter was reported to the Commissioner-cum-Secretary, RDM department in July 2011; Reply of Government had not been received (January 2012)'. When such a long silence in response to indicting audit findings becomes a routine strategy employed by an audited entity, Public Accounts Committee must reconfigure the norms and prioritise picking up such alarming report for discussions and follow-up action.

Performance audit of land acquisition and management in Kerala (2015)

During the fiscal 2013–14, CAG of India carried out a special audit titled 'Land Management by the Government of Kerala with special focus to land for Aranmula Airport and Smart City Kochi'.[4] The report was placed in the Kerala legislature in July 2014. The report pointed out that three PSUs, namely, Kerala State Industrial Development Corporation (KSIDC), Kerala Industrial Infrastructure Development Corporation (KINFRA) and Kerala State Information Technology Infrastructure Limited (KSITIL), had acquired 5003.78 acres of land of private land during the period 2008–13. Particulars of land available and allotted as of March 2013 were shown in Table 13.1.

This audit revealed that out of the total land, 2,290 acres were allotted to 558 entities and the balance was yet to be allotted. Jacob and Arun (2015) point out that 'even though the allotments were at throw away prices; 41 persons did not utilise (March 2014) the allotted land measuring 180.57 acres defeating the very objective of setting up industrial units'. The audit report had also pointed out grave failures on the part of KSIDC. Audit scrutiny found that KSIDC acquired a total area of 1096.12 acres of land for setting up of four Industrial Growth Centres (IGC), out of which 447 acres were allotted to entrepreneurs. Of 258 acres of land acquired for IGC at Mallapuram, 243.97 acres remained vacant for 12 years due to non-creating of infrastructure by KSIDC. The joint venture partner, a private company called Infrastructure Kerala Limited (INKEL), was allowed to possess 60.95 acres of land through sub-lease. It is such a grave failure of governance that the MD of INEKL who decided to transfer 60.95 acres of land was simultaneously holding the position of secretary of industries department!

Table 13.1 Particulars of Land Available and Allotted, as of March 2013

PSU	*Total area (acres)*	*Allottable area (acres)*	*Allotted area (acres)*	*Percentage of allotment*	*No. of allottees*
KINFRA	3283.47	2292.49	1842.12	80.35	489
KSIDC-IGC Mega	1096.12	1009.78	447.14	44.28	68
Projects/Other	219.29	Not estimated	–	–	–
KSITIL	404.90	Partly estimated	1.00	–	01
Total	5003.78		2290.26		558

Source: CAG 2014

The CAG audit also showed cases where 39 allottees were holding on to plots measuring 176.51 acres in eight parks even after failing to commence commercial production within two years from the date of license agreement. CAG auditors pointed out to KINFRA that the period of non-utilisation ranged from two to seven years. As per regulation 26 (5) of KINFRA Act, such non-compliance would result in cancellation of allotment and resumption of plot. When CAG auditors pointed out these cases of non-compliance, KINFRA management claimed in its reply (January 2014) that it had cancelled allotments and resumed 154.30 acres. CAG of India report stated that 'the reply is not correct since the unutilized area of 176.51 crores pointed out by audit is *above and over the area mentioned by the management as already resumed*' (emphasis added). This reply and the incorrectness of the same indicted by CAG points out the lax and casual attitude with which the audited entity was dealing with the audit findings. CAG auditors also concluded in unambiguous terms that 'there was no system prevailing in KINFRA for post allotment verification to see that the allotted land is used for specified purpose, within the period stipulated and for resumption of land in cases of violation of conditions of allotment'.

Audit scrutiny showed that at the time of the enactment of the Kerala Conservation of Paddy Land and Wetland Act, 2008 (i.e., August 2008), the process of survey and hearing of objections filed by landowners was going on in the case of land acquisition for setting up a Knowledge Park at Ramanattukkara in Kozhikode district and 'KINFRA could have discontinued the acquisition process'. However, as the audit reveals, KINFRA had gone ahead with land acquisition process and indulged in willful neglect of the provisions of Paddy Land and Wetland Conservation Act and handed over compensation amount worth Rs 24.24 crores for 77.78 acres of land during April to October 2010. Since 69.67 acres of the acquired land belonged to the category wetland, KINFRA requested the government of Kerala to grant exemption from the provisions under Section 10 (1) of Paddy Land and Wetland Conservation Act. In November 2011, the state government had rejected the request based on the recommendation of the State-Level Committee. Thus, CAG auditors found the expenditure worth Rs 24.24 crores as wasteful. On this being pointed out, KINFRA in its reply (January 2014) stated that it had fielded a fresh application for exemption under Section 10 (1)! One fails to understand if section 10 (1) of the Paddy Land and Wetland Conservation Act allows for multiple applications for exemption. Also it would have been helpful if CAG auditors would have told readers on whether this case of land acquisition had impacted paddy cultivation and what livelihood options were adopted by those farmers who lost their cultivable land.

Jacob and Arun (2015) voices a general opinion that 'acquiring agriculture land for unjustified industrial activities and for creating infrastructure ended up in drastic fall in cultivable land', but it would have helped researchers if CAG auditors had given statistics on the impact on the paddy cultivators of such acquisitions.

Performance audit of land acquisition by IDCO (2014)

This performance review takes a comprehensive look at land acquisition by Odisha Industrial Infrastructure Development Corporation (IDCO), a PSU set up by the Odisha government in March 1981 with a mandate to facilitate rapid industrialisation. This performance audit (CAG of India, 2014: 7) puts under scrutiny land acquisition carried out during a 10-year period (2002–2012), when 'Government acquired 29769.482 acres of private land for industries and provided 20795.814 acres to 52 industries that had signed Memorandum of Understanding (MoU) with state government and other 8973.668 acres to 54 industries that had not signed MoU'.

The audit (CAG of India, 2014: 7–8) pointed out that 'in 190 LA cases test checked, RDM department approved acquisition of 14296.56 acres of private land for 33 industries (non-Government companies) at Rs 912.45 crores during 2002–2012 under "public purpose" clause even though the circumstances did not permit the land to be acquired under public purpose'. Audit (CAG of India, 2014: 8) also stated that this had resulted in a violation of provisions of LA Act, 'in bypassing the safeguard available in the LA Act, 1894 and LA (Companies) Rules, 1963 to protect the interests of the land owners'. Replying to this audit finding (CAG of India, 2014: 8), RDM department stated in April 2013 that 'IDCO was acquiring private land for industrial purpose, which is very much a public purpose under section 31 (1) of OIIDC Act 1980'. Department had also sought to argue (CAG of India, 2014: 8) that 'the public purpose clause as defined in LA Act has been fulfilled, as the cost of acquisition was fully borne by IDCO, which is a corporation owned and controlled by the State'. Having taken note of this reply, CAG auditors (CAG of India, 2014: 8) stated, 'the reply is not acceptable since IDCO was acquiring land for private promoters and the entire cost of acquisition was borne by the promoter concerned' and pointed out that 'land for these industries should have been acquired under Part VII of LA Act'.

The audit (CAG of India, 2014: 8) noticed that 'in respect of 92 out of 225 test checked cases relating to 20 companies, 7025.535 acres land was acquired at Rs 205.65 crore during 1995–2008, by invoking emergency provision', though none of the conditions required to be met was fulfilled. Audit scrutiny (CAG of India, 2014: 8) had found that 'in respect of acquisition of 4370.330 acre land in 58 LA cases, RDM department took six to 34 months for issue of order for acquisition under section 7 of LA act'. The audit (CAG of India, 2014: 8) also found that 'in case of acquisition of 1241.070 acre land for two industries, the entire land remained unutilized/vacant (as of March 2013) even after four five years of handing over the possession'. All these cases prove that the application of emergency provision was clearly arbitrary.

Performance review (CAG of India, 2014: 9) underlined that 'under section 5A of the LA Act 1894, the owners of land have the right to file an objection to the proposed acquisition within 30 days from the date of publication of preliminary notification under section 4(1)'. The major concern that emerged from scrutiny of records (CAG of India, 2014: 10) was that in case of

> 132 out of 190 test checked LA cases, involving acquisition of 9926.23 acre private land (LA cost Rs 751.02 crore) for 30 industries, copy of the section 4(1) notification which was served in the locality, did not mention any clause/ provision inviting objections under section 5(A) of LA Act from the land owners. Reason for such omission was not found on record. Besides, individual notices were also not issued to the affected land owners, as required under Executive Instructions of the Department.
>
> (emphasis added)

Such a systematic lapse and the extent of cases in which such a lapse was observed makes us wonder if LAOs in Odisha worked overzealously to ensure that there were no objections to the land acquisition process, even if that meant denying the little breathing spaces that LA Act provided to oustees.

Similarly, examination of records of 55 LA cases test checked (CAG of India, 2014: 10) revealed that, 'in 10 out of 15 LA cases relating to four MoU based industries, the RDM department received collectors' reports citing objections like existence of fertile land, inadequate compensation, lack of provision of employment and other things, but these reports were not considered by the secretary and declaration to the effect that the land is required for a public purpose under section 6 of LA Act was issued' (emphasis added). The audit (CAG of India, 2014: 10) also came across another instance of 'collector, Bolangir disposing off 718 objections filed by land owners in seven LA cases, though the Secretary RDM department was the competent authority to consider and dispose of the objections filed by land owners'. The audit didn't find any instance of LAOs, collectors and secretary, RDM department, attentively engaging with the objections filed by landowners against land acquisition process rendering section 5(A) meaningless.

Replying to this audit observation (CAG of India, 2014: 10), state government stated in July 2013 that 'all collectors were instructed in June 2013 to strictly adhere to the provisions of section 5A of LA Act and directed that the public notice served in the locality under section 4(1) of LA Act must contain provision for calling of objections within 30 days.' The reply appears to be a mere half-hearted effort to suggest that there are some directions issued and doesn't inspire confidence that the state government looked at these instances as serious mal-governance. After mentioning this reply, audit report (CAG of India, 2014: 10) goes on to state, 'the reply does not elaborate any action which would be taken in cases cited above by Audit'.

Performance review (CAG of India, 2014: 11) pointed out that 'as per Rule 4 of Land Acquisition (Companies) Rule 1963, acquisition of private land for companies was to be allowed only after the company had made its best endeavor to find land in the locality suitable for the purpose of acquisition and made all reasonable efforts to purchase such land by negotiation with the person interested therein on payment of reasonable price and such efforts have failed' and added that 'in such cases, the collector is supposed to hold an enquiry under Rule 4(2) and submits a report on the above to Government for consideration'.

Examination of records (CAG of India, 2014: 11) pointed out that 'though IDCO/IPICOL was aware that, three out of 89 industries had directly purchased 327.81 acre land from the land owners, yet the same was not reduced from the land requirement finally assessed (1295 acres) for these companies by IPICOL'. There was also a shocking revelation (CAG of India, 2014: 11) that 'in the remaining 86 cases even the extent of land acquired directly by these industries wasn't available with IPICOL as well as IDCO'. So in the course of performance audit (CAG of India, 2014: 11), 'a joint inspection was conducted with RDM department and IDCO officials during which seven industries intimated that they had purchased 1324.343 acres of land from owners'. Both scrutiny of records and joint inspection results exposed the failure of both administrative and RDM department to exercise oversight on land acquired by industries through direct purchase.

The audit (CAG of India, 2014: 15–16) observed that 'in case of seven MoU's based industries, 4210.419 acre private land were acquired between May 2003 and March 2012 at the cost of Rs 159.22 crore' and 'verification of records of Sub-Registrars concerned revealed that the LAOs under assessed compensation of Rs 55.05 crores in 33 out of 55 test checked cases due to fixation of market value of land at a lower than the highest sale value'.

Performance audit of implementation of Odisha R&R Policy, 2006

A performance audit by CAG of India on Resettlement and Rehabilitation of people affected by industrial projects in Odisha is part of an audit report (No. 7 of 2014, See Para 2.1, chapter 2, pp. 07–32) that got tabled in the state assembly on 12 February 2015. The 27-page-long performance audit presents some startling findings. This performance audit (CAG of India, 2015: 9), which looked at the implementation of the Orissa Resettlement and Rehabilitation Policy, 2006 (ORRP), test-checked records related to 32 industrial projects spread across 13 districts.

Appendix 2.1 in the audit report (CAG of India, 2015: 143–144) gives the list of the 32 projects sampled and shows that as per official estimates, 6,533 families were displaced by way of loss of cultivable land and 3,5632 families were affected by loss of homestead land and livelihood. These projects had taken a toll of 36555.18 acres of land, some of which haven't witnessed the realisation of 'public purpose' even after a decade!

This performance audit (CAG of India, 2015: 25) states that 3,790 acres of land were acquired by the government for the TISCO steel plant in Gopalpur in the year 1995. When the steel plant on the acquired land couldn't take shape, the government decided in 2007 that this land would be used for a multi-product SEZ. However, even after a lapse of 18 years, no development has taken place on the acquired land. The audit also talks about a government decision dated July 2013, wherein an enhanced rehabilitation package was proposed for displaced persons, but the same was not acceptable to industry. Audit scrutiny (CAG of India, 2015: 25) revealed that displaced families submitted a memorandum in December 2013, asking for enhanced compensation as per the July 2013 government decision and that 'the decision was pending till date'. There were two other projects – the Aditya Aluminium Project, Rayagada and Kalinga Nagar Industrial Infrastructure Project, Jajpur – which jointly displaced 312 families. The CAG's performance audit (CAG of India, 2015: 11) brings this under scrutiny and states that these 312 families were 'identified but not given R&R benefits due to non-setting up of industries' though they were supposed to get R&R assistance under the ORRP.

Responding to this audit finding (CAG of India, 2015: 11), the Revenue and Disaster Management Department stated in a reply dated October 2014 that since physical displacement of Project-Displaced Families (PDFs) had not occurred, industries did not provide resettlement grants. Having recorded this lame-duck reply, the CAG audit observes that 'the PDFs had nevertheless lost a perennial source of income from land, for a period ranging 6 to 17 years, and their issues had still not been sorted out'!

This performance audit also imparts lessons indicating why social impact analysis must be a crucial component. It reports that as per the ORRP provisions, socio-economic surveys (SES) were primarily intended as guides and bases for preparation of relief and rehabilitation plans. However, audit scrutiny (CAG of India, 2015: 14) revealed that these SES were deficient in many ways. It was observed that the SES were not made public in all cases, and hence this mechanism had failed to invite objections, thereby leading to diminished scope of public hearings. The performance audit (CAG of India, 2015: 14) noticed that 'in seven projects, developers directly purchased 726.94 acres of land in 19 villages, without conducting any SES'. The CAG audit (CAG of India, 2015: 14–15) tells us that this shortcoming resulted in 'identification of affected people and their entitlements under R&R policy' getting short-circuited. The audit (CAG of India, 2015: 7) also shows that 'in respect of 15 out of 32 industrial projects, SES reports were prepared but were not approved by the Rehabilitation and Periphery Development Advisory Committee (RPDAC) and hence, the R&R plan for affected families was not prepared'.

The gaps in accountability over resettlement and Rehabilitation

If an affected person is not rehabilitated as per the provisions of the ORRP, then should it be regarded as a violation or a mere grievance emerges as a moot question after reading this performance audit. Audit report (CAG of India, 2015: 30) showed that 'even as Para 20 of the ORRP provided for setting up of an effective grievance redressal mechanism at the district level, no specific mechanism was followed at the Collectorate level to receive grievance petitions'. It was found (CAG of India, 2015: 30) that the collectorate merely acted as a post office from where 'grievances related to R&R were forwarded to the project authorities for consideration, but no follow up action was taken'. Audit findings (CAG of India, 2015: 30) showed that there existed a huge backlog of unresolved grievances: 'out of 2222 grievances received, only 880 were settled'!

How regularly did those various committees that were envisioned to have performed review and monitoring of the implementation of the ORRP meet? Audit report (CAG of India, 2015: 30) states that 'Para 17 of the ORRP lays down the requirement of a council headed by the Chief Minister to advise, review and monitor implementation of R&R policy in the state'. But a scrutiny of records (CAG of India, 2015: 30) revealed that 'the State level Council of Resettlement and Rehabilitation has met only once on 18 June 2008 in all these years'. Scrutiny of records (CAG of India, 2015: 30) of meetings at the department level also revealed that review meetings were convened mainly to discuss land acquisition. Audit (CAG of India, 2015: 30) reported that 'during the nine departmental meetings held between April 2012 and June 2013, 294 issues related to land acquisition were discussed, while only 42 R&R-related issues were taken up'! This clearly shows the bias of the department towards facilitating land acquisition for industries, while it fails to care for displaced.

Auditors (CAG of India, 2015: 30) came across a government circular (August 2012) stating that a 'review meeting on R&R should be held at least once in a month by respective district collectors and district magistrates and once in two months by Rehabilitation and Peripheral Area Development Committees (RPADC)'. But audit scrutiny (CAG of India, 2015: 30) revealed that the collectors or RPADCs of none of the sampled districts could show any record of any such review meeting having taken place after August 2012! There was no comprehensive database of project-affected families available with the department for effective monitoring of R&R.

These performance audits by CAG of India on land acquisition and resettlement processes and the ways audited entities and legislators responded to audit findings tell us a lot about many a slip between policy statements and performance on ground. It also points out the need for an analysis of the audit reports of constitutional institution carrying out its mandate to ensure accountability in order to seek pro-people reforms. These audit findings appear to bolster the amendments that were sought in land acquisition processes before the enactment of amendment bill in August 2013. In the face of such hard evidence, the efforts of further diluting the provisions of Right to Fair Compensation and Transparency in Land Acquisition, Resettlement and Rehabilitation Act, 2013, by NDA government through the route of ordinance appeared to offer an unconvincing argument.

Notes

1 See CAG of India (2007) CAG of India's Report on West Bengal (Commercial) for the year ending March 31, 2007, especially first 28 pages of chapter 2, titled 'Performance Reviews'. Also see 'Crores wasted in HIDCO flop show, says CAG', *The Financial Express*, 28 March 2008. www.financialexpress.com/archive/crores-wasted-in-hidco-flop-show-says-cag/289854/ last visited 21st September 2017. For a brilliant academic account of Rajarhat Township Project and the issues encountered in land acquisition and allocation process, see Dey, Ishita; Ranbir Samaddar and Suhit K. Sen (2013) *Beyond Kolkata: Rajarhat and the Dystopia of Urban Imagination*, Routledge, New Delhi.
2 See CAG of India (2014) CAG of India's Report on West Bengal (General and Social Sector) for the year ending 31 March 2013, pp. 76–79. www.cag.gov.in/sites/default/files/audit_report_files/West_Bengal_General_and_Social_Sector_2_2014.pdf. Accessed 21 September 2017.
3 See CAG of India (2009) CAG of India's Report on Goa.
4 See www.cag.gov.in/content/report-no-6-2014-performance-audit-land-management-government-kerala-special-focus-land. Accessed 1 August 2016.

References

CAG of India. (2011). *Report of the Comptroller and Auditor General of India CIVIL for the Year Ended 31 March 2010*. Bhubaneshwar: Government of India.

CAG of India. (2012). *Report of the Comptroller and Auditor General of India CIVIL for the Year Ended 31 March 2011*. Bhubaneshwar: Government of Odisha.

CAG of India. (2014). *Report of the Comptroller and Auditor General of India General and Social Sector Volume 2 for the Year Ended March 2013*. Bhubaaneshwar: Government of Odisha.

CAG of India. (2015). *Report of the CAG of India on Government of Odisha (General and Social Sector), for the Year Ending 31st March 2014*. Bhubaneshwar: Government of Odisha.

Jacob, Biju and I. P. Arun. (2015). Issues in Land Management in Kerala. *Journal of Government Audits and Accounts*, no. 2, January. www.cag.gov.in/sites/default/files/cag_pdf/january-2015/featuring-an-audit-report.html. Accessed 21 September 2017.

Upadhyaya, Himanshu. (2015). CAG Report on Odisha: Will Legislators Take Note Please? *India Together*, 9 March. www.indiatogether.org/cag-audit-of-odisha-rehabilitation-for-those-affected-by-mining-and-land-acquisition-government. Accessed 21 September 2017.

Index

Note: page numbers in *italic* indicate figures and page numbers in **bold** indicate tables.

Taylor & Francis Group
an informa business

Taylor & Francis eBooks

www.taylorfrancis.com

A single destination for eBooks from Taylor & Francis with increased functionality and an improved user experience to meet the needs of our customers.

90,000+ eBooks of award-winning academic content in Humanities, Social Science, Science, Technology, Engineering, and Medical written by a global network of editors and authors.

TAYLOR & FRANCIS EBOOKS OFFERS:

- A streamlined experience for our library customers
- A single point of discovery for all of our eBook content
- Improved search and discovery of content at both book and chapter level

REQUEST A FREE TRIAL

support@taylorfrancis.com

Routledge
Taylor & Francis Group

CRC Press
Taylor & Francis Group

For Product Safety Concerns and Information please contact our EU representative GPSR@taylorandfrancis.com
Taylor & Francis Verlag GmbH, Kaufingerstraße 24, 80331 München, Germany

www.ingramcontent.com/pod-product-compliance
Ingram Content Group UK Ltd.
Pitfield, Milton Keynes, MK11 3LW, UK
UKHW020146200926
475702UK00016B/2579
9780367504779